Broads Books

The Nine Horizons

Mike Robbins is a journalist turned development worker. He is also the author of *Even the Dead are Coming* (2009), a memoir of Sudan; *Crops and Carbon* (2011), on agriculture and climate change; and two works of fiction, *The Lost Baggage of Silvia Guzmán* (2014) and *Three Seasons* (2014). He lives in New York.

The Nine Horizons
Travels in sundry places

MIKE ROBBINS

broadsbooks@gmail.com

Design by Jasiek Krzysztofiak / www.jasiek.co.uk

Cover photo: Avik Chakraborty / Shutterstock

Suggested cataloging data:

Robbins, Mike, 1957-
Nine Horizons / Mike Robbins. - 1st ed.
p. cm.
ISBN 978-0-9914374-1-2 (paperback)
1. Voyages and travels--Anecdotes. 2. Sudan--Description and travel. 3. Bhutan--Description and travel. 4. Ecuador--Description and travel. 5. Syria--Description and travel. 6. Economic development. I. Robbins, Mike, 1957- II. Title.
G465 .R63 2013
910.924--dc23

Contents

Author's note

This book is not an autobiography. It is a series of snapshots.

A snapshot is random, and excludes everything that the writer did not see. But it may also capture what might otherwise be dismissed as of no value. I have not ignored wider issues, but you can find these in *The Economist* or journals of foreign affairs. What they won't tell you is why the 1931 *Miss Ecuador* competition was a failure, why Bhutanese pigs are happy, or what the Speaker of the Kazakh Parliament thinks about pornography.

The years covered by this book were a time of change in the developing world. There were winners and losers; many countries, especially in the former Soviet Union, have undergone dramatic and sometimes traumatic change. The Syria I knew has ceased to exist. There have also been enormous political changes in Bhutan and Ecuador since I lived in those countries. I have not attempted to reflect those changes. Each is a snapshot of a time as well as a place.

The first chapter of this book, *A Small Town in Africa*, is adapted from a previous book, *Even the Dead are Coming*.

Acknowledgements

Many people have have helped me in the countries I have visited. It is not possible to acknowledge them all. I do wish to thank Piet van der Poel, Melissa Richardson and Linda Rosalik for their endless hospitality and friendship in Bhutan. I should also thank Britain's VSO for twice giving me the chance to work abroad, in Sudan and later Bhutan.

In more recent years, Hazel Marsh and Lisa Sutton have been great sources of support, and the pieces in *Uptown and the Bronx* were originally written for Hazel. Last but far from least, Sandrine Ligabue has somehow tolerated my angst as this book has finally become a reality.

A small town
in Africa

You do not need to know much about me. In 1987 I was 30 and had lived for some years in London, where I had been a traffic broadcaster and business reporter, worked for a rock-music publisher, and finally joined the weekly paper for the fishing industry. I had always struggled, and besides, London in the 1980s felt more and more soulless. I decided it was time to see the world, of which I felt ignorant, and applied for a two-year volunteer post overseas. I heard nothing for months, then they contacted me about a post on Java; at the interview, Java was not mentioned, but Thailand was, briefly; and then I got a letter posting me to the Sudanese government's Refugee Settlement Administration on the border with Eritrea and Ethiopia. After some thought, I agreed to go. In November 1987 I set out from Heathrow with an Irish fellow-volunteer. I knew I had started a long journey, but did not know how long.

*

It was a night flight and we arrived in the small hours. We slept briefly, then Khartoum had burst upon us like a blow on the head the moment we stepped out of the hotel early the next morning.

The impact of light in a desert land, upon one who had never seen it, was spectacular. It lit everything so brightly; the dust, the concrete, the broken black pipework and cables sticking out of the cracked pavements, the men in their startling white *djellabiyas* crouching by the side of the road drinking tea; traffic, donkeys pulling water-carts made out of old oil-drums lashed to worn-out lorry differentials, and bright yellow taxis that were 20, 30 years old and honked and bucked their way round the souk-trucks that stood in the middle of the streets to discharge their loads or change wheels. The roads were sealed in the main thoroughfares, but they were badly broken, and where there was a pothole, it took the form of a savage little trench across the road, with jagged tarmac lips. As for the buildings, they all seemed to be of cheap, square concrete, discoloured, never white, never brown; just indifferent, with dingy doors set behind pillars of tiles or plaster. Between the two would be galleries where you could walk, but there was no pavement as such, and where there were gaps between buildings, pedestrians were forced to leap into the traffic and back again. Dogs slept, unperturbed, amid the chaos. My eyes hurt. You have a choice, I told myself; take an interest, or consign yourself to two years of misery. So I took an interest, and slowly the city of Khartoum started to resolve itself into districts and faces, older buildings as well as cheap new ones, roundabouts here and there decorated with hibiscus, the odd dusty neem tree; and a few *hosh*, or yard, walls garlanded with bougainvillea that flowed across their parapets like a slow, fiery waterfall.

The city, I observed in an early letter home, seemed grim on first acquaintance, but every now and then one wandered into little squares, the walls of which were so garlanded... Did one?

It must have been the heat. I was right the first time. Khartoum was a mess.

But there were oases in the capital. One such was the suburb of Mogren, where the British organisation that had recruited me had its own office in a one-storey building surrounded by trees. Mogren means "the meeting of waters". It was here that the Blue Nile from Lake Tana in Ethiopia met the White Nile from Uganda; they came together in a great sweep of water several miles wide. Near here, the flying boats of Imperial Airways swept down to refuel on their journey to the Cape, and it must have been a sight after hours above the desert; an inland sea. The riverbanks at Mogren were partially wooded, and you could walk across a short stretch of field from the ring road, beside rows of date-palms, watching oxen plough and small boys in dirty *djellabiyas* drive herds of goats just as they did in the countryside. And the earth just here was a rich dark brown. There was a timelessness about Mogren, despite its location in the inner city; even the pick-ups roaring down the dual carriageway beside the Blue Nile towards the heart of Khartoum often had livestock in the back, old-fashioned brown sheep with woolly coats and long ears, standing stupidly upright, ignorant of the knife that awaited them on the morrow.

Away from the river, Mogren was leafy, a place of trees and frangipani and quiet yards like VSO's own. Rich people lived there, and there was an embassy or two. The river frontage was dominated by Friendship Hall, built for the congress of the Organization of African Unity in 1978; a splendid modern air-conditioned building with assembly halls, cinema and cafeteria, a total lunacy in a poor country, even when it was built. But I could understand why the Sudanese had built it.

Follow the road from Mogren on the banks of the Blue Nile, towards the city centre, and you travelled back into another world. The bank was again lined with trees; opposite was Tutti Island, a place that belonged to those that were born there, and sold their houses to no-one who couldn't trace their ancestry back on that little patch of land. Ferries disgorged them on the beach from time to time, and shoals of white figures streamed up to the May Gardens, where a restaurant served well-prepared dishes of meat or of fish in batter, and the attractive young aristocrats of Khartoum came to meet their girlfriends. Romance pervaded the May Gardens; I even saw couples kissing in the darkness.

Walk on from the May Gardens, if you could stand the heat and the sand that made walking slow, and you came to the Grand Hotel, where the British stayed in their heyday. The hotel was still elegant, with its terrace where a sugared lime-juice cost what the average Sudanese earned in a fortnight. Still with its marbled colonnades, too; its cool, dark entrance hall with its whiff of fresh bread from the on-site bakery, and the classical bar where you could buy as many cigarettes as you wanted, even in times of shortage.

On from the Grand, and the Ministries began, overlooking the leafy corniche; the most spectacular of them all was a great red stone building, once the British Sudan Club but now the Department of Protocol of the Foreign Office. Finally, a gateway appeared across the road; the presidential palace, two sentries in decorated frock coats and ornate headdresses, guarding the entrance to the staircase on which the Mahdi's men had done for Gordon a century before.

That was to your right; to your left, across the broad, grey-blue waters of the Blue Nile, you saw the enormous paddle-steamers, white behemoths with stern-wheels that for much the century slewed slowly through the murky waters of the Sudd, the enormous swamp in South Sudan, bearing the District

Officer northwards from his lonely hell towards Khartoum, dinner, dancing and the train to Port Sudan, whence he would take ship for Suez and sail home on leave. One could almost see the wheel rip the surface of the White Nile and break it into a thousand fragments that caught the evening light as you smoked your pipe, watching the Nuer and Shilluk sleep peacefully on the decks below. But now the huge boats stayed where they were. The war had blocked the river route south, and only the odd armed convoy staggered as far as Malakal in the early part of the year with ammunition and food for the besieged. It had been thus for five years. To walk along Nile Avenue was a trip back in time, but the people of the city had no time to make it with you. If you opened your eyes a little wider, you saw the usual black pipes sticking out of the broken pavements, even here; and the groups of Southern teenagers with their flat, African faces, scratching along as best they could, selling cigarettes and washing cars.

But the chaos and glaring light of Khartoum could be oddly deceptive. I was struck by the private nature of a house in Sudan; it was surrounded by a high wall, and the street outside was no-man's-land. The distinction between the general, which did not matter, and the particular, which did, was often very strong. Thus the streets around fellow-volunteer Hannah's home in Omdurman were typical; they were a mess, with the usual accumulation of discarded plastic bags, cartons, bits of peel and, alarmingly, used needles. Yet as soon as she opened the door of the *hosh*, we were in a different world. It had been smartly swept; there was not a bit of rubbish anywhere.

Like many Sudanese houses, it was of one storey and was built around the courtyard in a rather rambling way. On the left was Hannah's room, with a patio outside that was covered over and fronted by two rather nice Doric columns that sat well with the light-coloured stone. Inside, the ceilings were high, and supported fans that turned slowly on long shafts; it was dark, with zinc shutters that took the place of glass being firmly drawn shut to keep out the heat and dust of the day.

One Friday, the Sabbath, the Irish volunteer and I went to visit her, taking the bus across the very long steel bridge that linked Mogren with the Omdurman bank. The bus had been clearly been bought secondhand, for its interior bore advertising slogans in Dutch; once or twice I even saw buses with destination boards from Amsterdam. Buses were an experience in Sudan. Unless you were lucky enough to board one at the terminal, there was no way you were getting inside, and when visiting Khartoum for work I often travelled downtown hanging out of the door, holding onto the railings in the doorway, hoping that my rear end would not strike a passing lamp-post. The fares were collected by agile young boys who crawled through whatever gaps they could find, but as the fare was only a few pence, it was not uncommon to hand over a note and indicate that one was paying for one's neighbours; the next day someone would do the same for you. That day, however, the bus was quiet, and we had seats as we rattled across the long bridge above the grey-blue midday surface of the Blue Nile, admiring the vast sweep of water to our left where the two great rivers met.

In Omdurman we sat on the patio in the shade, drinking lime-juice and eating fruit. I remember watching the doves that played on the wall, white between the light-brown stone and the deep blue of the afternoon sky; bit by bit the sunlight retreated up the wall towards them, the line of shadow moving with deceptive speed as the sun's hot rays left us in peace to enjoy the last brief hour of daylight, while Hannah made some *karkadee* – hibiscus juice – in a jug, with lots of sugar. There was little sound in the *hosh*.

As darkness fell, Hannah announced that she would have to go soon to the bakery, and I went with her. We made our way through the unlit, unpaved streets, past the abandoned combine harvester (what was *that* doing in the middle of Omdurman?); across the stretch of waste-ground where the children played football in the afternoons; over a drainage-ditch and down an alleyway to where a gaggle of people, mostly women, waited in front of the closed shutters of a low mud-brick building. I remember that it was almost the only place where I ever saw the Sudanese form an orderly queue. The women reached out and smacked children who tried to push in front of us. If they were surprised to see two foreigners queueing for bread with them, they didn't show it. The women were dressed in multicoloured, swirling *toabs*, the loose-fitting layered robes that women wore in Sudan; they were mostly middle-aged, large, fat, rather fierce, many of them with tribal scars. A typical scar, that of the Sheguy from Northern Sudan, consisted of three vertical slashes down the cheek. There was nothing unusual about this, or about the scars on the wrists or temples that many people had from medical treatment given by the traditional practitioner in their villages.

At 6.15 the shutters opened, and a smell of new-baked bread flooded across us; immediately, everyone was pushing and shoving. Behind the counter, two or three men in dirty *djellabiyas* moved quickly, carrying long loaves very like French baguettes. I never did see bread like this away from Khartoum; every region had its shape, and this was the capital's. When we got to the counter, Hannah bought eight loaves for 15 piastres each. But they were too hot to touch, and when she tried to pick them up she was forced to drop them back on the counter.

"Perhaps you can make an apron of your dress and carry them that way," I suggested. Doubtfully she did so and I dropped the hot loaves into it, much to the amusement of the other customers, who laughed—not rudely—at the sight of the *khawajaya* marching off with eight long loaves bouncing in her makeshift apron. As we crossed the waste-ground, we started to eat the hot bread. I have never had bread like it since. As we walked, laughing, munching, the moon lit our way. It had been rising since an hour or two before sunset, first pale silver against the light sky, then bigger and more distinct as the blue mellowed into night. Now the disc was yellow. Later we went down to the river; a breeze had come up, as it sometimes did after sundown, and the surface of the Blue Nile was covered with a million tiny ripples. The moon, ahead and a little above, cast an immense pathway of gold across the water towards us, so that it seemed one might walk down to the water's edge and along the beam to the Presidential Palace on the south bank. The moon shone through a canopy of date-palms and acacias, lighting, to our left, a series of low embrasures built by the Mahdist forces to defend the city against Kitchener in 1898. They were a monument now, but people lived there in lean-tos made of cardboard and corrugated iron; now and then, as we walked slowly across the packed earth, we would see a flash of white in the gloom as someone moved silently around them.

There was something ancient about this place and the mood of it held me, even after my companion and I had an argument with a taxi-driver who, after being given twice the normal fare, demanded yet more. (The Sudanese are less mean than almost anyone, but taxi-drivers can be an exception, as they can in any big city.) That night I didn't sleep early. I lay there and thought of a thousand things; of white walls against a rich blue sky; of Dutch buses, displaced, rattling across a great steel bridge past oxen that ploughed dark earth in the heart of a city; of a vast yellow moon tipping liquid gold across a river between the date-palms, and the whiff of charcoal from the stove in Hannah's yard; of hot fresh break and Doric pillars, of doves on a wall and *karkadee*. I will like it here, I told myself before I finally fell asleep, untroubled by the clangs and scrapes of zinc doors opening and closing and echoing through the bare corridors of the hotel. I am going to be happy here.

*

The Khartoum interlude ended quickly. One day my companion left on the long journey to his post at a small town some 36 hours to the south. Two days later I left too. I had an early start. I rose at five, in black night; when I left the hotel half an hour later it was light, a very delicate pink from the sun beginning to spread across a pale, luminous blue. It wasn't cold; it was only mid-November, and the mornings would be chilly for only three or four weeks at most, right at the bottom of the year, Still, it was mild, and as I lifted my heavy suitcase down the steps of the small hotel, I barely broke into a sweat.

I hadn't slept much. The sound of the zinc doors of the hotel clanging and scraping had reverberated all night, mingling with the relentless hawking of the Saudi in the room next door. My other neighbour was doing something with a number of steel pails and much fluid, a performance that continued until after three. I suspected he was producing bootleg liquor (Sudan had introduced strict prohibition four years earlier). Or maybe it was something worse. He was a sinuous man, rubbery, creepy, hairless, like an eel; I had passed him once or twice in the corridor and felt a faint tang of evil. After an hour or so I had started to feel uncomfortable, and tossed and turned in bed; I told myself not to be absurd. But then the sounds of shots rang out in Abdel Rahman Street, and continued for half an hour. They were shooting stray dogs, a guess confirmed by a squeal of shock and pain as some unloved animal died in the dust of the pavement, such as it was, outside the hotel. All in all, I had closed my eyes for less than an hour.

A taxi took me to the main bus-station, and at seven I boarded the bus. By that time the temperature had risen into the 90s Fahrenheit (low 30s Centigrade), and the inside of the bus got warmer and warmer and the passengers quieter and quieter as we headed south-east from Khartoum, through the cotton area of the Gezira and into the arid flatlands beyond. The endless baked-earth plain that accounts for most of Eastern Sudan is not what it appears, springing to life in the rains; but in November the dry season had begun, and it was like a sheet of grey marble broken only by a skein of very fine cracks. Moreover it stretched, uninterrupted, as far as the eye could see, so that one had the impression that the earth had been turned inside-out, and you were crossing what had been the inside and was now the skin. Both earth and sky were infinite, leaving the eye to search for some point of reference—and find none.

Except the mirages. These began at mid-morning, and seemed always to be on the horizon; at first, I thought that they were lines of trees. They were not simple shimmers such as one sees on an English summer's day, but great expanses of water floating across the landscape. So realistic were they that reflections of real objects, when there were any, could be seen as they passed. That included the *jebels*, small hills, that appeared near Fau, in the fourth or fifth hour of the journey. The *jebels* were hauntingly weird; some round, and some jagged like snaggle-teeth of witches; small ravines full of stones ran down their flanks. One of them, two or three miles from the road, was so distinctive in shape that I dubbed it Cathedral Rock, and in months to come it was a landmark on many journeys that I made along this road.

In the meagre shade of the *jebels*, man and beast took shelter from the furnace of the day. This was where I saw my first camels; first just two or three, hobbled, one leg tied in an angle at the knee so that it wouldn't wander far. Then there were more and more, and there were goats too, and stupid brown sheep with their long, silly tails and ears. Always these animals seemed to be in the care of a single boy, who looked about 10 to me but was probably 14; he was armed with nothing more than a stick, and dressed in a simple white *djellabiya*. He would squat below a solitary, windswept acacia, if he could find one, and would be alone but for the herd, which might be a hundred strong. I have no idea how he controlled them. Probably he did not know himself, and would have been surprised that anyone should remark upon the matter. Sometimes, he would be at a *hafir*, an artificial lake or pond 50 or 60 feet across, constructed of banked earth on the surface of the plain. They collected water in the rains, and held them a few weeks—no more; already, after three weeks of drought, they were reduced to a few murky puddles in a bowl of churned earth.

After the *jebels*, there was again nothing to either side of us. By lunchtime, there wasn't even much traffic; at one in the afternoon, many drivers had chosen to break their journeys. We had ourselves been travelling for six hours. Even the souk-trucks had rumbled off the road for an hour or two. They were beautifully-kept, these souk-trucks, and would work on for several decades. They were built mostly on the Bedford TJ chassis; their round, postwar-style cabs were usually a bright royal blue and their bodywork had been painstakingly constructed in the souk, great slabs of steel painted matt-black, studded with a thousand rivets. Sometimes steel hoops protected the cargo, which might be loaded to twice the vehicle's height. The bodies were extremely heavy, and the lorries were said to be net consumers in the economy, so profligate were they with precious diesel. But they were impressive, polished to perfection, interiors tastefully upholstered in crushed velvet and hung with tassels; doors cut away and replaced with wooden balustrades as armrests; slogans painted, with care and symmetry, in a million designs that include expressions of religious faith, national flags, eyes — all overshadowing the drabness of the buses, which offered nothing more than posters of Bob Marley and, more frequently, Michael Jackson in their rear windows.

There were truck-stops in this wilderness. They were tumbledown shacks lining the road, teahouses and restaurants, with a few shops selling cigarettes and groceries; others sold petrol or diesel from 44-gallon drums from which the fuel was pumped by hand. Other shacks were brothels. Prostitution was not rare, and the truck-stop was a good place for a brothel. A lorry-driver's life in Sudan was a lonely one, and never more so than on the long sealed road that stretched a thousand kilometres from Khartoum to Port Sudan. The journey could be completed by coach in 19 hours, often with a single driver, who would go hard to make time. The truckers did likewise. It paid well, if one stayed awake. There was only one way for many of the drivers to survive such a punishing schedule—dope, or *bango*; a rolled leaf full of the stuff (which was strong) could be had quite cheaply. I was told that many of the lorry-drivers were more or less constantly stoned out of their brains. Even if this were untrue, fatigue and heat together would have wrought havoc on this road. Every mile or two there seemed to be a burnt-out coach, overturned souk-truck or flattened car. The coach in which I was travelling would itself overturn at speed and burn out a year or so later, with terrible loss of life that included the brother of a colleague.

The evidence of carnage did not discourage people from travelling at 150kph and more in the daytime. At night, they couldn't, for you were lucky if a lorry had more than one headlight. That would be pointing in the wrong direction, anyway. Tail-lights were often neglected; a problem, as the big Fiat trailer-trucks often rumbled through the night at 35-40kph or less. Any faster, and the one dim headlight would have been inadequate. But the truckers' most disconcerting habit was when they broke down; a cairn would be erected some way behind the disabled vehicle, to warn oncoming drivers. The matter resolved, the truck would pull away, the cairn being left where it was—normally under your sump.

With the afternoon came an uncomfortable dryness and a caking of dust upon the face, so that the eyelids felt as stiff as card. The passengers were quiet. Earlier, there had been a cheerful group at the back of the bus. One had cried out: "Sudan *niish—aragi!*" Sudan finished—*aragi!* The latter was the local firewater, distilled from dates and, like all alcohol, illegal. Perhaps the cry was for my benefit. But now those passengers, too, were dozing. The sky was pale blue and empty, although I believe that once on that journey I did see a tiny white cloud; I can't be sure. An empty pan beneath a dome. Occasionally, however, the featurelessness was broken. Every half an hour, we would drift past a small corral of rush fencing, often broken or sagging. Within would be a group of perhaps four or five round straw huts, with conical thatched rooves tied at their peak. The walls of the huts, too, were often thin or damaged. These were called *tukls*, or *goateas*, depending on the region. Nothing stirred within the compounds; and there was just nothing there, save for an occasional yellow moulded plastic jug with a handle and a long spout. This was used to keep water handy for washing, and was found in every house.

The journey ended eventually. I recognised the town from the cylindrical water-tanks that towered above the United Nations compound like Wellsian tripods. There was nothing else; I could see few buildings apart from the odd shack. By the time I had realised where we were, the bus was well past the bus-station—itself a series of broken-down shacks in the plain.

"Showak!" I gurgled.

"Showak!" cried my neighbour, a clerkly figure in razor-crease slacks and shirt, waking suddenly from the deep sleep in which he had been for the previous eight hours.

"Showak! Showak!" yelled everybody, snapping their fingers and stamping their feet to attract the attention of the driver, who, they realised, had forgotten to stop for me. Now he did so, with reluctance, a kilometre or so beyond the bus-station. The riding boy helped me to take my suitcase from the locker in the vehicle's side. I did not tip him—it was not the local custom—but thanked him; he grunted and climbed aboard again, and the blue bus pulled away, and out of my life forever.

I looked around me. There was no traffic whatsoever. Nothing stirred. The landscape was not so flat as it had been earlier, but it was still plain, and for the most part featureless. I could see the bus-station in the distance, and wondered if I could walk to it with my luggage in the sun that beat down on the parched earth. There was no sound. It was peaceful, as it must be for a chicken when it is finally in the oven.

Far away, a white shape detached itself from the bus-station. It came slowly towards me as I watched, standing in the dust beside the empty road. It did not speed up but approached in third gear, the whining of the transmission coming clearly to me through the emptiness. It was a pick-up truck. I wondered if I had arrived, by mistake, in a small Texan town; and whether the driver wore a stetson.

He wore no stetson, but looked thoroughly evil. He was a driver for a Government workshop in the town. He was also, it was said, a part-time secret policeman and was rumoured to carry a gun in his glovebox. I never confirmed this, but he was certainly strangely wealthy, with a penchant for European three-piece suits that he wore on cold winter mornings—the only time when they did not boil him to death. But he was always kind to me.

I digress. I knew nothing, then, of this; nothing indeed about anything much. It was three in the afternoon of Saturday, November 14, 1987. It was 110 deg F in the shade. There was no shade. There was nothing much of anything. I could see no town.

"Oh, my God," I muttered. "Am I spending two years *here*?"

*

Had I looked carefully when I climbed into the pick-up's cab that blazing day, I should have seen a slight hollow in the ground, four or five kilometres away towards the cleft made by the Atbara river. Therein lay the town of 15,000 that was Showak, a word that meant either yearning, or a fork. No-one seemed quite sure which.

It was the tree-shaded compound in which I lived that was the saving grace. Built at the top of a slight rise, it consisted of four *tukls* that had been built of brick, instead of the rush construction normally used. This was not uncommon; if someone could afford to build of brick, they did so, and sealed it down afterwards with a mixture made of donkey-dung. The rooves were thatched. Our *tukls* were oblong rather than round, and had originally been divided into two, giving eight rather cramped little homes. The decline in the number of volunteers since the 1985 Horn of Africa famine had made it possible to knock them all into one, although mine retained a partial divide, so that there were two rooms. It was just the right size for me, cool, dim, with concrete floors that were easily swept clean of the dust that deposited itself on every surface. Some plywood furniture, crude but adequate, completed the picture, along with an enormous concrete slab of a bed built by my predecessor; at first, this had been hollow, but had been filled in, as the roof was never quite watertight and he had found that the mattress was always damp in the rainy season, the water collecting in the concrete depression. What was now left was a sort of platform with ample room for three. Over this, he had rigged a mosquito-net, made from two single ones; I kept this, and in the night, when the room was lit by a single low-watt lightbulb, the effect was that of a translucent tent into which one could slip and dream.

Sometimes a hedgehog came in the evenings to bask in the pool of light outside the door; once, it got into my room at midnight. I was puzzled by a scuffling, snuffling sound, and turned on the light. Then I looked under the plywood cupboard, and saw the hedgehog, rolled tightly into a ball. I fished it out as gently as I could and deposited it outside; it had been looking for the exit.

This was not the only nocturnal noise. The chickens could fly well enough to reach my roof, and spent many happy hours nesting in the thatch. Any droppings were deflected by the mosquito-net, and the rustling in the straw above became almost a comfort. I was less happy with the dogs. Every house had a guard-dog, and at night they ran wild, barking incessantly, so that towards the end of my time there I took to going out in the early hours and lobbing stones, not to hit or hurt them, but to drive them away.

Dogs were not the only animals to intrude. The compound was surrounded by a scrappy hedge of mesquite, a tough, wiry bush that thrives in desert lands. It ran round the outside of a rush wall that was constantly falling down or being split or ruptured, a process assisted by the goats, who have a liking for mesquite; a goat will eat anything. In the day, when Hamid, the guard, was absent and the steel-and-mesh gates at the entrance to the compound were left open, goats would come into it in twos and threes until chased out with much waving of arms and cursing.

There were other uninvited guests. Donkeys were frequent intruders, wandering up the driveway past the car and, unseen, round the back of my neighbour Ian's *tukl*. In truth they did no harm, but out of habit we drove them out too; not difficult, for they are surprisingly timorous and a war-whoop or two would send them cantering, shocked, little spurts of dust shooting from their hooves as they clattered on the baked-earth surface of the drive.

They were less stubborn than the sheep which came in one day, looking for good grazing. Sheep do not roam freely in Sudan; this one must have detached itself from its flock on the way through town, either while being taken to market or driven across the Atbara River in search of richer pastures. I found it chomping happily near Hamid's string bed one clear blue afternoon in winter, and it was quite placid until I tried to shoo it out. Then it rebelled. A stupid, trusting creature with shaggy brown coat and long ears and tail; as I tried to push its rump it stood its ground, and I felt rather a fool, shoving as hard as I could while it turned and looked at me, betrayal and reproach in its big, liquid, dark-brown eyes.

We did have one pet I would have been pleased to see the back of. Bernadette the turkey liked to crap in the shower. And when not harassing the six or seven chickens who also lived in the compound, she would pick and peck her way towards the *rakuba*, a wide canopy of woven rush which provided shade; there, she would find an iron chair that was occupied, and peck at any flesh that was exposed through the gaps between the slats of the upright. Often after I returned from work at 2.30 I would slump into one of the white-painted seats with a glass of tea, only to feel Bernadette's beak upon my buttocks.

When darkness fell, Bernadette always retreated to the top of a six-foot-high wall of woven rush that bordered the chicken-run. She perched on top and went peacefully to sleep; the chickens flew one by one to join her and I watched them rest peacefully, the electric light outside the latrine shining through their feathers so that they seemed incandescent in the hot, velvet night. By now Hamid, the *gafir*, or guard, would have arrived, and said his prayers for sundown; a series of mutters were delivered softly towards Mecca as he knelt on the ground, having completed his ritual washing. His sword hung on the wall of my *tukl*, ready to repel invaders. When he had fnished I sometimes brought him tea, strong and sweet, served in a glass, without milk; then he settled down on his bed, which was made of string woven in a fine pattern across a wooden frame, cool in the heat as it let the breeze, such as it was, blow against your skin through the gaps in its skein.

*

Besides Hamid, there was Miriam. If she was not in the compound, then one of her children would be. Ian and I paid her S60 a month each to do our washing-up, washing and ironing. Later, when two new volunteers, Wayne and Simon, arrived, they paid her the same amount. A princely £20 a month to support a family. "We're exploiting her," Ian would say in one mood; then, in another, he would remember that his own boss paid less than half that to the woman who looked after his own household. Probably Miriam did do better than most, but she was desperately poor.

She was about 27, and lived in a *tukl* across the yard behind our compound with her children, Ahmed, Awadea and Noora, aged nine, eight and six; a new baby arrived in February 1988. I only met her husband once; he was rather older, and very quiet. They joined us for tea one evening, but he said little. Not long afterwards, he divorced her.

I doubt if it made much difference to Miriam. He already spent most of his time in the city of Gedaref, 60 kilometres away, with the other of his two wives. In Islam, a man may divorce at will, provided he has witnesses; a woman has little say in the matter. But he is not supposed to acquire a further wife if he cannot already meet his obligations to those he has, and must treat them all equally. Neither does he rid himself of this obligation on divorce. So Miriam went to a *Shari'a* court and took her husband to the cleaners, much to our delight.

Of all her children, I suppose I got on with Ahmed the best, perhaps because he was the oldest and easiest to communicate with, despite his painful shyness. One day, as the rains were beginning during my first summer, I went round the corner of the chicken-run to go to the latrine and saw Ahmed, immobile, crouching on the ground and apparently staring into space. What was odder yet was that Ian and two other fellow-volunteers, Simon and Wayne, were also squatting on their haunches and looking in the same direction.

I moved forward, but Wayne motioned me to stop. Without really knowing why, I crouched on my haunches beside them. Then Ahmed, smiling slightly, scattered breadcrumbs on the ground some way in front of us, stepped back, and waited. So did we.

First one or two, then several birds descended. They were creatures the size of a large sparrow, with handsome yellow breasts that set off their grey feathers. They pecked at the crumbs for a minute or two before Ahmed jerked his hand, and I saw that he was holding the end of a fine wire. The wire ran out across the ground between the breadcrumbs and in several places had been carefully looped, so that when Ahmed pulled it with the right amount of force the loops closed up and caught one of the birds around the leg. Like a fisherman, Ahmed reeled it towards him. He neatly broke the bird's wings and it was laid, disabled, on the ground behind another, also unable to fly. It looked cruel, but I doubt if Ahmed thought of it that way; almost certainly they were destined for the pot.

That was in July 1988. The rains were gathering strength, and within a month the whole of Eastern Sudan was in the grip of a malaria epidemic that would kill ten thousand before it was done. In August it took Ahmed without warning. As soon as he felt unwell, Miriam took him to the local hospital. They discharged him the next morning, saying he would be fine. He sickened further the following day and returned to the hospital, where he died in the night.

I was away in Khartoum on business, and did not discover what had happened until I returned after a long absence, in October. Miriam had little to say about it, but looked older. I gave her a photograph I had taken of Ahmed with the birds he had trapped, and she seemed pleased. But she never mentioned Ahmed again. Later I heard that there had been another, much older, child that had died a few years earlier. Child mortality in Sudan was high, and I suppose she saw nothing unusual in her loss.

*

I had my own problems with malaria. One night in Khartoum, a few days after my arrival, I had enjoyed an illicit drinking session on Ethiopian cognac with friends on the roof of their flat; during the evening I was badly bitten on the forearms, but thought little of it at the time. I got malaria, and sometimes wonder if being exposed at that early stage caused the bouts I had later, for most Europeans didn't suffer that badly.

The disease struck early on my third day in Showak. I awoke at 5.30, feeling slightly unwell; half an hour later I felt suddenly sick and rushed for the latrine, but failed to get there in time and threw up all over the floor of my *tukl* instead. The suddenness of it shocked me. I took the emergency dose of six chloroquine tablets, then went to bed again and slept for 12 hours. When I woke up again, I felt much better. But it would be about 10 days before I really felt normal.

The attack left me weak; I also felt rather isolated. And hungry. I had hardly had time to get into the rhythm of shopping for food as it is done in Sudan, and anyway the souk was a mile or two away; too far to walk after malaria in a temperature of 110 deg F in the shade (and there was no shade on the way to the souk). I wasn't yet confident enough to ride the unreliable motorbikes we had in the compound.

Not without sympathy, Ian, who rarely cooked, took me to the souk in the evening in the white Toyota pick-up truck that he used for work. This had an instrument panel like a jumbo jet's, and a large pair of *dik-dik* (oryx) horns lashed to the grille. This journey to the souk in the evenings became a pattern. At six Hamid would arrive—a little earlier if he planned to water the trees; then he would say his prayers. When he was done, we would wedge back the gates and set off, the last light dying in the sky, our faces bathed in the surreal glow of the instrument panel, which included a turn-and-bank indicator with a neat little graphic of a car tilting alarmingly. We would bump and sway at 15-20 miles per hour past the concrete blocks of the next compound and onto the football field where the children of the district had just finished their afternoon game; then enter a long, narrow dust road, just wide enough for two cars to pass, although if a souk-truck came the other way you quickly ran the wheels up the verge.

Just over halfway to the souk, we arrived at Beshir's. A Pepsi at Beshir's shop was part of the evening ritual. Everyone drank Pepsi in Sudan if they could afford it, Coca-Cola having pulled out after a row about the repatriation of profits.

Beshir's shop was typical of the Sudanese store, a narrow shop-front across the width of the building, entirely spanned by the counter, and covered during the day by lurid zinc shutters that stuck out into the street and deflected the sun. On the counter stood plastic bowls of dried, flaked fruit, in a series of muted colours; there were also bowls of sugar and salt. An ancient set of brass scales stood beside them, and each purchase was carefully measured with a series of weights—kilo, half-kilo and *rottl*, which was about a kilo. The commodity requested would be poured off the measuring-tray and down a funnel of newspaper which, shaped like a cone, would be neatly closed off at the top so as to make an easy-to-carry vessel. Beshir himself, slim and young—not more than 25—and usually smiling, with a thin pencil moustache and white *djellabiya*, would be laughing and joshing as he rolled up the newspaper. Sudan imported cast-off newspapers for wrapping goods. One day, one might have one's sugar or *karkadee* wrapped in the *South China Morning Post*; the next, in the *Straits Times*. Dutch, Danish and Indonesian newspapers were also common. Beshir would lay down the newspaper, ready to be rolled; and while he stacked his brass weights on the scales, one could read the television schedules for Copenhagen, or the racing programme for Nairobi or Hong Kong while standing in front of a tiny shop in a small town less than 100 miles from the mountains that rise out of the Middle Eastern plain to the fabled lands of the Queen of Sheba.

If one demanded a Pepsi, Beshir would hold out a bottle by its neck, the glass glistening with condensation from the refrigerator, so that Ian or I could lay a hand on it, test its coldness, and nod our approval. "No *Peps*," Beshir would say gloomily if the electricity had been off, and he thought the Pepsi wasn't cool enough to sell. That often happened that autumn and winter, and we would instead load our pockets with *bazooka*—cheap chewing-gum from God knew where—and slope off to the souk, feeling vaguely cheated. But more often, everyone saw each other at Beshir's; a familiar face would appear, ambling slowly into the pool of light cast by the fluorescent strip across the top of the shop; or a small motorcycle would sweep into the glow, its rider sitting well back, *djellabiya* streaming in the wind; or some schoolgirls would saunter by in pajama-suits and headscarves. Now and then women would float by in their *toabs*, the younger ones drawing our wistful glances.

After the aperitif, it was time for dinner.

The approach to the souk was through a side-street that was completely dark at night. The souk itself, about half a kilometre long and 100 metres wide, burst upon you as you rounded the corner from blackness to see row upon row of fluorescent lights across the tops of shops, restaurants and soft-drinks bars. At seven it was always busy. There were many shops like Beshir's; there was an ironmonger or two selling nuts and bolts and Bulgarian lightbulbs, and a cycle-shop, outside which were rows of small, heavy, old-fashioned Flying Pigeon bikes from China. In the centre of the souk were rows of four-wheel-drive vehicles; old Land-Rovers belonging to local businessmen, new ones from aid agencies, new Land-Cruisers driven by UN personnel and Government officials, and ancient ones belonging to the local traders who flogged them up from Gedaref in the early morning, laden with vegetables and fruit. Sometimes there were souk-trucks, though these usually parked in an impressive phalanx behind the meat-market. There were pale blue Mercedes lorries with the UN crest; they carried food supplies to the refugee settlements in the region. And there were donkeys, apathetic and immobile.

In front of the soft-drinks bars stood the men of the town, out to meet their friends and talk. Women scurried between the little knots of men, laden with heavy bags of shopping, bags of coarse fibre that for some reason often bore the mark of a Romanian cement-factory. Here and there a European drifted along in slacks and sandals, looking for cigarettes. Meanwhile the fluorescent lamps lit the whole souk in a series of shadows and electric glows so that when a large group of men came towards you, the fluorescence shone through their white cotton *djellabiyas*, shilhouetting the body and the baggy pants beneath; and these ghosts walked in clouds of fine dust that filled the air and also caught the light, like snow.

Beside the cars in the centre of the souk there crouched or squatted women with trays of nuts or *taamiya*, small hard balls of fried *ful*-beans that were salty and sharp on the tongue; and curious, plasticky envelopes of field-beans that one squeezed so that the seeds shot out into your mouth, bitter but full of calcium. The women in this and other souks that crouched over their trays of peanuts always looked exhausted and apathetic; it was a job for the very poorest.

We might, on arrival in the souk, decide on a takeaway, and go to one of the many *ful*-stands.

Ful beans resemble kidney-beans and taste similar when eaten on their own, but are a little more bitter. Often spelled *foul*, they are an important part of some Arab cuisines, especially in Egypt. In Sudan they were cooked for hours, and kept warm in large vats that reached a man's waist and were shaped like milk-churns. One asked for however many ladlefuls of *ful* one wanted, and that number was placed in a plastic bowl. Then sesame-oil was poured on them, and they were crushed with the end of a coke-bottle. That, for many people, was all that was eaten, once a day; nothing else. The cost was about 20 pence for two.

In later months, when food ran short, that was sometimes all that was available at any price. In November 1987, however, few people ate *ful* on its own unless they really were quite poor. In our case, it was always a luxury *ful*. The beans and the sesame-oil went into the bowl, and were given a preliminary crushing with the base of the coke-bottle, which was grasped by the neck and worked round and round. Then salad—grated green vegetable and chopped fresh tomatoes—would be scattered on the surface, followed by a fierce local cheese that couldn't be taken on its own, but lent spice to many things. This, too, would be grated vigorously and then powdered all over the *ful*. Sometimes one would ask for an egg. Hard-boiled, it would be peeled on the spot and then grated with equal enthusiasm. Finally a little *kumen* would be sprinkled over the surface, and then the bottle would be grasped by its neck again and pummelled hard into the bowl until everything was reduced almost to a purée. Two loaves of round, flat Showak bread would then be slapped on top.

Unless you'd brought your own bowl with you, the *ful* was poured into a thin plastic bag. It was advisable to use two or three *kiis*, as these bags were called, unless one wanted steaming hot *ful* pouring down into one's crotch on the way home in the car. The *kiis* were sold by small boys who darted around the souk and were onto you with cries of *kiis! kiis!* as soon as you reached the *ful*-stand.

Before pouring the goo into the *kiis* you might have added, not only salt, but a large amount of red pepper, of which the Sudanese used lots. Ethiopians of all groups used lots more. It was an essential source of vitamin A, and shortage of it was what had caused Tigrayans refugees to suffer from poor night vision on their terrible journey across the mountains two years previously.

I liked *ful*, but it could get monotonous, and if we had the money we would go for a sit-down dinner. The Green Valley restaurant, the largest and most fashionable of several in the souk, was a brick building with a shack-like frontage; there was an inside room but we generally ate in the enclosure in front, in the open, where we could watch the world go by and where Ian's many friends could see and join us. The Green Valley was known to Europeans as Al Green's, as all but the a and l of Valley had disappeared from the English version of the sign tacked to the wall.

Al Green's did do *ful*, but not particularly well; you didn't go there for that. Instead we would treat ourselves to a half-chicken (very small, scrawny, but with taste) or *kostaleti*, little cutlets of lamb that were dipped in a secret sauce, different everywhere, and deep-fried. These were excellent. Better still, money permitting, was *chaya*, small lumps of meat braised on stones heated directly by charcoal. Everywhere I saw *chaya* prepared, it was done by a man working on his own, outside the main restaurant. You paid him separately; he had no direct connection with the restaurant. *Chaya* wasn't always available at Al Green's, because the chaya-man was in and out of prison all the time.

The tables were unsteady, flat tin devices. They were shoved together, so that you would often find yourself eating with several other people. "*Fadl*," you would then say. This is a word which has no direct translation in English—it means go on, help yourself, have some of mine. Two people in a doorway will politely *fadl* each other (after you). In a restaurant, it means, share our food; and I don't think I ever sat at a table with a strange Sudanese, even in Khartoum, without hearing this word that English does not have. Often, in the Green Valley, our *ful*-bowl would be replenished by the contents of someone else's, which would then be tossed aside; and they would share some of our *chaya*. It was automatic and pleasant.

I was often ill in Sudan but not usually with stomach-trouble. Customers washed their hands very thoroughly before entering the restaurant, using taps mounted on an old oil-drum and the coarse purple soap provided. In the restaurant, they ate strictly with their right hands (though you could use both hands to break bread). Probably the men who prepared the food were just as scrupulous. My first sight of the restaurant's interior horrified me; the kitchen looked especially dingy. But there was a view that dirt was quite harmless unless it got into your food, and my stomach seemed to agree.

*

Once, when my Arabic teacher in Khartoum, Abdel Moneim, was trying to explain to me what I would find in Sudan, he described an incident before independence, in the Law Department in Khartoum. A British administrator had read details of a case in which the appellant was, in his view, being importunate. He scrawled across the margin: "This reminds me of the case of Oliver Twist!" Some hours later, his Sudanese assistant was found searching the files for the case of Oliver Twist, which he assumed must demonstrate a precedent in law.

Now the boot was on the other foot, with foreigners as bewildered by the Sudanese administration as the Sudanese had ever been by theirs. Over the next two years I was to be offered numerous reasons why my wages were late, or there was no diesel, or we could not obtain advance expenses to travel to Khartoum before Ramadan, or we could not obtain advance expenses to travel to Khartoum after Ramadan, or there was no money to pay my wages. Sudanese colleagues would insist that this was the result of three centuries of corrupt and lazy Turco-Egyptian administration over which the British had presided only briefly. Moneim himself argued that the British had promoted people who would get the job done without asking too many questions—that is to say, efficient, perhaps honest, but lacking in imagination; and that this legacy had come down to modern Sudan. Personally, I thought it was just the heat.

Richard Dowden, Africa correspondent of *The Independent*, once addressed the subject in an engaging piece called *On Carrot Soup in the Bath*. (The title referred to the water filtration in Khartoum's Grand Hotel.) Bureaucracy in Sudan, he explained, was as lousy as everywhere else in Africa, but it did at least come with charm. I will endorse this. Even as the official sat behind his desk explaining (quite sincerely) that something could not be done until there was a Z in the month but would then be no problem, he would be knocking his palm against the spring-loaded, chrome-plated bell that adorned every official desk in the nation, summoning a secretary who would enter, *toab* swirling gracefully in any breeze there might be, with your glass of hot sweet tea spiced with cinammon.

More often than not, one's interminable waits in offices were occasioned by the need for a *warriga*. A *warriga* was any official piece of paper. To obtain a travel permit, a foreigner or a refugee had to collect two or three from local officials or employers, and take these round to be stamped by several different officers at the city police station, 60 km away; at a certain stage these documents had to have a revenue stamp affixed, and a whole cottage industry had grown up to supply these stamps outside Gedaref police station, which demanded but did not supply them. Boys at these stands also supplied tissues, cigarettes and tea to sustain the hopeful traveller.

Neither were travel permits the only *warriga* one needed. Requisitions for diesel at the Commissioner for Refugees office for which I worked had to be signed by the General Project Manager, the chief driver, the head of administration, the head of the workshop and one other whose function I do not remember. All were quite reasonable men, but were hardly likely to be in one place at the same time. Thus it was not uncommon to rejoice in getting a *warriga* signed, only to find that all that had been achieved was to get permission for it to be signed by someone else.

Physically, at least, the Sudanese office was uncluttered. There would be a bare floor, thick walls to keep out the heat, and a high ceiling. There might be a tin cupboard, and there would be plain steel desks, the drawers of which never seemed to run smoothly. There was a plain steel-frame chair with a plastic wove body on seat and back, and around the edges of the offices—always the edges, with geometrical precision—there would be steel-framed easy chairs; low, comfortable, with thick cushions. There would be as many chairs as could be placed with their backs against the wall. In any office, there were normally several people sitting, chatting, drinking tea, reading the paper or, towards midday, simply slumped over with sweat pouring down their cheeks, comatose.

There was rarely, if ever, any paper on the desks. This puzzled me at first, until, always untidy, I left a few papers on my own desk. Paper in Sudan was always foolscap, and unbelievably light. It tore easily. Worse, a slight breeze was enough to send it floating into the centre of the room, and picking it up was felt to be undignified; I never saw any Sudanese official do it himself. Even on still days, the electricity in Showak cut in and out so often that I kept leaving work on my steel desk while it was off, and then coming back in to find that the fan had re-started and documents were scattered all over the room like confetti.

There was little else on the desks. There might be the stainless-steel clockwork bell for summoning the messenger, as they called the office-boy. In Khartoum there might be a telephone as well, but there was no line to Showak (we were linked to the refugee settlements, and to Khartoum and Gedaref, by VHF).

In any case, the telephone was of limited use, as many numbers were unobtainable. It was often easier to ring London from Khartoum than it was to get Omdurman. After a catastrophic flood in 1988, many more lines ceased to function altogether, so that it was common to ask someone for their number and be told gravely that the 'phone hadn't worked "since before the flood". Even before that, an office worker in VSO's London headquarters picked up the handset and dialled the number of the field director's private home in Khartoum, only to be told by the international operator in Sudan that it was unobtainable. Why? she asked. "Well, all numbers beginning with seven are unobtainable, of course," replied the operator.

"Of course," replied the worker, and rang off, feeling rather foolish.

*

All this could leave you in need of a drink.

Booze was not a problem in Sudan at that time. It had been outlawed four years earlier and the legal supplies poured away. However, across the border in Eritrea there was the Melotti brewery and distillery, founded by the Italians in 1939. This was busier than ever, despite the Eritrean war of independence that was raging around it. In 1987 camel-load after camel-load streamed across an unguardable border into Sudan, where the price rose depending on one's distance from the frontier. In Khartoum it was more expensive; the supplies had to run the gauntlet of the police roadblocks that dotted the main roads to the capital, so that it cost about S120, around £20 ($30), for a bottle of Asmara or Baro's Ethiopian gin. A small premium was charged for Melotti, which was better. In Showak, we paid about S90. Excellent and very strong Melotti beer in small bottles was sometimes seen, and Melotti also made *zabeeb*, a strong ouzo. For the homesick there was Ethiopian cognac. I rather enjoyed that, but most Europeans thought of it as industrial alcohol. For highly-paid expatriates in Khartoum, who did not like Ethiopian spirits, there were supplies of Johnnie Walker and Red Label and the odd crate of Carlsberg. These all dribbled through cracks in the diplomatic bag. Personally, I always thought that the Ethiopian distilleries did us well; the gin was especially enjoyable when mixed with strong lime juice that we made in the blender.

When cash was short (it usually was in our compound), we resorted to the local alternatives. The usual social drink for rural Sudanese, and for many others in the provinces, was a thick, heavy beer called *marissa*. This was probably rare in Khartoum. Brewed from wheat, it was greenish and had bits floating in it which tended to distract you from the full, soft, slightly sweet flavour. At least one guide-book on Sudan had praised *marissa* for its nutritional value, pointing out that farm-labourers sometimes drank it before starting work in the fields: "A nourishing way to begin the day," it said, with slightly smug approval.

Marissa was Sudanese, but the Ethiopians and Eritreans had an equivalent. This was *tej*. In the highlands of Ethiopia, it is brewed from honey, and at its best it is clear, sweet and potent. Lacking honey, the refugees in the settlements of Eastern Sudan used to brew it from dates, but it was still enjoyable. Supplies reached us from the *tej*-houses in the big refugee camps such as Safawa, a couple of hours' drive along the dirt road to the Ethiopian border. It would be brought back in five-gallon cans and held against a rainy day.

If one fancied something a little harder, there was always *aragi*. This was the indigenous Sudanese spirit, distilled from dates. This could be dangerous (and *tej* and *marissa* were notorious for spreading hepatitis). But *aragi* was at least cheap and plentiful. And it really was strong.

Sources varied. My favourite came from a house some way away; and once Ian took us to a compound of south Sudanese people, where they sold us a gin-bottle-full, measured out in the usual Pepsi-bottle quantities. This then had a twist of paper put in the top to stop the fluid from slopping. I remember that African compound for the foul-tempered mongrel dog that guarded us, snarling, while a young woman filled the bottle. We crouched on the ground and gazed back, and it never quite had the nerve to spring.

Sometimes we mixed two gin-bottles'-worth of *aragi* with the juice of *karkadee* and lime and made a pleasant punch— though this masked the strength of the alcohol, sometimes to very ill effect.

But although *aragi* was relatively cheap, it still cost about $20 for a full gin-bottle. The other answer was homebrew. I was no expert at this, but did my bit on a journey to Khartoum by begging a consignment of equipment off a departing expatriate and bringing it home to Showak, complete with a five-gallon jerry. This nearly misfired. The expat had been making some awful brew of his own in the jerry; I brought it back across Khartoum from his flat in a taxi, but as the top was clearly designed for brewing purposes, I put it in a bag, along with the various bungs and tubes we would also need. I didn't realise that the jerry hadn't been properly washed. I had had trouble finding a taxi that afternoon; when one did stop, the driver, pulling away, sniffed and glanced at the jerry and asked if it had contained *aragi*.

God forbid, I replied hastily. I had been using it for petrol.

Apparently satisfied, he drove on for 20 yards before seeing a police officer standing on the corner. To my horror, he pulled in and picked the officer up.

"My brother," he explained pleasantly. "Do you mind? I can give him a lift on to Omdurman after we drop you."

"No, of course not," I said quickly.

Another 20 yards or so later the police officer said to his brother, "Is that *aragi* I smell?"

"He says it's petrol," said the taxi-driver, a note of doubt creeping into his voice.

"Oh," replied the officer, and, after an interval, "Good."

I got the taxi to drop me some way from the rest-house, and fled.

*

In late May, it became hotter and hotter until one could scarcely breathe. Normally, the lack of humidity made the extreme heat tolerable, but as the rains approached, it did become humid. Worse still, there were the *haboobs*, or dust clouds. These were harbingers of a storm. As the season wore on they were sometimes accompanied by a clap of thunder, and finally a few drops of water. Then, in early June, it started raining in earnest.

I remember one such storm, the first proper one of 1989, a few months before I left the country. The sky was overcast from lunchtime onwards; at half-past three the dust-storm started, and was so fierce that normally one would have taken shelter in the house. But I sensed that this one would be different, and stayed outside to watch. After 20 minutes the dust died down suddenly, and almost immediately I heard a strange, rustling sound like a curtain being dragged along the ground towards us. It was the rain, and it swept across the compound, beating the last dust from the air.

It is a cliché but a true one that tropical rain comes in jets, not the dribs, drabs and drizzle of the English variety. In half a minute, the compound was awash. First I saw dark dots appear on the dusty ground, then they joined up, and finally the earth disappeared altogether beneath the weight of water as yet more came in perfect rods that appeared to be boring holes in the earth. Then it was finished; the dust was damped down and cleansed from the air, and black clouds split to reveal, first perfect white ones, then a deep blue such as I had not seen for days. The water made the straw rooves of the *tukls* glitter in the new sunlight against a skyscape of black and iron-grey, alternating with patches of blue and white. And that day, as sometimes happened, there was a fine rainbow.

Four in the afternoon was the time to expect such storms. Sometimes there was another deluge at eight, and there might be one or two more in the night. The evening storms would lower the temperature incredibly quickly, and I once watched in disbelief as the thermometer in my room dipped from 40 to 200C in just 15 minutes. The impact of this after a day of extreme heat and dust-storms may be imagined.

The thunder and lightning that accompanied these storms were equally spectacular. One night, I opened my door at about 8.30 to watch; at that moment there was a thunderbolt that made my ears pop and, simultaneously, I saw three great forks travel from heaven to earth. In that instant, the town power supply failed, plunging us into darkness until the morning.

Any inconvenience cause by the rains was, for me at least, compensated for by the change in the landscape. It hardly ever rained in Khartoum, but on my way back to Showak in July after a work trip, I realised that something fantastic had happened as soon as we left the Gezira. Out of the deep brown earth, itself a change from the baked dry dust, rose blades of green that seemed to have been sown in drills like a farmer's at home; there was always space between them through which the ground could be seen. Yet those blades were a luminous green, for when there is sun as there is in Sudan, a little rain will make everything grow with a vengeance. In the wood between Gedaref and Showak, the leaves were reappearing on the trees; I felt it was spring although the word *khareej*, for the season that begins on June 15, is more usually translated as autumn.

The sky was better still. Where there had been glaring pale blue, almost white at midday, there was now a variegated patchwork of black, grey, white and strong, bright blue; a journey from Showak to the Shagarab refugee camp in late July felt more to me like a trip across Norfolk, the light bouncing this way and that on patches of water and wet earth and cloud, the great plains alive with grass and the patterns in the sky constantly changing as the wind freshened. And it was cool; sometimes you could walk about in the open quite normally at midday.

Indeed, in the night, I found myself using a blanket, something which in winter was only needed for four or five weeks around Christmas.

But the rains had their drawbacks. The most obvious was that travel off the one tarmac road became nearly impossible for two days in three. There would also be a plague of insects; in the dry season, the great camel-spiders were a hazard and so, now and then, were the scorpions, but one watched one's step at night, kept the mosquito-net down during the day and need otherwise not worry. In the rains, it was different; amongst the seasonal hazards, there were the blister-beetles.

These little bastards were round, jet-black and perhaps half the size of a man's fingernail. They crept up your trouser-leg. When one felt something moving and automatically brushed it away, it in its fright discharged urine that stung the skin, and would continue to do so for some days if you were unlucky. In extreme cases, they could cause painful injury, and scarring; a friend of Ian's had several blister-beetles crawl up his *djellabiya* one afternoon as he slept, and when he awoke they peed on him. The scars covered much of his chest. There were also the stink-beetles, which were about the same size but narrower. Instead of discharging poisonous urine, the stink-beetle released a pungent marker-scent. And the mosquitoes, ever-present even in the dry season, multiplied horribly.

*

On the last night of June 1989 several of us gathered over a bowl of punch in the compound. The base for this punch was industrial *aragi*, the taste disguised by *karkadee* with lashings of sugar. It was Thursday night; no-one was working on Friday, that being the Moslem sabbath. It rained heavily. There was much thunder and lightning, and we took shelter in Simon's *tukl*. The dog joined us—an unpopular move, as she stank horribly. At about nine, the power went off. This was unusual; it had done so far less that year.

At about midnight I decided that I had had enough, and dashed through the heavy rods of rain to my own *tukl*, where I balanced my torch on a shelf and got ready for bed. As often happened during the rains, it was cool. I had a good night's sleep.

I awoke on the morning of July 1 to find the sun shining cleanly; it was hot, of course, but there was a freshness, as the rain in the night had evaporated and cooled the air somewhat. Ian was was just outside my *tukl*, working on one of the motorbikes.

"Did you hear, there's been a coup or something," he grunted.

"Oh," I said. Then: "Would you like some tea?"

Friends in Khartoum were closer to events. As one, an Englishman, wrote:

I had gone to bed, as usual, in the front yard, completely sober, and about three in the morning was woken by a tremendous rumbling sound... I attempted to get up... but was...restrained by my mosquito-net in which, in my haste, I got tangled up (James Bond never used a mosquito-net and now I know why). I got to the wall in time to see a British-made Ferret scout car bringing up the rear. It did cross my mind that it might be a coup but it seemed a bit of a cliché to be doing it that way so I put it down to some Sudanese tank commander... going to visit his relatives...

He went back to sleep.

The coup brought my work to an end, and I left Sudan some weeks later.

At the time I was saddened. I had finally thrown off recurring malaria about six months earlier, and my work had eventually gone well; in fact, I had thought of extending my post. But although Sudan inspired me, it also wore me out. I was down to about eight and a quarter stone (about 62 kilos), and was so thin that I had recently leaned into the boot of a car to retrieve some papers, and had bruised a rib on the spare wheel. Moreover the coup brought chaos; in their zeal to destroy the black market, the new rulers of the Eastern Region insisted that everything be sold at its official price, which was often unrealistically low. Many commodities simply disappeared, and we were reduced to eating stews of okra alone or, on one or two occasions, fried locusts (they were not so bad; rather crunchy).

Two weeks after the coup I hitched a lift over to the United Nations compound on some business or other. On the way back, we followed the main road into the town centre through the red-light district. The road there was blocked by a large green lorry, surrounded by troops. Women were being herded out of the *tukls* opposite and onto the back of the lorry, carrying what possessions they had; occasionally a cassette-player, or a bundle or two. They seemed to enter the lorry without fuss, but were heavily guarded.

I mentioned this to a Sudanese colleague in the office when we got back. He said he doubted if the women would come to any harm. "Perhaps the army is having a party," he said with a grin. Then the grin was replaced by a frown.

"You know what all this means for us," he said quietly.

"What?"

"We will have 20 years of this before we try democracy again," he said. "Another 20 bloody years."

I nodded. In fact, 24 years later, democracy has still not returned to Sudan.

I left not long afterwards.

*

I last saw Showak a quarter of a century ago. I have been busy, and have not often looked back. When I have, it is not malaria I have remembered, or struggles with food or bureaucracy, or even the heat. Rather, I have thought of the afternoon, when the sky turned to blue from the merciless white of midday, and the heat ceased to oppress you but became instead a velvet cloak, draped across your shoulders.

One day, a fortnight or so after I first arrived, I was sitting in a garden chair outside the kitchen, recovering at last from the malaria that had floored me on my second morning in the town. I had so far mostly seen only the inside of our compound, and, at night, the souk. My fellow-volunteer Ian kindly offered to drive me to the river in his Government pick-up. Two miles from us, on the other side of the town centre, the river went under various names; on the world atlas it is called the River Atbara, but I often heard the name Settit mentioned. It rose in Ethiopia and wound its way across Eastern Sudan to join the Nile at the city of Atbara itself, many hundreds of miles away to the north of Khartoum.

We left the compound at a quarter to five. The afternoon was softening, and the sky was turning a darker blue. Beshir hadn't yet reopened after the afternoon siesta. People were just beginning to stir after their sleep. The sun, starting to slant, slowly turned the dust surface of the road from light grey to brown, and the grubby bricks of the *hosh* walls took on a new life. We rattled and bumped past the tree at the entrance to the souk, where men sometimes sold fish—Nile carp, or tilapia; and turned right through a similar street, instead of going left into the souk itself. The street narrowed, then opened out into a wasteland, after which the houses gave way to huts. We picked our way between them, the track very narrow now, and the flanks of the Land-Cruiser almost scratching the mesquite hedges; and then started to go down, down, a steep hill with switchbacks and troughs in which four-wheel-drive was needed. The huts gave way to poorer ones, and finally to hovels of cardboard, some with a slab of corrugated iron to deflect the sun. There were one or two goats; men and women lay on string beds in front of the hovels; and then they, too, were gone and we were heading down yet more steeply, towards a wide, flat valley in which the blue ribbon of the Atbara glittered in the distance. Beyond it, the bank rose just as steeply towards the refugee camp of Abuda, which was over the horizon; the road twisted its way up through a cleft. Of dirt, deeply rutted, and just wide enough to accommodate a Bedford truck, this track was shown on the Michelin map of north-east Africa as an international highway. It was.

On our own side was a beach of packed mud, perfectly flat, and we bounced down to this and levelled out towards the water's edge. The river was falling, for the rains were well over. It was only four hundred yards wide, and was not too deep to ford. In the shallows near the beach stood two souk-trucks and a pair of small Hilux pickups. The royal blue of the souk-truck's cabs gleamed richly in the lowering sun as boys, stripped to the waist, moved around them with rags to remove the dust of the day. Meanwhile the drivers of the Hiluxes were disconnecting their fanbelts, ready to plunge across the river to Abuda.

It was a ford, but when I saw a truck go across from our side, I noticed that he did not go direct; instead, he zigzagged, guided by two men in long shorts and, for some reason, woollen skull-caps, who took a few pounds from the driver for providing this service. They were descendants of West Africans who had stopped on the way back from the Haj, instead of braving the return crossing of the desert. The Sudanese knew them generically as Hausas, and many will have spoken that language. Guiding cars across the ford was just one of the odd jobs that the Hausas did. It was best to trust them, for at least one UN official attempted to cross without their guidance and dumped his Land-Cruiser nose-first in an enormous underwater pothole. It took a couple of camels to haul him out.

On the bank some yards down I saw, to my surprise, an old-fashioned boat—large, some 40-50 feet, complete with a separate wheelhouse. It was high and dry. I said to Ian that this was a bit like having the Queen Mary to take you across the Thames but he replied that this was not so; when the wet season began across the border in Eritrea, even that big boat would have to cross with care. And when the river was really flowing strongly, it wouldn't be able to cross at all.

For now, however, the river flowed gently. Behind us, where the dunes came down to the beach, there were patches of violent green; these were irrigated by single-cylinder Lister diesels whose chugging could just be heard in the stillness of the evening. These patches were the work of men who had found employment building the trunk road when it came through to Kassala in 1979. They had sunk their earnings into a plot by the river and a Lister to make their vegetables grow. It was a good business.

The sky had now deepened further in colour, and the water with it. From the east bank came a man on a camel. The camel stepped cautiously into the water; behind it, it dragged an enormous clump of brushwood, like several bushes. It was for heat and fuel, but I later learned that illicit liquor also crossed the border in these branches. On the camel was a man of the

Hadendowa border tribe, carrying a whip. He knew the way and needed no Hausa to guide him. The camel's legs broke the surface of the water and sent little droplets into the light; the current, such as it was, tugged at the dun fur, and the water rose in rounded crests around the legs. The beast seemed to take a thousand years to reach us, but was unworried about this, as was its rider. His face was impassive, his whip unused in his hand. He greeted the truck-cleaners quietly as the camel stepped onto the bank, and then he passed us, the camel rolling to port and starboard with a pitch that must have been as familiar before the coming of Islam as it was to us. We could see man and camel for 10 or 15 minutes afterwards, slowly climbing the winding track to the town.

On another afternoon, months later, I was sitting in one of the cushioned garden chairs, outside the kitchen. Once again, it was about five. Another volunteer was with me, and we were leaning back gazing at the sky. Its colour, during the day, had as usual been bleached almost white but had now become vibrantly blue and had a transparent air to it, as if you could look straight through to Heaven.

There were snowy egrets in the town, nesting in the neem-trees in the souk. Every now and then something would startle them and they would scatter into the sky above the Green Valley, wheeling and darting. Today, there were eight or nine of them flying in neat formation, line-abreast, then wheeling around so that the line formed a shallow half-oval, then partly straightening, so that they were like a flying question-mark. They held this shape, and soared higher and higher; we could see them clearly for perhaps a quarter of an hour, and because we knew they were there we could track them for longer, higher and higher, clean white birds against a sky as blue and translucent as layered lacquer. To the end of my life, I will always look forward to that time on a summer's day when the afternoon mellows, and the sky comes slowly to life between full day and sunset.

Easter in Quito

At Christmas 1990 I had to leave my job in London; it seemed best to treat this as an opportunity, so I went to South America. It was not hard to get a ticket, for it was the winter of the first Gulf War. I went to the Avianca office in Linen Yard. A beautiful girl with dark-blonde hair and olive skin took calls in the corner. A few posters of South America brightened the rather bare room. I was the only customer. A friendly Colombian sold me a ticket for half the price I had been quoted elsewhere, then pressed a thick paperback into my hands. "This is our guide. I do hope you find it useful," he said. I flicked it open. I saw a picture of a great cathedral of shining marble. Its twin towers soared against black clouds lit by sunlight, and a rainbow arced across the dark green mountains behind. I shook his hand warmly and strode off down the corridor, clutching the ticket and the guide.

Late in January I arrived at Gatwick Airport for the first leg, to Paris. I had a green canvas bag. In it were two changes of clothes, a spare pair of shoes, two guidebooks, a very cheap personal cassette paper, a tape of Mozart's C Minor and Coronation Masses and a small copy of the *Rubaiyat of Omar Khayaam,* given to me by my editor when I left to work in Africa three years earlier. I stood at the check-in with my green canvas bag, wearing an old tweed sports-jacket and rather baggy jeans and an open-neck shirt and an old pullover. I would return when my money ran out. The British airline that took me to Paris ran out of money before I did and collapsed before I returned.

A few hours later I sat with 20 or so others in a bleak turret in Charles de Gaulle, watching the Avianca plane lumber slowly to the gate like a huge basking-shark. Joining a handful of passengers who had come from Frankfurt, we stopped briefly at Madrid, then soared over the snowy Guadarrama and crossed Andalucia. I looked out of the window and saw the lights of Malaga shining in the calm waters of the black winter sea.

*

We followed the path of Columbus, aiming for the same landfall, Hispaniola. It is a dark journey – you chase the sunset. There was little to see out of the window, and I settled down with a good Rioja, which dissolved Avianca's steak. There had been a series of incidents on the region's airlines at that time. A friend, contemplating the same journey, also rang a South American airline. "I am thinking of travelling to South America," she said, "but I am told that your planes keep falling out of the sky. Is this correct?" "Oh, no, that only happens on internal flights, Madam," said the voice at the other end. Avianca seemed fine; it was, at least, an excellent airline on which to get pissed, and it always arrived promptly although by the time it landed, I rarely cared.

A sea of seatbacks stretched before me, one in 50 occupied. One of the few passengers was an Englishman of perhaps 20, on his way to spend six months with an uncle in Chile. We talked quietly for an hour or two and then I returned to my seat and stretched myself out on a row of three and closed my eyes. Then great marble towers reared against black but sunlit clouds, and I fell into a light sleep.

When I awoke we were an hour or so from landfall. I had a wash and took some coffee from the galley at the rear. Outside it was still dark, but after a few minutes I realized that the clouds were tinted here and there with light blue; later, warmer tones of peach and orange started to appear behind us, and to come closer. Around me the few other passengers stretched and rubbed their faces and farted and wandered to the toilets with towels and toothbrushes. We were losing height. Dawn was here now. The sea came much closer, a calm surface with small waves, light green-blue; as it rose to meet us, it was first emerald, then transparent, the sea bed clearly visible below as the nose pitched up and the tail fell back and we prepared for Santo Domingo. The runway ended a few feet above the water. The aircraft was a huge shadow on the surface, like a vast bird of prey; then, in the path of Columbus, we swooped down on the New World and the undercarriage thumped out, dark against the luminous sea, like claws.

The airport wasn't awake yet. We taxied through a series of curves, each marked by an armed man lying peaceably on a string bed, seemingly unaware of the Boeing 747 screaming past their heads.

The young Englishman unclipped his belt and came and stood beside me.

"There's nothing here," he said.

There wasn't then. There must be now; the Dominican Republic has become a popular tourist destination. That morning, however, we approached a low building surrounded by very old aircraft, a few Dakotas and their Czech-built equivalent; they must all have been 30 or 40 years old, but what caught my eye were eight or nine huge piston-engine aircraft that towered above the little terminal. Several had arched backs and triple fins and vast cowlings; postwar Lockheeds. Others, even bigger, with round noses like cigar-tubes, were Stratocruisers, evolved from the Superfortress that bombed Japan.

Our engines had stopped now and we sat by the window in a sticky tropical silence. There was a sense of peace after the long hours in the air.

"It's a museum," said the Englishman.

"So it is. I wonder when one of those last flew," I said.

Then I heard a dull bass roar which swelled, and caused the plane to tremble a little. A giant shadow swooped across us and turned and banked and slid smoothly onto the runway; a triple-finned Lockheed Constellation in the white and light green Dominican livery, morning sunlight flashing off its giant propellers. It was magnificent. I spent a happy hour or so gazing at the flying fossils.

We crossed the short stretch of Caribbean to South America. "Look, look. Your country. Colombia," the woman behind me kept repeating to the lively young child who kept squirming free of her arms. The woman was in late middle age and looked nothing like the child. I wondered if she might be a nanny or a grandmother. Perhaps she was snatching the child from his wicked English mother and taking him to the safety of his wealthy father's ranch, where he would learn to ride horses and shoot guns and would one day hear about his mother's evil ways, her lipstick and her socialism.

Colombia, glimpsed now and then in gaps between clean white cloud, was uniformly mountainous and green. Once we passed across a high peak with a lake in the bowl of its summit. There seemed scarcely to be a road, or a town. The sun bounced off the top of the cloud and filled the cabin with light, so much light that it hurt the eyes. For a few minutes the cloud fell away, revealing yet more high forested mountains. Then, as the cloud built up again below us, there was a perfect aureole of orange and yellow that chased us for some time. They say that aureoles are harbingers of change and luck.

At Bogotá I strode up the corridor from the plane, glad to stretch my legs after 20 hours travelling. I shook hands with the young Englishman, who was boarding another plane straight away for the long journey to Santiago. Before long I left myself. I had only another hour or two to go. I felt strangely lightheaded after the long journey. I exchanged courtesies with a well-dressed elderly businessman in the seat next to me, but my Spanish was very limited then, and after a while we gave up and I stared out of the window instead. The mountains were getting higher.

We crossed a ridge so high that it was only just below us. Then we lost height rapidly, turning in a tight spiral. The mountains disappeared above us; a deep valley spun below as we turned and turned, the ground half-hidden by cloud that thinned to reveal a steep hill rising through the vapour on the valley floor. The hill was crowned by a mighty grey-white statue of the Virgin, arms outstretched, and then a city appeared at her feet as if she had conjured it into being.

*

One day the previous autumn I had been alone in the office with a colleague who was an enthusiastic traveller. Prior to joining the company she had been on the road for some months in India and the Far East. Besides being a colleague, she was (and still is) a friend, and knew I was about to be fired.

She asked me what I intended to do. There was a recession starting in 1990, and I had had little luck with a new job, apart from an interview for sub-editor on the *Illustrated London News*. I did not get it. In any case, London felt like a prison after Africa, in which I had just spent two years. I told Joanna that I had vague plans to go abroad again, this time to learn Spanish. I would not go to Spain, I explained; far too expensive. I had been thinking of Guatemala.

"Go to Ecuador," she said at once. "The teaching's as good, it's only a little more expensive – and it's a bit safer. I'm going myself in the spring."

She had a friend who was about to return to Ecuador and who had contacts with a language school there. She suggested I ring him. I did so that afternoon, and we met in a pub not far from Hammersmith Broadway. I don't really remember much about that evening, except that Andy was very tall and thin with blonde hair, about my age (early 30s), and seemed all right. He was going to a language school in Quito, which taught Spanish and Quechua to development workers as well as tourists. One could find one's own accommodation, in which case one paid $35 a week for eight hours a day one-to-one tuition – a bargain, even then; or one could live with a local family who would speak only Spanish, in which case one would pay twice as much for full board. Andy had studied there before, and told me frankly that he would get a small commission for introducing me. "But I'll buy you a pint when you get to Quito," he said. "All right, I'll come then," I said, and I did.

*

In the mornings Norma would send me off to school with a lunchbox. Celso would have gone downstairs by then, to the small liquor store he ran in a sort of converted garage that ran out to the pavement. I would say goodbye to the two little boys, Celsito and Pablo, and to Norma, a pretty woman in her twenties with black wavy hair and white, smooth skin. Then I would descend the concrete stairs outside to street level, pausing at the little concrete enclosure to greet its occupant, a shaggy white guard dog called Willy who barked and wagged his tail at anyone who passed. Then off along the street swinging my lunchbox on its little strap. I should have worn a cap and blazer and grey serge shorts, too.

There are two Quitos, the Old Town and the rest, and Celso and Norma lived in the rest. The school was near where the two halves met, perhaps a mile and a half from home along a busy main road. I would reach this from the Mariana de Jesus, a short dual carriageway with a grassy central reservation; I would stop on the way to buy cigarettes, of which I then smoked 20 or 30 a day, and a newspaper. Sometimes the newspaper would be the rather old-fashioned broadsheet, *El Comercio*, but more often I chose a lively, attractive paper, also a broadsheet, but tabloid in style, called *Hoy* (*Today*), which strongly resembled its English namesake. Then I would walk along the main road.

My clearest memory of that city, it seems now, is the quality of the light. Besides being very high, Quito is just 15 miles south of the Equator. Indeed, on my second day in the city, Celso and Norma had taken me there and stood me before the monument the Ecuadorians had erected to the fact that gave their country its name. I stood with a foot on either side of a painted line and Celso took a picture with my camera. I still have it; I look younger than I was, my hair is very short, I am wearing a checked shirt and white trousers and I look horribly pleased with the world.

But my face is very red. The previous day I had gone with Celso and Norma to Celsito's school, which held a ceremony to celebrate the opening of its new building. It was a pleasant occasion. The parents – like Celso and Norma, well-to-do people of mostly European descent – gathered in the grounds outside, informally attired in slacks or jeans and open-neck shirts. The teachers recited prayers and then played songs with a guitar accompaniment and the children gave a display of sports. I suppose I stood there for 45 minutes without a hat in the cool mountain air, unaware that the equatorial sun was cutting me like a laser. By Monday morning, 48 hours later, the skin was falling from my face in great white gobs. From then on I always wore a locally-made sombrero or, more often, a baseball cap, which was what urban Ecuadorians usually wore. Sombreros were more common in the countryside, where the pure-bred Indians – the *indígenas*, as they were called by other Ecuadorians – wore them from the age of three or four to protect themselves, even when they had been accustomed to the sun since birth. Working at 12-14,000ft in clear air on the Equator, they knew better than to dispense with them. Oddly, I never heard anyone in Ecuador mention skin cancer, but perhaps that is why.

The route to school was unattractive. Four lanes of traffic roared by along the main road, the Diez de Agosto; and the buses, as broken down as any I had seen in Africa, belched great gouts of black diesel smoke which took on a hard edge in the clear, direct sunlight. (The bus companies had been privatized not long before, but the fares had not risen, I was told; few operators could afford more than the most basic maintenance.)

Raise one's eyes to the horizon, however, and there was a different world. Quito is surrounded by the Pichincha range; although the city lies at over 9,000ft, the mountains that hem it in closely on every side soar to twice this height, giving one the impression of being at the bottom of a vast crevasse. The mountains began to climb away steeply only a mile or two from the centre of the long, narrow town, so that one was never far away from green slopes and meadows dotted with trees. Often, harsh weather could be seen to touch the upper valleys, for it was the wet half of the year. Quito has no seasons in the European sense, lying as it does on the Equator, but six months of the year were wet, the remainder completely dry. I had arrived at the beginning of the rain; the mornings were clear and warm, but the cloud arrived at midday, and by late afternoon it was sometimes raining quite heavily. It became cold then, too, and nights could be chilly. So I walked to school in shirtsleeves and returned in a hooded anorak.

On the Monday after my arrival I sat before my first teacher, whose job it was to cope with new arrivals for the first day or two. Young, he was powerfully built with an Indian's face. He was friendly but his face was closed. He taught me the Spanish alphabet and the pronunciation of the letters' names, and gave me one or two other tools I would need in the weeks to come.

With each student having a teacher to themselves, we sat in pairs, five or six to a floor. No one had the same teacher for more than a week, except by special request; I would do that with Adriana. The teaching was good. The school operated on the principle of total immersion. No English was used at all. This worked, especially if one was lucky with one's 'family'. I was; Celso and Norma were charming and endlessly patient, and took pride in my growing skills.

The teachers' attitude to us was detached; I do not think they either liked or disliked us much. They were not unfriendly, but we would spend as much in the bar after school as they would on several days' food for their families, and they knew it. I don't think they saw much of the fees we paid. Every now and then the school organized dance parties in the basement after school. Everyone drank rum out of pink plastic cups. You could dance with the teachers if you wanted to, but they were happier dancing with each other. They usually left early.

Yet they could also show unexpected warmth. They loved to talk about Ecuador and later, when I had acquired some Spanish, lessons often took the form of long conversations about the economy, history, the *indígenas*, the oil industry and religion. Interest in South American literature was especially encouraged. Magic realism was at its height; its roots were Latin American, and I think that for some educated South Americans it had become an assertion of cultural identity.

School ended at five. I would meet Andy at the street door. A restless man, he had been working as an accountancy clerk in England but it bored him; his interest was travel. He had embarked on a six-month language course in the school that would, he hoped, fit him for a career in the tourist industry. He was serious about this, but was motivated by curiosity as much as ambition. I found him easy to get on with from the beginning.

We would walk the mile or so through the side-streets to Quito's main shopping street, the Amazonas, and the Scottish.

The Scottish was kitsch. A six-foot plastic figure of a Scottish piper towered over the entrance. Waitresses wore short tartan skirts, rather fetching tartan waistcoats and tartan cardboard eyeshades; they dashed about between the gloomy interior and the cluster of blue tin tables on the wide pavement outside. Now and again, when it had been raining and the air was cold, we would be forced inside; more usually we sat outside and watched the world go by while drinking good local lager at 25 pence a pint. The clientele included young American tourists, clearly identifiable from their locally-made sombreros, which Ecuadorians, as I have said, rarely wore in towns. The Germans wore frayed jeans and tee-shirts. There was a

scattering of Ecuadorians, mostly smartly-dressed young people. Now and then one of the tables would be taken by a pair of
tarts in risible skirts and vertiginous heels, mouths glistening
red, earrings like hula hoops and big hair to the waist, dyed
blonde, a little black showing at the roots.

Every night, Maria would pass by the tables. A middle-aged
Indian woman in bowler and shawl, she brought a large wood-
en box, lined with felt, of the sort in which one might expect
to see rows of butterflies, transfixed with pins. In this she displayed the jewelry she sold to the tourists on the Amazonas.
She said she made it, and perhaps she did; I rather liked it, buying earrings and pins as presents from her before I left. There
were beggars too. One, a thin man of perhaps 30 with dark skin
stretched tight across his wide cheekbones, came most nights,
hauling himself along the pavement, his bent and shattered legs
dragging inertly behind him; now and then one of us would
give him something and he took it without thanks. The poor do
not thank you for being rich.

The people on the pavement varied in appearance, for Ecuadorians are not homogenous. Some people, like my hosts,
were of clearly European descent. But most of the people of the
cities in the Cordillera – that is, the country's Andean backbone
– were a mixture of Hispanic and Indian blood and were not
unlike Southern Europeans in appearance. They dressed and,
in some ways, lived much as Southern Europeans do.

The costeños were different. They were the people of the
coastal belt, of the flat country where they grew bananas, of
the ranching country, of the great coastal cities, Guayaquil and
Esmeraldas. Many were of Afro-Caribbean descent. They were
all markedly livelier than the people of the cordillera, and much
easier to get to know. The difference was exemplified by the
fiasco of the first Miss Ecuador competition, sponsored by El

Comercio 60 years earlier, in 1931. The *costeña* women paraded past the judges without a second thought, dressed in bathing suits; those from Quito, however, did not even turn up, sending their photographs instead. Eventually, the director of *El Comercio* was reduced to touring the contestants' homes with the Mayor, trying to persuade them to make an appearance.

With some people having African looks, and the rest varying widely in skin tone, no-one used the words white or black. One was more or less *moreno* – that is, dark-skinned. One of the teachers, a petite young woman who taught me soon after I arrived, introduced herself thus: "My name is Flor, I'm a *costeña*, *morena* – and I like to dance." (Most *costeños* and *costeñas* liked to dance.) Indeed, Ecuadorians seemed to accept their racial differences without anxiety.

But I wonder if that was really true. In March the 1991 Miss Ecuador competition burst forth on TV, breaking the stranglehold of football and Brazilian soap operas. For weeks Ecuavisa ran trailers for it every ten minutes, and it became clear that this was a less inhibited affair than it had been 60 years earlier. But it was strangely pale for a multiracial society, with contestants sometimes bearing anglophone names – which were rare in Ecuador.

If any racial group was really distinct, however, it was the *indígenas* – that is, the indigenous people of the Andes, the descendants of the Cañars and the Incas, with their shawls, their bowler hats and their closed, unsmiling faces, who lived in the countryside: the peasants. Some of them crowded into the cities, for all was not well in the countryside. Then they swapped their hats for baseball caps, and exchanged one set of problems for another.

*

After some weeks, life in Quito had become oddly normal. I would go out at half-past eight swinging my little lunchbox, spend the morning with my tutor for the day, break mid-morning for coffee and meet whoever was around, and eat lunch in the little park behind the school. In the afternoon one's teacher would shift the emphasis from grammar to literature or culture, reflecting the decline in concentration as the day went by. At five I would wait on the steps for Andy and anyone else who happened to feel like a beer. I am sorry that after nine years I cannot remember many of these fellow-students; I mostly only knew them for a few weeks. But there was Graham, an English rock-music entrepreneur who had sold his company and taken early retirement (he was 31) and wanted to do some travelling. Sadly the buyers of his company betrayed him, forcing him back to work a few months later, and he had to make his fortune a second time. We remained friends for several years. There was a slim German in her twenties whose name I can't remember; she had a brown bob and round cheeks, a sharp nose and big glasses, and always wore a sombrero and ragged jeans, and a check shirt outside her waistband. There was Greg, a kind, friendly young physiotherapist from Long Beach. There was Ellen, a tall, gentle midwife in her mid-thirties from New Jersey; she was a friend of Andy's, and I would get to know her well. Later there was Joanna, my friend and colleague from London, who arrived in Ecuador in April. You couldn't stop her travelling for long.

And there was the man from the Welsh borders who had taken time off to cycle from Tierra del Fuego to the Bering Strait. He was still recovering from the journey through Peru.

67

He had left the bike locked up in Lima and taken the train to Cuzco with an American, one of those casual acquaintances you make when travelling. Leaving Cuzco, they were walking to the station when the American stopped to buy cigarettes. It was a moment before the Englishman realised that he had done so. Stopping himself, he turned to see the American set upon by three youths; to his horror the American simply pulled a gun and shot them. "I ran," said the Englishman. "We believe you," we said. Peru was rough then.

We would head for the Scottish. God knows why we all liked it so much, with its high prices and high-heeled tarts, but it was home, and we knew we would find each other there. The talk was of buses to Santiago (96 hours), planes to Los Angeles, safe ways through Colombia (rare), rumours of muggings (common) and of plans for the weekend. You would announce that you were going to Otavalo for the weekend and some Dutchman or German you had never seen would announce he was going with you, and he did, and you had a good time.

After an hour or two in the Scottish I would get a taxi, slightly pissed, and arrive home with half an hour to spare before dinner. I spent this playing with Celsito and Pablo. After dinner Celso and Norma and I would chat over coffee, a habit that became more regular, and pleasant, as my Spanish improved. I would finish the evening with homework, or watch a little television, or listen to the Mozart masses on my cheap stereo. Somehow they matched the white churches.

In fact, I was very happy.

One weekend we travelled back from Otavalo in the late afternoon. Just before sunset we passed across a wide valley, and away across the fields a rainbow arced across it just as I had seen it do in the book – the clouds behind it were grey, yet there was evening sunshine, and below the rainbow in the distance I could just make out the characteristic white twin towers of a church. Then, as the sun finally set, we saw the extinct volcano of Cayambe, its snowy summit glowing pink in the dying light. As we passed it, the coach dropped a gear and strained past an old American-style school bus; in it, ten or 15 young people were holding an impromptu disco, clapping and dancing and laughing.

We had an earthquake. It was morning; Celso had already gone downstairs to the shop, and Norma and I were finishing our coffee after breakfast. Celsito and Pablo were playing quietly on the living-room floor. Then the cups and cutlery started to move. We grabbed a child each and stood in the doorway to the corridor. As we did so the house started to rock. The tremor lasted for perhaps a minute, although of course it seemed longer. It was a modern house, and was designed for earthquakes; I was dumbfounded to see the doorways around the room become completely rhomboid in shape, and could not believe that they would not break. But when it was over, the house was quite undamaged.

*

It was now the week before Easter. I had a new teacher. Adriana was very small, clever and gentle with a round face and enormous brown eyes. She was about my age (I was 33) and was married with a daughter. That week, she taught me with great tact and charm, and I learned much. Instead of switching at the end of the week, we decided to work together for a little longer. I found myself looking forward to school in the morning.

One day Andy and I were sitting in a bar (we did a lot of that). It was somewhere in the mountains south of Ibarra, on the Pan-American Highway. I think we had gone up there looking for places to hill-walk. We had not found any. (The Andes, unlike the Himalayas, are rather conical; one is either on a mountain or off it, and they are not such good walking country.) At night, in search of beer, we had walked down to the main road from the village where we were staying, along a narrow country lane, across a little steel bridge that clanged back at us in the dark, the sky a mass of stars.

"I like Adriana," I said.

"You like Adriana," he repeated.

"Looking into Adriana's eyes," I said, "is like sinking into a hot bath on a winter morning."

"Oh, good *Lord*," he exploded, with something between mirth and exasperation.

Andy was not a romantic, although women certainly liked him. At the time he was just embarking upon a relationship with one of the teachers at the school, but he said nothing about it and I did not ask. He returned to England at the end of summer, but in 1993 he moved back to Quito, where they started a family; he went to work for a bank. I last heard from him in 1995. I suppose he is still there.

Adriana and I remained in contact for a little while but there was nothing between us; she was married, anyway. Two years later she travelled with her husband to Belgium, and thence to London, where she did look for me; but I was no longer there. One day at school she had asked me if I had a dream, and I said that it was to see the Himalayas. That was where I had gone. Later Andy told me that she got divorced. I do have a picture I took of her on the roof of the school one afternoon. The wind is blowing her very dark brown hair. She is wearing a blue denim shirt and jeans and smiling, and I have bounced a little flash into her eyes, but I wonder if they needed that. Behind her is yet another white church with twin towers; beyond it, the green of the Pichincha range can just be made out below the startling blue of the sky. But I am older now.

"If you drink tonight, you'll turn into a fish," she said one Thursday afternoon. "That is what our people say of those who drink or dance before midnight on Good Friday. And I know that the English students are always drinking on the Amazonas after school." This was true. There were only a few of us but we had teamed up with the German dropouts.

"Will you go to the processions tomorrow?" she continued. "You should do. You'll see the *cucuruchos.*"

I said that I would certainly go to the processions, although I was sure it would be raining. The weather had been bad lately; the previous day had been cold and wet. Walking home at dusk down the Mariana de Jesus, I had turned and looked up at the Pichinchas to see patches of snow creeping into the higher gullies. Today had been grey and cold. But it had not rained.

After school, I headed for the Scottish. But I did not stay long there that night. After a beer or two I left alone and hailed a taxi on the Amazonas. The driver was about 60; unusually, he wore a suit and tie and was very polite, even switching on the meter. "Hasn't rained today," I remarked. "No. First dry day in two weeks," he replied. "It's a miracle," I went on. "A miracle!" he confirmed with enthusiasm. "A miracle, for Semana Santa. Will you go to the processions tomorrow?"

Celso asked me the same question as we drank our coffee after dinner. He had studied in a seminary for some years before abandoning the priesthood because the church took too much from the poor. In fact, the Second Vatican Council at Medellín had changed much, and in South America these changes had taken root, leading to a more liberal, compassionate church that was closer to the people. Celso had a new occupation anyway, running an all-night off-licence. But I do not think he had lost his faith.

"Have you seen the uniforms of the Ku Klux Klan?" he asked. I nodded. "That's what you'll see tomorrow. The *cucuruchos* are purple – well, sometimes brown – and they've got those same high pointed hoods that cover their faces. The hoods are pretty heavy, they're lined with card. They'll parade slowly through the city for some hours, carrying heavy crosses. It's an act of penitence for the suffering of the *Señor*. Sometimes they will whip themselves and those without hoods may wear crowns of thorns that make them bleed. One year, instead of a heavy cross, one man carried a huge cactus instead of a cross. He bled. And they will walk in bare feet."

"Good Lord," I said. "Do they heat up the surface of the road as well, just to make things more interesting?"

"Oh, no," he replied without smiling. "If the sun shines it should be hot enough."

My flippancy was misplaced. The custom of penitence is an accepted part of Catholicism. Its expression in this form arrived from Spain with the *conquistadores*, who in 1534 founded the city of Quito on the ashes of the old Inca capital, which had been burned by the retreating forces of Atahualpa's last general, Rumiñahui. The penitents' parade endured, but got out of hand, as those who sought public office chastised themselves to excess in order to curry favour with the faithful. So the Church had insisted that all the participants disguise their identity. Today, it was said, many a senior politician might be found beneath the sinister pointed hoods. "Including President Borja?" I asked an Ecuadorian acquaintance. "I doubt it," he replied, "though God knows he's got plenty to repent."

The penitents inspired the respect of many, but the puzzlement of others. With 61% of Ecuadorians attending church regularly, this was still a deeply religious society; but it was not monolithic. Agnosticism and Protestantism were gaining ground. Amongst those who did believe, the strict tenets of the Church were no longer law; the Church in Rome had turned its back on the liberalizing spirit of the 1960s, but in South America it had not. Adriana was not unusual in getting divorced, and many priests no longer opposed contraception. The public observance of Holy Week lacked the deep solemnity of thirty or even twenty years ago. Today, the *cucuruchos* had their critics. They were aware of this.

"Why make fun of us?" one penitent asked a journalist from the daily paper *Hoy*. "It really worries me that people of some faiths should think they have the right to deny us our manner of worship." He added that he wished more young people would take part. "This year, I'll do their penitence for them."

But the *cucuruchos* weren't all old. Another article quoted a 23-year-old driver as saying that, ever since he began taking part, he felt more secure behind the wheel. Many a near-accident, he claimed, had been suddenly avoided without explanation. He was not alone in believing such things. The bus traveller in Ecuador soon got used to the stickers of Jesus in his crown of thorns, displayed above the seat of almost every driver; around the figure was written the words *Dios guia mi camino*. I wished at times that the drivers would rely on more than divine intervention.

"What, really, do you think of the *cucuruchos*?" I asked another Ecuadorian.

"I think they're very religious," he said cautiously.

"But these guys whipping themselves?" I pressed.

"Oh well, I think they're *sádicos*."

The next morning we met at the Monastery of San Francisco to see for ourselves.

*

Brother Jodoco Ricke arrived in Quito in 1536, hot on the heels of the conquistadors, and started work on the extraordinary Monastery of San Francisco. Built over the succeeding 50 years, it now stands proud above the Plaza of the same name, its white twin towers shining in the direct equatorial sun, the structure clearly visible from the hills far above. Inside, its finery is a tribute not only to its artisans, but to a culture that was prepared to expend such monstrous sums in the name of God that nothing of the sort could be built today; even the basilica of Yamoussoukro in Côte d'Ivoire cannot quite be judged in the same context. It was said that if just two of the gilded columns in the church of San Francisco were stripped, they would pay off Ecuador's burgeoning external debt. But there was no chance that this would be done, for the treasures of colonial Quito were a source of justified pride. Here and there one saw notices or stickers proclaiming *Quito – Patrimonia de la Humanidad*; UNESCO apparently agreed.

I did. One day I wandered quite by chance into one of the lesser-known colonial churches in Quito's Old Town. The church was lit by beams of sunlight that streamed through arches around the nave, creating patches of vibrant light and cool, dim shadow; a priest swung a censer on a rope, and the smoke from the censer drifted in and out of the sunbeams, which caught the metal of the censer so that a dull gleam flew backwards and forwards with the rhythm of a hypnotist's pendulum.

The magnificence of the San Francisco was not solely a product of Renaissance Europe. Brother Ricke arrived in Quito just 44 years after the Moors had left Granada. The craftsmen who accompanied him brought influences that were as much Islamic as they were Christian, influences reflected by the courtyard within and its alabaster fountain. The Islamic and Christian traditions had combined Islamic decorative and Christian figurative influences to form one of the most striking buildings I have seen.

At ten in the morning on Easter Friday, I stood with Ellen and Andy in the courtyard of the San Francisco. It was not raining. It was a miracle. For Semana Santa. Knots of soberly-dressed worshippers were holding spontaneous services in the courtyard, sheltered from the sun in cloisters that looked out onto clumps of bright red flowers, contrasting with the white stonework and the brilliant blue of the sky. Deep within the building, in the headquarters of the Brotherhood of Jesus of the Great Power, the *cucuruchos* prepared body and mind for the six-hour ordeal ahead. Outside the Brotherhood's door, a sign pointed to the studio of Stereo Radio Jesus del Gran Poder, the sign surmounted with a cartoon of a monk DJ in headphones with a turntable. Through this medium, the Brotherhood spread its message; but the sign pointed, too, to the dispensary, a boon in a city where the public hospitals lacked basic things like needles and sterile dressings.

We shouldered our way through the crush and out into the Plaza below. Here the faithful ambled across the cobbles, pausing now and then to inspect stands selling hats and craftwork. In the cat's-cradle of ancient streets behind the San Francisco, market traders sold everything from digital watches to brightly-coloured rucksacks, stereos smuggled from Colombia, jewelry, cheap jeans and whole roast pig. On the steps of the monastery itself, four or five peddlers provided devotional images of the Virgin, votive candles, and postcards of Christ. Two aged beggars sat against the great, open wooden doors of the main church, hands outstretched for alms. No-one bothered them, the odd priest or monk stepping around them with something like respect. We sat on the steps in the growing heat. Everyone was waiting for the same thing – gringos, city families and the pious *indígenas* of the Cordillera, for some of whom there was Christ alone and not much else.

At midday, the penitents emerged. The first one saw from the Plaza below was the high purple cones, the *cucuruchos*; they advanced slowly, two by two, preceded by a military band that belted out stately music, the brass notes with that curious Hispanic balance on a knife-edge of melody and atonality. The rims of the trumpets and tubas caught the fierce sunlight and refracted it, hurting the eyes. Then, very slowly, the huge statue of Jesus of the Great Power was borne shoulder-high from the doors of the San Francisco, ablaze with gold.

We made for the Calle Guayaquil. Here, an hour or so later, the procession moved slowly down the slope towards us, still escorted by the band, which would continue until the end at half-past six. Behind them came the first *cucuruchos*. They had a strange humanoid appearance. I raised my camera; normally shy about photographing people, I felt strangely detached from these curious creatures with their high pointed heads, their eyes just visible behind slits in the hoods. Then, as I focused my lens on the leading figure, I saw the eyes staring back at me, distorted by the fresnel screen in the viewfinder. My finger froze over the shutter and I did not take the picture, waiting until he had gone by before raising the camera back to my eye.

Many *cucuruchos* passed by, some of the penitents carrying vast crosses. Later I was to hear that one penitent, Humberto Bautista, who was 89, was carrying a three-metre cross that weighed a quintal – about 46 kilos, just over 100lb. Many were bigger. One or two of the penitents, stripped to the waist beneath their conical hoods, whipped their backs. Behind the *cucuruchos* came 15 or 20 Roman centurions, driving before them penitents dressed as Jesus who they were beating with cats-o'-nine-tails. Others walked past in simple robes, patches of blood showing as crowns of thorns bit into their foreheads. They too were lashing their naked backs with the same short, evil little whips. I saw more than one man who already had what must have been stinging weals between neck and waist. There were children in the procession, too, although certainly no-one was whipping them. Some were dressed as Christ; a few wore purple robes to match their fathers, and one child, three or four years old, was a mini-*cucurucho* complete with cornet hat and cape. Some of the children carried small crosses.

The procession moved slowly, and stopped often. It must, for a man with a 100lb cross on his shoulders does not run, even if he is not 89. The number of spectators grew. In the Calle Bolívar, just after two, I had one of the very few ugly moments I had in Ecuador; part of the crowd, which had swelled to 500,000, about 200,000 more than expected, rushed the statue of Jesus del Gran Poder in a display of mass piety. We were forced backwards and forwards and half-crushed as a moan of devotion arose from the worshippers. Gringos were now less in evidence.

Later we walked through the quieter streets of La Ronda, further behind the San Francisco, where beautiful houses of neat square proportions with white walls and blue window-frames recalled the elegance of colonial Quito. But the paint was flaking. An *indígena*, one of the new urban poor, lay against a dirty white wall in the sunshine; he was insensible, but his hand still clutched the neck of an empty rum-bottle. A teenage girl passed us. "They rob you here," she warned us, whispering. Later I would hear that the fine streets of the Old City, hamstrung by planning and conservation laws, had become havens for the poor, and that people slept in shifts so that up to six could use the same bed. But maybe they were lucky. The following week an unexpected hailstorm caused the collapse of some corrugated-iron shacks on the edge of the city, killing nearly 30 people. Many Ecuadorians, whether religious or not, believed that religion was the cornerstone of the country's tranquility in the face of such poverty.

Oil in Greeneland

In August 2013 Ecuador's President Correa announced that the country would permit drilling for oil in the Yasuni National Park. It was a controversial decision both within and outside the country. The Yasuni National Park, in Ecuador's rainforest region, is one of the world's treasure troves of biodiversity, home not only to predators such as jaguars and harpy eagles, but also to a giant otter and to multiple species of bats, frogs and insects. According to the Wildlife Conservation Society, a conservation group based at New York's Bronx Zoo, just 2.5 acres of the Yasuni contain nearly as many tree species as in the U.S. and Canada combined. It is also the home of indigenous people from the Waorani group, some of whom have had little or no contact with the outside world.

In 2010 Correa had announced a scheme to leave 840 million barrels of oil below the ground in the Yasuni National Park, if the international community could raise about $3.6 billion – roughly half the value of the oil. Very little of this was raised. "The world has failed us," Correa told a news conference in August 2013 when he announced that there would be permits to drill.

Not all Ecuadorians approved of this decision, and at the time of writing (October 2013), a petition had been started to force a referendum on the issue. Under Ecuadorian law, if 5% of the electorate sign this, such a vote must be held. The result could have gone either way. Most Ecuadorians apparently supported the original decision to try to preserve the Yasuni. But the Park may contain as much as 25% of the Ecuador's oil reserves, and between a third and a half of the country's revenue is from oil (these figures vary, depending on where you look).

The story that follows recounts journeys may years earlier, in March and April 1991, to the region where the Yasuni National Park lies. It passes no judgment on President Correa's decision; Ecuador is a democracy and its voters will do that.

*

Our journey to the jungle began in the mountains above it. In 1991 I was studying Spanish in Quito. In January of that year my friend Andy, a fellow student, and I flew for the weekend to the beautiful Andean city of Cuenca.

In the town centre we pushed open the double doors of a hotel to find ourselves in a marble hall at the bottom of an enormous light well. Four storeys above us light flooded through panes of glass set in an iron framework, then shone through a filter of ferns and other plants, which softened it so that the pink and grey paintwork seemed to glow.

We dropped our bags in our room, and went slowly down the staircase through the cloud of light that suffused the central space, and went to see the city. Later, after a number of beers, we returned to our baroque hotel, flung ourselves down on our beds and ordered more beer from room service. Then we discussed travelling to the jungle.

Ecuador has three distinct areas. Behind the Pacific coast lies an area of banana groves and plains; in the latter cattle are raised for export. Then the Andes rise from the plain. The mountain area is usually referred to as the Cordillera; for much of its length it is divided into a western and an eastern ridge, and Quito, the capital, lies in the fault between the two. Then, beyond the eastern ridge, the mountains tumble down in a series of foothills, becoming progressively more forested, until they end in the westernmost reaches of the Amazonian rainforest. Here begin rivers that feed the Amazon itself. This region is known as the *selva* (jungle), or Oriente.

In late 1941, fighting between Peru and Ecuador ended with Ecuador's loss of an immense area of jungle, including Ecuador's stretch of the upper Amazon. (Peru had in fact occupied much of this area for many years, but Ecuador had always claimed it.) Fifty years later this area, which included the populous city of Iquitos, was widely accepted by the rest of the world to be part of Peru. But the Ecuadorians had never accepted it. Each student at our language school was issued with an exercise book. On the back was a map of Ecuador and the words of the Ecuadorian national anthem. More to the point, above the map was printed a legend in bold: *Ecuador has been, is and will be an Amazonian nation.* The matter did not rest and fighting, on the ground and in the air, had broken out again briefly in 1981 and would do so again in 1995. It was after the second conflict that Ecuador and Peru did reach an agreement of a kind. In 1991, however, the two countries were heading for another war.

The war of 1941 had left the Ecuadorian Oriente truncated. But the country's *selva* was still an area the size of England. In the *selva* lived the indigenous Amazonian peoples, most notably the Shuar, the Achuar and the Waorani; many of the latter two groups were uncontacted, while many of the first group, although in contact with the outside world, neither had nor needed much to do with it.

However, they shared the Oriente with two forms of economic activity from outside. First, *indígenas* – indigenous, Quechua-speaking people from the poor and overcrowded Cordillera – were being settled there by the State land agency, IERAC. (Ecuadorians tended to use this word *indígena* for the Quechua-speaking people of the Highlands; the word *indios* was more used for the peoples of the *selva*.)

Second, there was the oil industry. This worked almost entirely in the northern Oriente; the Shuar and Achuar lived in the south, and the two halves were separated by a large river, the Río Pastaza. But the oil companies had their eyes on the south. And the Río Pastaza was being bridged.

Andy knew at least some of this. "We can get to the Oriente," he said, picking up the phone to order beer. He put the phone down and turned back towards me. "Not just the north. It's not hard to get into the north. I want to see the southern Oriente before it ceases to exist."

I tried to imagine the Oriente on a map, and asked him what the largest town in the southern half was. "In the south? Macas," he said. "The jumping-off point for Macas from the Cordillera is right here. Cuenca. It's about 12 hours by road."

I groaned.

"Does Macas have an airstrip? Does anyone fly there? And if we get there, what do we do? Hack our way through the jungle and hope no-one puts a poison dart in our arse?"

Yes, he replied, we probably could fly to Macas. As to how one got around an area of impenetrable jungle, this was simple. We would go by boat. He was expanding on this when our beer arrived, ice-cold. I drank it and listened. In the Amazon basin one could then still – just – travel to the edge of what we know as civilization.

I wanted a cigarette. Andy did not smoke, so I went out on the balcony. It was quite cool, but the air was calm. Nothing moved, for it was after ten, and people slept very early in the Cordillera. I looked down to the street three floors below. The silence was broken by an aged police car, one of its indicator lights broken, a rifle moving about loose on the rear parcel shelf. It halted briefly at the traffic light, which cast a dull red glow on the shiny cobbles. I looked up. The great blue marble dome of Cuenca's New Cathedral floated above the rooftops, floodlit, as it was every night from sundown. I stared at it, forgetting to smoke my cigarette, which burned down nearly to the filter.

The next day, we made for Ingapirca. This ancient city, on the edge of a valley over 10,000ft (3,200 m) in the mountains several hours' drive from Cuenca, and had been the home of the indigenous Cañari people, who were taken over by the Incas not long before the Spanish invasion. It was a beautiful place; pale blue skies were interspersed with soft white and grey clouds above a sweeping green valley, the fields and mountains bathed in a soft, hazy light. Vicuñas grazed peacefully near the ruins. I loved it. Yet I remember the day now chiefly for two things we saw that I would remember later, when we were in the Oriente.

The first was the sheer density of the cultivation we saw as we drove, first up the Pan-American highway in the bus, and then on the dirt road up to Ingapirca, which we covered on the flatbed of a small pickup. Every steep bank that shadowed the road would be overhung with maize that clung almost horizontally to the earth.

The second thing I would remember later would be the fight in the village square. Andy and I had gone to the village's only restaurant for beer and *churrasco*. The latter word, in Latin America generally, just means grilled meat; but in Ecuador it was a large oval plate with a medium-sized steak, an inverted cupful of rice, an avocado, tomatoes and other bits of salad. The beer was a large bottle, cold and good. Looking back, it seems to me that Andy and I had *churrasco* and beer for lunch every day we spent travelling in the mountains.

Outside the rather dark restaurant were the people who did not get *churrasco*. These were the local *indígenas*. They were short and dark and their skins seemed wrinkled by the sun, despite their black felt fedoras; because it was Sunday they wore shabby suits and trousers and they drank. I was later told that the villages all over the Cordillera were full of drunken men on Sunday. There was little else to do, and it was their only escape. That afternoon, two middle-aged *indígenas* were lurching and sparring at each other in the muddy village square; their wives hovered around them, trying to stop them, their faces contorted with misery. Later I would think of those two men in the muddy village square, and of the maize that grew on every last clod of earth in the Cordillera, and I would think of what it all meant for the rainforest below.

*

Back in Quito, Andy and his teacher, Alfredo, started to plan the journey to the Oriente in earnest. Andy was determined to see the Southern Oriente before the oil industry, and the settlers from the Cordillera, changed it forever.

Alfredo was Andy's teacher for much of the time he was there. He was short, stocky, in his late twenties, with jet-black hair and beard and a sardonic cheerfulness. Yet, like many Ecuadorians, he always seemed slightly detached with us; I think the disparity in income was a wedge between us, the elephant in the room that one never discussed. Still, we were to travel long distances together and get on well enough.

Alfredo knew the Southern Oriente and had a friend, Carlos, who ran tours on the river near Macas; as there were few travellers in the region, he must also have had other activities, perhaps connected with the nearby missions. We would fly to Macas and from there we would somehow reach a particularly isolated mission at Maizal, deep in the rainforest, where Carlos, who was half-Shuar, had a compound. If all went well we would then travel down the remote Río Mangosíza to the ceasefire line with Peru, a three-day journey through Shuar territory. A friend of Andy's, Ellen, a tall, gentle midwife in her mid-thirties from New Jersey would join us. So would two Swiss tourists, a middle-aged woman and her daughter of about 21; this would spread the cost, which Andy thought would be about $450 each.

I had to think about this. I had quite literally to sit down in my bedroom and count the remaining dollars. I had brought about $2,000 with me, and had hoped to travel on to Chile later in the year. But the money was already running down, and I knew now that I wouldn't. Besides, the Southern Oriente was an untouched part of the Amazon basin that contained uncontacted human beings. It was already hard to travel to the frontier of the known world; today, I suspect, it is no longer possible. I told Andy that I would come.

So it was that on March 15, 1991, when Graham Greene had about two weeks to live, we came to a place that he must have invented. Macas, cantonal capital of Morona-Santiago, was a town of about 5,000 people. As Andy had said, there were two ways there; 12 hours by bus from Cuenca, or one hour from Quito in the weekly Fokker. We took the Fokker.

It was uncrowded and comfortable; drinks were served, and the morning's newspapers were hung neatly over the armrests, looking as if they had just been ironed. At Macas we stepped into a different world. The mid-morning heat and the humidity could be felt at once. We were surrounded by mountains; not the bare towering peaks of the Cordillera, but steep, heavily-wooded peaks of 2-3,000ft. A casual little group unloaded our bags from the tail end of the Fokker. Cows and farm-workers wandered together across the runway between the overgrown fields on either side, ignoring the Fokker as it turned at the end of the tarmac. Scythes across their shoulders, wearing T-shirts and tatty cut-down denims, they scarcely looked like the ben-eficiaries of a new oildorado.

Yet Macas was in transition. Much of it still consisted of *ad hoc* wooden houses of one or at most two storeys, raised slightly off the ground; most were painted cheerful, if faded, colours. But they were on their way out. "There are fewer and fewer every time I come here," said Alfredo as we took an after-noon stroll through town. The new church, finished a year or so earlier, was actually a small cathedral. It was built on a hill from which one could see the greater part of the town, with its mostly low buildings, rambling through the valley between the moun-tains that rose steeply above it. Wisps of cloud drifted along their wooded flanks. In the late afternoon, the trees caught the low rays of the sun, and the top branches were brightly lit as shadows crept in below. One building did dominate the sky-line: the Hotel Peñon del Oriente, in which we were staying. The rest was pure Greeneland.

We needed to reach the mission at Miazal, which would be our departure point for the river. But the only practical way there was by light aircraft, and no-one at the airstrip was sure when one would be available. Certainly nothing would happen that night. We slouched off back towards the Hotel Peñon del Oriente.

On the way Andy and I stopped at the barber, not to have our hair cut, but so that Andy could satisfy his craving for comic-books. I never knew why comic-books were sold by barbers in Ecuador. They just were. Andy loved comic-books, arguing that they helped his Spanish, and a walk through a strange town would often be interrupted as Andy popped in to see if there was anything new. He made a selection. I settled for a Colombian strip called *La Bestia Roja* (The Red Beast).

In the Peñon del Oriente I tried to take a shower, but the water went off. Brushing the soap off my body, I noticed the posters that had been stuck at random on the bathroom wall. All were home-made, and religious; mostly photocopies of Jesus's face with, beneath, roughly typewritten in capitals, dire warnings of what would happen to us if we ignored the teachings of *El Señor*. I felt a spasm of irritation at being preached at in an hotel that at $12 a night was expensive for Ecuador, and appeared to have no water. I threw myself down on the bed to read *La Bestia Roja*. On the first page a thug in a quilted dressing-gown was waving a cigar and a brandy-balloon at a flunkey. "Tell them to mind their own business, accursed coward, or I shall have Chinatown razed to the ground!" he rasped.

There was a knock on the tin door and it scraped open to reveal Alfredo, carrying two plastic bags.

"I just saw Carlos," he said.

"OK. So what happens tomorrow?"

"He thinks he can sort the plane out for the morning. Depends."

"On what?"

"On weather. And other things."

The light plane was based at Macas, he explained, but the

87

pilot had plenty to do, delivering medicine, mail and other supplies to the missions in the *selva*; some of these might be only
30 or 40 minutes' flight away, but to reach them on the ground
could take days. He tossed the two plastic bags at me. "Put everything non-essential in one of these," he said. "Everything
you can. We'll leave it here. Use the other to line your rucksack.
Arrange it so that it folds over the contents at the top. You're going to get very wet over the next few days." He leaned forward.
"What are you reading?"

"It's Colombian. Magic realism."

Alfredo left, nonplussed. I returned to *La Bestia Roja*. A
tightly-clad blonde was talking to a Chinaman with long baggy
sleeves and a moustache. *Sheila, priestess of the Children of Satan, is cementing her alliance with the patriarch of the China-
men.* I dropped the book on the bed and opened the window. In
the street below, the yellow light of sundown caught the faces of
the children who circled around on bikes on the cinder surface
of the road. A few adults sat outside the tatty covered market,
in front of a wall daubed bright red with political slogans. On
the other side of the street, there were low wooden buildings,
one of them the post-office, painted bright blue. Bricks lifted its
structure from the soft, damp ground. Greeneland.

The next day, pillows of grey and white cloud hung between
the dark-green, forested mountains. There was no clear sky at
all until after 11, when a pale sliver of blue appeared to the south-
east. We gazed up at it, encouraged. At 12 we were called away
from an early lunch to be weighed, with luggage, beside the
informal structure where the 'airline' had its office. The airline
was one man, a piratical barrel-chested individual with dark
skin, a large moustache, longish black hair and deep eye-sock-
ets that were further shadowed by a baseball cap; he wore jeans
and a red T-shirt. He was sorry about the delay, explaining that

it was not the cloud that had held him; he had had to fly to two missions that morning. But he was ready now. We flung our rucksacks into the back of an elderly American-built, single-engine, high-winged cabin monoplane. The two Swiss, mother and daughter, waved us off; they would join us in the jungle later in the day. An Indian climbed in with us, a portable stereo on his knees. Bit by bit the long, narrow plane hauled itself off the tarmac and Macas swung away below us, threads of cloud still twined round the decaying wooden houses, the concrete slab of the Peñón del Oriente sticking up like a pile of Lego bricks that has survived a child's tantrum while the remainder lie scattered around it.

The dragon's-teeth mountains barely fell away from us at first. When they did do so, it was sudden. The aircraft wasn't climbing; rather, the last foothills of the Andes were disappearing and we were over the Amazon basin, with no land so high again between here and the Great Lakes region of Africa. The airspeed indicator read 90 knots as we crawled across a skein of silver rivers that criss-crossed the light blue-green surface of the forest. Here and there, we crossed a smaller stream that was directly below us, so that it was possible to see the brown gravel bed below the clear water where it wasn't broken by rocks and rapids.

The cloud never cleared. But it thinned, and we turned slowly through a patch of sunlight two thousand feet above the treetops. Away to our right, a long, narrow strip of emerald grass appeared, hacked out of the dark-green jungle. It seemed to take us hours to reach it, and then we came down suddenly, our wheels skimming just above the highest branches as we dropped onto the airstrip; below us was a pile of bleached aluminium, the bones of a visitor that had not made it. Then the plane bounced gently and slowed down, and we were turning at the end of the strip. There was nothing here; just trees, and a knot of three or four Indians waiting at the edge of the cleared area.

The pilot stretched. "Welcome to Miazal International," he said, grinning. "Please do not forget your belongings. Please do not smoke until you enter the terminal building."

He opened the door and we clambered out. The climate hit me at once, even more than it had at Macas – which was two or three thousand feet up in the foothills. Moving out from under the shade of the wing, I felt as if I had had several cans of strong ale.

Two of the welcoming committee were for us. Pedro and Bartolo were Shuar Indians, members of the fiercely independent local tribe who lived in the Southern Oriente, and were said to still shrink heads when the mood took them. There was a myth among foreigners that, if you knew the right people and had a few hundred dollars to spare, you could still – so to speak – visit the factory. This will not have been true. Historically, Shuar and Achuar Indians had shrunk the heads of enemies killed in battle, but they had done so for complex ritual reasons and would not follow the practice when not at war. The Shuar did reject much that came from outside, not because they didn't understand it, but because they did. But I would learn more of them later.

Pedro and Bartolo did not look as if they shrnk heads. Dressed in T-shirts and cut-down jeans, they escorted us to the bank of a nearby river, where our transport was waiting, guarded by a mongrel dog. The transport was a pair of crude dugout canoes. Long – 20ft or so – and very narrow, they seemed almost to clasp your hips. They were awash with an inch or so of water and oscillated wildly from side to side with each thrust of the oars. The dog jumped ship and swam to the bank. I wondered whether I should follow his example. But then we slid out from the shade beneath the trees. The sun was warm on my back; the water of startling clarity, each light-brown pebble distinct on the riverbed. The banks were thickly forested, but now and then a tree would twitch. Birds darted across the water and there were butterflies, too – bright splashes of yellow and blue and purple in the thick, still air. I liked it here.

*

Carlos's father had helped to found the Catholic mission at Miazal. Two decades on, Carlos himself had founded a different sort of mission on the other side of the river. It was a staging-post for the travellers he guided around the wilderness of the Southern Oriente. The building itself resembled a Wild West stockade, wooden walls surrounding a small open space where one could sit and eat; basic wooden cubicles lined the outside walls on the side nearest the river, with slatted shelves for beds. As we arrived, a large bright-green parrot sat peacefully on the stockade. Later it would take flight in the night and crash about in the rafters, causing a domestic crisis.

The mission itself was a mile away on the other side of the river. The latter ceased to be navigable here, shooting out from a series of cataracts into a deep pool below high, steep banks; it was spanned by a wood-and-rope suspension bridge 40 or 50 feet above. The walkway was just three feet wide. I was good with heights but did not like this, and strode across quickly, unsettled by the way the bridge pitched and swung from side to side. For Ellen, who feared heights, it was too much and she inched across with Alfredo guiding her, his hands on her waist.

We were not on our way to the mission just now. We wanted to swim. The humidity had increased as the day wore on; it had clouded over, and the air felt threatening and close. We scrambled down the bank to the pool below the cataracts, and stripped to our underpants. I was slower than the others and by the time I got into the water, they had nearly reached the opposite bank. I set off in a relaxed breast stroke, enjoying the cool clean water after the sticky day. I was not in a hurry, but wondered why I was making so much less progress than they had. I looked across the surface to see Andy sitting on a log on the opposite bank, looking rather grave. The current seemed very strong as I approached the other side. I looked up again. All three of them looked rather concerned. As I approached them the current began to tug at me. I grasped the log, remarking only that the undertow seemed strong. Then I saw that the level of the river was already two or three feet above where it had been when I entered the water; the log was almost submerged now, and Alfredo was scrambling onto the riverbank. We had been caught by a flash flood; our Wellington boots were with our clothes on the other side. I was marooned in the jungle in my underpants.

Two or three locals from the mission appeared on the opposite bank. Grinning, one of them gathered our clothes and moved them up the bank, while the other picked up our Wellington boots and made a signal to say that he would bring them across the river. Some 20 minutes later they appeared with the boots and we followed them rather sheepishly through the jungle. It was a tricky route, hanging onto roots and lianas that often came away in one's hands, threatening a plunge into the still-swollen river 30ft below. I did not know, but suspected, that there were five days of this ahead of us. Back at the lodge I changed into clean clothes, but I could feel damp sand still sticking to my body.

Later that afternoon, we visited the mission. There we met two priests, one young, one old.

The young one was tall, brusque, smartly dressed in dark trousers and black vest with clerical collar, although he was far from anywhere. He wore glasses and had neat, short, thick brown hair. I guessed he was in his early thirties. Must go, he was saying; we have a class to prepare for first communion; and with that he shook hands with Carlos and strode off, calling to some Shuar student in clear, ringing tones. He did not look Ecuadorian. He was probably European.

We knew Raoul was. In fact he was Belgian, but had been in the region for 35 years. He wandered slowly towards us, smiling; his rough hair was down below his shoulders; he was deaf and was probably 70. Carlos talked to him in a loud, clear voice. He talked for a little while about the mission's vaccination programme, and then wandered gently away. Later we passed the little shack where he lived on the edge of the mission. The Shuar children had chalked a huge shining sun on the door.

The Miazal mission was oddly like an English public school. Rows of buildings edged a large open space which was marked out for football; gaggles of 11-18 year olds ran through the dust from class to class. In the kitchen, cheerful cooks prepared the evening meal. Under their feet, two quiet, immensely shy little girls gazed up at us with vast eyes. When greeted, they giggled and covered their faces, pleased but confused. Carlos, who was short, barrelly, pugnacious, strode towards the dressmaking class with us in tow. The teacher politely broke off to allow us to explain why the girls were there. Shuar men, Carlos opined (and he ought to know as he was half Shuar himself), treated their wives as useful machinery, summoning them from bed to fetch bowls of *chicha*, the local home-made beer, at whatever the time of night. The mission taught girls to produce items they could sell for hard cash, making them more important in the economic life of the community, and raising their status.

Later he talked more about the spirit of the mission. The Catholics, he said, trod carefully in the jungle. The children prayed, but it was explained to them that the God they praised was the same one as their own Creator God, who sits at the head of a pantheon of five. The four lesser gods, which include an anaconda and a bird of the jungle, were, they learned, unique to the Shuar – but not therefore wrong. "Everything possible is done to ensure that what they are taught here does not undermine their own tribal life," Carlos continued. "When they've finished their schooling here they'll go back to their own villages, where they'll have spent much time anyway during their education. We don't think it's a good idea to split people apart from their communities and they're not encouraged to head for the town."

I found it hard to reconcile Catholicism with the beliefs of the Shuar, whose priests and elders must drink a hallucinatory drug in order to induce nightmares; their struggles with the demons therein will earn them the respect of their people. And they do have five gods, even if one of them is paramount, and interchangeable with the Pope's. Why did the Catholics come here at all? But the missionaries could have argued that they had no alternative, and there was good reason to hear them out.

The hold of the Catholic church was being undermined in Ecuador. In the Cordillera, nonconformist evangelists were gaining ground, while evangelical Protestant missionaries had been in the Oriente for some 30 years. As yet, they were confined to the Northern Oriente, across the Río Pastaza. They had a simple purpose. A few weeks earlier, staying in an hotel in the northern town of Otavalo, I had found the magazine of an American missionary group. Clean-cut faces of young missionaries off to spend 40 years in the Third World shot penetrating stares from the well-produced pages; their dedication, their desperation to save souls was screamed from every headline. There was little else. The traditional Catholic missionaries, by contrast, showed a quiet determination to spread vaccines with the word of God.

Should they all, Catholics included, just leave the people of the forest alone? The Catholics insisted that the rest of the world would come here, whether they did or not, and that they should come here first and help the Shuar build up their own defences in their own way. Some weeks later, across the Río Pastaza, I would understand this better.

That night, we sat around the wooden table in the stockade, lit by hurricane lamps.

"Music," said Carlos. "You want music?"

He asked each off us in turn and we all said yes, although I was not sure what he meant. I expected to see a ghetto blaster appear but no, he meant to get the older children from the Mission to come over and sing. So he and I and Alfredo and Andy went off into the night, crossing the swinging bridge in the dark, and walked through the blackness until we saw dim lights in the mission ahead. We pushed open a door and a chorus of voices welcomed us. Someone passed us a bowl of *chicha*, and we drank. Then several of the students stood up; one held a guitar; another, a slim girl of perhaps 15, led the way back down the path towards the stockade. She laughed and sang as she walked and when she reached the bridge she moved swiftly across it. She was singing *El Condor Pasa*. I followed her, watching her bare heels and her strong, slim calves by the light of a hurricane lamp; this time I crossed without fear. Still singing, still laughing, she led the way into the stockade, where bottles of banana liquor waited on the rough wooden table.

*

The jungle was no place to have a hangover. The morning light had a gentle gold quality to it, but it wasn't cool. The rash of damp sand on my skin combined with the banana fumes to produce a real malaise as I sat on the slatted bed, listening to Alfredo address us on jungle realpolitik. He was stretching my Spanish, but I understood. Before we started out on our journey down the Río Mangosíza, probably tomorrow, we would have to pay a bribe.

"It's quite sudden," he said. "Carlos went to see one of the local Shuar chiefs yesterday, before we flew in from Macas. This man announced he needed $50 to get one of his children to Quito for medical treatment."

"And we've got to pay this?" asked Andy. "Was that actually said?"

"It was strongly implied."

"It's blackmail," said Ellen. "We want to pay blackmail?"

"Do we want to travel down the river?" Alfredo shrugged.

"Has anyone said we can't anyway?" I asked. "We aren't asking him for any favours, are we?"

"No. But we've got a long way to go through his territory."

"And that's all we get for the money?" said someone.

"Maybe a good meal," said Andy.

At this, everyone laughed; $50 was a month's wages in Ecuador, two months' wages for some.

"Oh, let's pay the bloody thing," I said snappishly. I started burrowing in my rucksack for my matches. They were wet.

Alfredo handed me his lighter. "Sorry," he said, smiling ruefully, and went off to find Carlos and tell him the gringos would stump up. I worked it out in my head and felt mean. We were assuming that the chief did not really have a sick child. If he did, $7.50 a head was absolutely nothing.

My pique dissolved along with my hangover as we walked through the jungle on brown earth paths sprinkled with pools of light. After an hour or so, walking turned to clambering, up and down steep river banks; and then to wading, through rivers that came up to our necks. It was not an easy journey. The currents in the river were strong, and the scarps above the river were high enough to worry Ellen. More than once I put my weight on a dodgy root. But two or three hours of this brought us to one of the loveliest places I had ever seen. We were at a point where the river flowed between high, rocky banks. It was crystal clear, cool, about 40 or 50 feet wide, and it curved past a small pool into which three waterfalls plunged 30 feet or so from the rocky cliff above. Clouds of spray rose from the pool, catching and refracting the midday light which shone down into the gorge. Butterflies drifted through the warm air in profusion. I realized that there was not only spray, but steam. The waterfalls were hot springs, gushing out at about 550C. Hunks of bread appeared from Pedro's sack, along with tins of tuna and beer. We settled down, fully clothed, in the warm water. I offered Alfredo a cigarette. He took it with pleasure, as his own were soaked.

"How did you keep them dry?" he asked.

"An English gentleman always keeps his cigarettes dry," I replied loftily. I put them back in my hat and put the hat back on. He laughed, and launched himself backwards into the water. I took out my camera. "For the London *Times*?" he called, grinning. I fired the shutter. I still have a slide of Alfredo floating cheerfully on his back in the warm water, the sun glittering off its surface; he is wearing his white sombrero, shirt, trousers, boots and cravat, and there is a cigarette between his lips. He looks very cheerful. I think we all were. We were only the second group of outsiders to see the falls; three Swiss had reached them the previous year, presumably with Carlos's help.

We returned straight down the river. The best way was to float down, lying back suddenly in the water so that air was trapped in your shirt and boots; then you aimed feet-first through the gaps between the rocks. Now and then you needed to swim, so you turned over and around, hoping you didn't bash yourself too badly on the river bed as you did so. Once I lost concentration, and found myself floating out of the slow current I had chosen and towards a fierce little rapid. I wedged myself between two rocks for a minute or two, and then Pedro and the younger of the two Swiss women came across the rocks and pulled me onto a boulder. I felt a bit of an ass.

I felt a much bigger one later. Back at the stockade, I took off my shirt and plunged it into the water to get rid of the grit. As I did so I tumbled off the bank and into the pool, bashing myself on the side. I was then very thin, and the blow bruised a rib. I had done this many times; with a sinking heart I realized that this meant some weeks of discomfort. Later that night, I lay on my thin, sandy mattress trying to breathe without my chest exploding. It would prove to be a mild bruise, but would still plague me for three weeks.

*

On our third day in the jungle we took to the river again, but this was a bigger one. It was the Río Mangosiza, and this time we had more than shirts to keep ourselves afloat. From the mission, a two-hour walk through the trees brought us to a bluff, down which we scrambled to a yellow beach on a wide, fast river. Two long dugouts were there with their owners, Shuar in T-shirts; they were not taking us, however. They watched, expressionless, as we embarked on two 12ft aluminium speed-boats with outboard motors, arranged ourselves with all our gear, and strapped on our life-jackets. The guides did not wear them. Even if they had felt comfortable with such things, the jackets would have impeded their movements when they were guiding the boats through rapids and shallows – something they would have to do often.

The engines started; a whiff of exhaust hung on the air, and then we headed east. There was no point in asking where. Alfredo said he did not know; Carlos either had not decided, or had not told him. The banks to either side were thickly wooded, but here and there we saw breaks in the vegetation, with oblong structures that had walls of narrow planks that had been turned at an angle so that the walls were actually grilles, allowing the air to pass through. They had steep thatched rooves. Shuar stood and watched as we went past. If we waved they waved back; otherwise they simply stared. Around us were small mountains of a few hundred feet, a sign of the Andes scarp which was still less than 100 miles away. The usual threads of cloud nestled between them, and as midday approached the mist deepened and the sky turned grey. But the rain did not break until about one, boring down as we climbed the steep bank to one of the longhouses to visit the Shuar.

The Shuar were a paradox. Their religion, their way of feeding themselves, their customs, remained much as they had for thousands of years; a self-limiting population, held down by health hazards and their environment. That was how they wished to remain. Their isolation was only partly a reflection of their ignorance of the outside world; it also reflected a healthy skepticism as to how much that world would really do for them. Beyond Macas, in Sucua, was the Shuar Centre.

Partially-funded by the Government, it was however an ancient, probably pre-Columbian, tribal meeting-place; now it operated as a cultural focus and campaigning tool, as well as mounting exhibitions about Shuar life and maintaining a small zoo for the visitor. Going to Sucua some days later, we would see a noticeboard on which were pinned items about threats to tribal life not just in Ecuador, but as far afield as Irian Jaya. "Do Shuars vote?" I asked Alfredo. "Good God, yes," he replied. "Their chiefs will organize a light plane to get to the polls if they have to." Unlike many peoples for whom it was already too late, the Shuar had the sophistication to protect their simplicity.

The house we had come to visit was perfect for its site. Not only did the slatted planks admit air and exclude rain; the earth floor was raised by an inch or two off ground level, and was perfectly dry. The head of the household presided over his court from behind a crudely-cut table, and was plump and jovial. His age was impossible to determine. *Cuys* – guinea-pigs, which have always been eaten in South America, and are bred for that purpose – scuttled, squeaking loudly, in and out of a small enclosure that had been built for them in the corner. Women and children remained behind the master, the infants looking gravely at us. A young woman held a boy of about two in her arms. She was smiling at him, rocking him, and there was much love in her eyes. But the child's belly was badly swollen, perhaps from parasites in the drinking water. The women brought us sticks of maize, which they served us on palm-leaves on the earth floor. With them were whole catfish, bony but tasting a bit like trout. There was also *chicha*, a drink made from maize in the Andes but from manioc here. The manioc is chewed by the women, spat out and fermented; it had a strong, cheesy smell and bits floating on the surface. I cannot pretend I liked it, but it did me no harm.

The Shuar were about as far as it was possible to get from me, both culturally and geographically. There was no direct communication. I could speak some Spanish, but they could not. Those in the towns who did, sometimes spoke it strangely, as they had only the infinitive in their own language. Neither, in line with their climate, did they have dates or years or seasons. What would they need them for? Ask a Shuar how old they are and you would not get an easy answer. They lived by fishing and planting maize in a place which had no fierce climatic changes, and plenty of rain and strong sunlight to make things grow. When, after a few years, the ground was exhausted, they moved on, and the jungle reclaimed the small patch of land they had used. They also hunted, and used poison darts, albeit with care – judging the amount of poison for a blowpipe arrow is an acquired art, for too much can poison not just the prey but whoever eats it. They liked personal ornaments and decoration, although the authorities, alarmed at the use of feathers from endangered species, now insisted that they only make these for their personal use, or use more common types of birds. Their technology had developed to the point they needed it; the houses and canoes were adequate for their uses.

It seemed an idyllic life, but of course it was not in every way. Later that day, we moored at the beach where we would camp for the night, and Carlos visited a nearby Shuar household to see if they would receive us. They could not, for the wife was so gravely ill with an abscess that it was not clear if she would last the night. Alfredo borrowed some tetracycline off one of the Swiss, and in the morning the woman was dramatically better. Carlos left a supply with her, hoping that she would follow the dosage he suggested.

A little tetracycline to save a very sick woman. It seemed simple enough, but the Shuar had no source of supply for such things; what would it have been? I asked Alfredo if it would really be so difficult to provide a community nurse who would travel through the area once a month by canoe, carrying a supply of simple medicines. His answer was that it did not happen. In Quito, another teacher told me that the public hospitals even there did not have supplies of drugs and dressings. Part of the reason was that no-one in Ecuador was even supposed to pay tax unless they were earning a salary that was quite high even by Western standards. Even then, it was rarely collected. (Like much else in Ecuador, this may now have changed.)

I had problems of my own, albeit less serious, that night. We pulled onto a beach to make camp. Ellen, Andy and I crammed into a tiny tent and slept in sleeping-bags on the hard, crumpled groundsheet. My rib hurt like hell. Pedro, Bartolo, Carlos and Alfredo did not help matters by drinking rum and talking loudly round the campfire until after three, despite attempts to shut them up. I was probably more fragile than they were in the morning.

But a memorable morning. By 11, I felt I was living a dream, roaring down a remote river in a speedboat towards the frontier with a cigarette in one hand and a can of beer in the other. It was not even raining; the clouds were thin enough for a weak ray of sunshine to come through now and then, and I felt pleasantly warm.

Although internationally regarded as a frontier, this was, as I have said, a ceasefire line. Fighting in the air and on the ground had broken out again only 10 years earlier, although cynics had claimed that the incident had been allowed to happen by the then Ecuadorian president, Jaime Roldós, to distract attention from problems at home. (In fact, Jaime Roldós is remembered today mainly for his strong support of human rights. He and his wife died shortly afterwards in a still-unexplained air crash that some believed to have been engineered by the CIA.) The war broke out again four years after I passed that way. After that the two countries did come to an agreement, and it seems the matter has been settled. In 1991, however, there was an uneasy peace. The nearest we went to the ceasefire line that day was a river junction about 20 minutes' run upstream from it. There was an army post on a cliff above the confluence. It appeared deserted, although there was an Ecuadorian flag flapping flaccidly at the head of a pole on the cliff above us, and scraps of toilet paper clung to the bank below. Carlos went ashore and obtained permission for us to pass. We pulled away; as we did so, 15 or 20 soldiers, suddenly visible, stood on the cliff and waved.

For half an hour we travelled up another river, the low mountains of what was now Peru rising on our right, before stopping at a beach that would be that night's campsite. On the opposite bank was a scarp of about 10 feet in height, beyond which lay a lagoon, where there were alligators. The afternoon was spent portaging one of the boats, minus its motor, up the scarp and through the forest – a messy business as it was now raining. Bunches of wild bananas appeared here and there through the drizzle. We rowed across the lagoon looking for the alligators; we saw little of them, but now and then the silence of the humid afternoon was broken by the sudden sound of a rifle-shot from the lagoon – in fact, an alligator's tail smashing into the water.

It was another fiercely uncomfortable night. I was now covered with damp grit, and it seemed to be in every orifice. In the small hours it rained heavily, and we piled up the gear at either end of our tiny tent, sleeping three abreast and trying not to roll over on top of each other. Attempts to shift position were met with a thunderclap of pain from my right side.

Tomorrow, we would leave early for the roadhead at Morona. I was sad to leave the jungle, but I was also happy. Few people had come this way, and I had seen the headwaters of the Amazon, and the people who lived there, very much as Francisco de Orellana must have seen them in 1541. A few weeks later, north of the Río Pastaza, I would see what might become of them.

*

There was nothing at Morona, simply the narrow gravel track that came down to a broad, shallow part of the river. Yet that startled in itself. Morona was, in fact, the end of the known world, the end of civilization; beyond it lay the tangled skein of rivers that only men like Carlos really knew.

We unloaded our rucksacks from the boats and walked up the shallow bank, to see an object from another world: an old bus, the hazy sun gleaming gently on its sun-dried paintwork. The driver greeted us briefly and we climbed the ladder at the rear to deposit our luggage on the roof. Then we shook hands with Carlos, Pedro and Bartolo and the bus pulled away. We were bound for Macas, and it would take many hours.

At first, the journey bored me, and I regretted leaving *La Bestia Roja* in my rucksack. I quickly forgot about it. The track twisted its way up into the hills in pouring rain; to the left lay an abyss, to the right a wall of scree down which cascaded a mini-Niagara, which seemed it might dislodge the rock and bring it down on our heads or, worse, soak the road away from its narrow toehold on the mountainside – there was no tarmac to hold it together. Later, on the long road from Papallacta to Lago Agrio in the Northern Oriente, Andy, Alfredo and I would spend five hours waiting for a landslide to be cleared, but today were lucky.

After a few hours we came to the first cluster of buildings. There was an airstrip there, and an Army roadblock, manned by military police in fatigues and caps, American-style. We descended from the bus with our passports. I expected to be nodded on after a brief inspection, but we were not. We were still in a sensitive area; looking back, I suppose it was not obvious what we were doing on the road from Morona. We were asked why we had no stamps to confirm that we had arrived in the *selva* from within Ecuador. We explained that we had arrived by air. Unconvinced, they ordered our rucksacks to be brought down from the roof of the bus, and inspected everything, even the packet of disposable razors in my bag; the covers were slid off the heads. There was an atmosphere of polite suspicion. *La Bestia Roja* was tossed back into my rucksack without interest, but the Arabic visas in my passport caused concern. At length we were allowed to go. We climbed back on board the bus, apologising to the other passengers for the delay. They seemed unsurprised.

But now the sun cut through the vapour, and improved my mood. Indeed it was one of the few days I spent in the Oriente when it did not rain in the afternoon. I had thought of Macas as remote, but compared with Morona it was the centre of the universe. The 10-hour journey from the deep *selva* to Macas would take us through settler country, where the overspill from the Cordillera was encroaching slowly on the virgin forest. Signs of habitation would appear slowly at first, then with increasing frequency. It was a strange and beautiful time-lapse journey through history.

Sometime around three, we passed through the first settlement of any size; Huambi, a small wild west town about 30 or 40 miles from Macas. There was a post office and a cluster of empty, sleepy bars, a Catholic church and an Evangelical chapel, all built of wood and painted bright, warm colours. The wall of the school was decorated by a vast, colourful map of the world.

As the bus wandered slowly through the forest in the warm, gentle light of the afternoon, the settlers climbed on and off with their children, a racial mix as anarchic as the colours with which they painted their houses. A woman of Indian descent had twin infant girls in identical red dresses, their faces similar; but one child was as brown as mahogany, the other blonde. A beautiful girl of about seven with Spanish eyes and ivory skin rubbed shoulders with a plump blonde teenager who could, like many in those foothills, have been of German descent; this had been a refuge from the Depression for many. There were squat men with *indígena* faces, an Afro-Caribbean or two. As we lumbered out of Huambi in the golden light, we passed mile upon mile of settlers' shacks nestling in the trees; some smarter than others, some just huts, others with two storeys, brightly-painted, with flowers in the garden. All were jacked up on bricks against the rain. Indeed, people had come out to enjoy today's sun. As the afternoon wore on and the light turned yellow and orange, girls with great flashing eyes perched on fences, wearing old-fashioned skirts and blouses and enormous cheap earrings. They were like proud sexy extras from *West Side Story*, transported to the jungle.

Back at the Hotel Peñon del Oriente I had a new room. There were even more religious slogans pinned to the walls, roughly typed on bits of card. The religious maniac had however not translated the instructions on the electric shower-head, which were in Portuguese. Sweating and grimy, I struggled to make the shower work, remembering that I was missing *Miss Ecuador* on television.

But we were done with Macas and the Southern Oriente. As flights to Quito were rare, we would return by road. I wanted to see Baños, a spa town in the Eastern Andes that was said to be most attractive. We decided that, rather than climb back into the Cordillera via Cuenca, it would be better to cross into the Northern Oriente, transit it briefly and climb the pass from Puyo to Baños. Puyo was only about 100 miles to the north, but before it lay the Río Pastaza, the major river that was being bridged. As the bridge was not finished, we would hire a car to take us to it (there were no buses along that track) and cross in an engineers' cage. On the other side we might, with luck, pick up a bus or a lift for Puyo.

We left Macas on a cold wet morning. A friendly driver took us northward through the *selva* in his decayed Japanese car; after an hour or two we arrived on the banks of a steel-grey river that ran between gravel banks and islands. In the distance, low mountains were capped with cloud. On the opposite bank was the Northern Oriente. The driver grasped our hands warmly and wished us a smooth journey; the tired car swayed away across the gravel, its exhaust mixing with the wet mist as it crunched towards Macas. Across the river was a tall two-span steel bridge, some hundreds of yards long; but there was no roadway across it yet, just a cable that carried a steel box. I could see Ellen turning pale.

"Oh God," she muttered.

"Will you be all right?" I asked her quietly.

"Yes, I think so," she said.

We crammed into the steel cage, which was only just big enough for the four of us; Alfredo pulled the steel mesh door shut and we pulled on the rope and rumbled slowly away from the bank. At first we were a hundred feet above the river, but then we slid close to the rushing, boiling-cold water below. Ellen seemed to be holding her breath. I glanced at her with real regard. She was no soft case; as a midwife, after all, she delivered children – I cannot stand the sight of blood. Yet there had been times during the journey when I had sensed that she had not signed up for quite this. Still, she never complained, until the night we returned to Quito, where she cornered Andy outside the toilets in the Hotel Colón and gave him a piece of her mind, while I sat in the bar nearby, watching the aftermath of the first Gulf war unfold on CNN. For the moment she held her peace.

After many minutes, we thumped into the north bank of the Río Pastaza and disentangled our limbs before stepping out of the cage. Here it was a building site, contractors' lorries churning all to a muddy wasteland, the rain collecting everywhere in light-brown puddles. In a small shack above, we found a tired young woman selling drinks. Yes, she said, there would be a bus to Puyo in two hours. She brought us coffee and Coke and retired into the shack to breast-feed her child, a speck of femininity in a sea of hard hats and rain-filled ruts. We settled down to wait, saying little. Alfredo and I smoked, exhaling clouds that floated slowly away on the thick, damp air. I watched the men being winched up to the final span of the bridge in steel cradles. In a week's time they were due to close that final span, and everyone in the Southern Oriente knew what that meant. Change was coming.

That night a truncated American school bus took us from Puyo to Baños on a vertiginous track that wound into the foothills and on up into the Tunguruhua range, climbing into the high Cordillera in just over two hours. By the time we arrived in Baños it was getting dark. Baños is a tourist town, and we had no trouble finding a small, clean, cheerful hotel, where we shaved and showered before going out in search of a good meal. The change in pressure, and temperature, had restored my appetite, and I devoured a huge pizza and swallowed half a bottle of smooth Chilean Gran Reserva before flopping into bed. We were all very tired.

We awoke the next morning to find ourselves in a peaceful and attractive town in a deep, narrow valley, surrounded by the peaks of the Tunguruhua range. There were white churches aplenty here, and many tourists, American and European; the local speciality, a type of toffee, was made in shops open to the street, and pyramids of colourful sombreros, red, white, black and purple, stood ready for sale on the street corners. We walked slowly up the nearest mountain, aiming for the white cross that towered 1,500ft above the town. Two hours later, we arrived at the foot of the cross. It was quiet; nothing stirred except the long stalks of grass. There was some hazy sunshine, and it was gently warm. To the east we could clearly see the crack in the Tunguruhua range through which the track ran back to Puyo and the Oriente. At the other end of the town, which was laid out like a relief-map at our feet, we could make out the white stone cemetery. A funeral was making its way slowly towards it. It had about a mile to go. I watched its progress. Later we descended to the town and visited the cemetery ourselves. The white tombs, crosses and small mausoleums were divided here and there by bright red poinsettias; in the distance, the white twin towers of the church in the main square rose against the grey-green peaks, themselves brushed by wisps of grey cloud that crowded into the steep valleys between the sunlit slopes. It was good to be back in the mountains.

*

I was running out of money now, and would soon return to England. But Andy and I had one last journey to make together.

The track that had brought us out of the *selva* to Baños had not been the main route into the Northern Oriente. That lay some way to the north, across the Papallacta Pass. We decided to take it, and see what was happening north of the Río Pastaza. Thus, a week or so after Easter, I arrived at the main bus station, the Terminal Terrestre, at five one morning. Alfredo and Andy were already there, sitting in the deserted cafeteria and sipping black coffee. They were discussing a plan, later abandoned, to explore riverine caves at Archidona, where you waded in through the entrance to find yourself in a huge colony of vampire bats. We boarded the bus for Lago Agrio, stepping over the boy who collected the fares; he was asleep on the transmission tunnel. Bit by bit the interior filled up with oil workers and their families. We nosed out of the Terminal Terrestre. Quito and its suburbs fell behind as we dropped some 2,000ft into the valley east of the city, and then began the long climb to the 14,000ft Papallacta Pass. Before long the bus pierced the clouds, and I turned round to look back across the carpet of white. Many miles to the west, beyond Quito, the serrated peaks of the Pichinchas punched through a pillow of clouds in the thin early-morning light.

Beside us ran the Trans-Andean pipeline. This thin thread of silver steel stood four or five feet above the ground on tripod legs, and wound its way over some of the world's highest passes, rising from near sea-level in the *selva* to the summit of the pass and dropping to Quito before running on up the Western half of the Andes, finally dropping to the Pacific oil-terminal near Esmeraldas.

Towards the summit, the sealed surface ran out. As the bus wound its way along the narrow dirt road, bodywork vibrating from the strain on the engine, we crossed and re-crossed the rivers that ran down from the Papallacta watershed. Two or three hours out of Quito, passing over a turbulent stream, I saw through the mist that the current was going the same way as we were. We had begun our descent into the forest.

It was a long descent. Sometime in the early afternoon, we were still in the foothills; then we were blocked by a mudslide. A grader arrived, but it was clearly struggling. Bored, we walked some way back up the road to a small wooden shack, to try and beg something to eat. In front of the hut we found a man of perhaps 30, with an Indian face, T-shirt, shorts and flip-flops; all four looked tired and worn. His wife looked older. Several children were scratching about in the yard with the chickens. The man greeted us politely, but he had no food to sell us. "You will have better luck at the house up the road, perhaps," he said. "Unless you would like me to kill a chicken for you. You see, we are a little poor." It was an understatement. But he took a forked stick and knocked some grapefruit down from his trees. He would accept no payment.

A nice man; but he was also a reminder that, if the oil companies had packed up and left the Oriente that year, nothing would have been solved, for the Shuar, Waorani or anyone else. There would still be internal migration from the highlands above. Since the 1960s, a failure to implement effective land reform had driven some *indígenas* in the Cordillera to occupy land unilaterally, sometimes with difficult results. In the meantime, there had been a policy of relieving the pressure of a burgeoning rural population by settling the landless in the virgin territory of the jungle, through the official land agency, IERAC. This had implications for the ecosystem in which the tribal peoples lived.

That system was and is delicate. There were several hundred species of trees, including mahogany and what used to be called cigar-box cedar, although it was now little used for that. The roots of such trees are long; tear them up, and there is little strength left in the remaining soil. And they were being torn up. I had always believed that this was being done by wicked capitalists from North America, Europe or Japan, but in Ecuador at that time, at least, apart from a little very selective commercial logging, they had little to do with it. Neither was large-scale farming or beef-cattle ranching a major factor, at least in this region (although it certainly has been elsewhere).

When I returned to London in May I was put in touch with an Oxford-based consultant who had worked with Britain's Overseas Development Administration (later known as DfID). "There is a certain amount of clearance by commercial palm-oil companies, but most of it is done by small farmers," he said. I had heard a theory that clearing land at the base of a valley could cause landslips above, especially in the mountainous Southern Oriente. He replied that landslips were more common below cultivation than above it. "The main worry is where you get gullies in cultivated fields, in which the water concentrates. It can then run down and destabilize whatever is below it. In fact in the lower slopes of the Andes, where you get landslips, most of the trees have already gone. I think that you can paint a dramatic picture in all the Andean countries," he said, citing the example of Santa Cruz in Bolivia, which faced real danger. In the case of Ecuador's jungle areas, he suggested, the lack of coordination and efficiency by Government agencies had much to answer for. "Given the appalling situation in the highlands, space does have to be found. The problem is that settlers are sometimes badly-advised by the land agency and their agriculture often fails. People then sell up to large owners, move on and start again – so you get maximum environmental damage and minimum economic gain." Whatever the oil industry may have done in the Oriente, it was far from clear that it had been the main driver of deforestation.

This was in 1991. Ecuador has of course moved on since. However, deforestation has continued in Ecuador. Terra-i, a collaboration between (among other institutions) the International Center for Tropical Agriculture (CIAT) in Colombia and King's College London, has apparently found that between January 1 and March 7 2013, some 9,075 ha of Ecuador's forests were cleared. Terra-i states that this represents a 300% increase on the same period in 2012.

*

We arrived in Lago Agrio sometime after sunset, the western horizon still glowing orange, the streets lit by shops that lined walkways below the overhangs of ugly concrete buildings. The shops were bursting with goods: portable hi-fi, clothes, luggage – especially luggage. There were expensive hotels in Lago Agrio, and many restaurants. Housewives, out shopping, were casually but expensively dressed by Ecuadorian standards. They looked cheerful. The odd Chevrolet or Nissan Trooper swept by, sometimes with a gringo in the passenger seat. This was oildorado. But the roads were mud and cinder.

In the morning an ancient taxi took us along the cinder roads through a jungle punctuated by clearings, in which there were Christmas trees atop wells for gas and oil. Just north of Lago Agrio stood the refineries of Texaco and CEPE, the state oil company. They had a clean, modern look here; lots of fresh paint and silver steel. Now and then an orange flame would rise in the distance, pretty against the blue sky and the bright green vegetation.

We waited to cross the mile-wide Río Napo on the ferry. As we stood by the landing-stage, large dumper trucks ploughed through the shallows half a mile away, probably building a bridge. The hot damp air was tinged with diesel. The ferry turned slowly around to drift down on the current. It was called the *Lord Alexandra*. I was reminded of some of the cocktail menus I had seen over the last three months; one might be offered a Gras Hoper, a Tonkollins or, in one alarming case, a Blood of Mary.

Our route beyond the Río Napo wound through the little settlements that now dotted the region. There was Proyecto, for instance, which was what its name implied – a few clapboard houses, the odd pile of rubbish in the streets and several bars. Shushufindi was similar, but a bit larger. It was also in the news. The following August, the government was due to allocate blocks for the secondary exploitation of the Shushufindi oilfield. The reserves were thought to amount to 3,045 million barrels, but not all of this would be recovered; this was secondary extraction, meaning that oil not extracted under its own pressure in the first phase would now be pumped out using gas, of which there was plenty in the area. Ecuador thought that about 44% of the Shushufindi reserves could be brought out this way, enough to make the field viable well into the next century.

But Ecuador would not benefit from this as much as it should. Later, in Quito, not long before I left at the beginning of May, I spent an evening talking to Radu. A Romanian by birth, and an oil engineer, he was a friend's landlord, and now and then we all had a beer. He ran an independent oil consultancy, and he thought that the government was making a mistake. "They're simply letting blocks to the overseas oil companies," he explained, "instead of having the state oil company contract them to extract the oil on its own behalf. This means less control over the process for Ecuador, and less revenue." Some Ecuadorians were very concerned about this. However, as one told me, it was not possible for Ecuador to extract the oil itself. Substantial capital would be needed to hire foreign companies such as Texaco and Conoco to drill on behalf of the government, instead of simply leasing blocks to them so that they could extract the oil for their own benefit. Ecuador was paying a third of its overseas earnings to service its debts, and could no longer afford it.

This was serious. The percentage of oil earnings clawed back from each barrel was crucial to this small country. In 1985, for example, oil revenues had accounted for 66% of for-eign earnings in $US. Then the price of oil dropped, and the oil industry's contribution to the exchequer dropped to 45%. In the past, OPEC had approved Ecuador's upping its exports in such a situation, but the country could only go so far down that road; the export infrastructure, like the reserves, was limited. In 1991 things were far worse, for the Gulf War had sent prices tumbling to $15 a barrel as the markets anticipated stronger US influence in the Middle East. By April 1991, projected oil rev-enue for the year was $130 million down on 1990 – and this in the middle of an economic crisis. No wonder Ecuador could not afford to incur further debt in order to exploit Shushufindi on its own terms.

But there was an optimistic slant to Shushufindi, one that might make it worthwhile nonetheless. What would come out of the field's secondary exploitation was light crude. South of the Río Pastaza, in the Southern Oriente, lay untapped reserves which were nearly as big. They were unexploited partly because of their location, but also because they were of heavy crude, and could not easily be pumped through the Trans-Andean pipeline. However, if they could be, they would become eco-nomic. If the heavy crude was mixed with the light crude about to come on-stream from Shushufindi, this would come to pass.

*

Like Lago Agrio, Puerto Francisco de Orellana was booming too. This tatty town, better known as Coca, was as far east as you could go in Northern Ecuador before coming to thick jungle that runs down to the Peruvian border about 200 kilometers away, close to the point where Ecuador met Peru, Colombia and, nearly, Brazil. This jungle had never been properly explored by outsiders. The frontier between what was known and what was not was mostly the Río Napo, an immensely broad river that eventually flows into the Amazon.

We stood beside the river at sunset. There were steel-grey clouds in the sky, but they finished some way above the eastern horizon, which was light and clear; silver and yellow flecks of light bounced off the surface of the river, and a little yellow sunlight filtered through to the landing-stage where the people of Coca's waterfront were washing and drying their clothes.

I wondered if they drank the water as well. Cholera had by then crossed the border in the south. Already the first case had been reported in Lago Agrio, where we had spent the previous night. In another week a number of people would die in Chimborazo province, in the high Cordillera. By July, 375 Ecuadorians would be known to have died from the disease.

Over there in the forest, other bad things might be happening. There was probably oil there too, and in the previous 10 years, more and more local tribespeople had been shifted off their land and onto 'reservations'. The London office of Survival International claimed in March 1990 that 700 of the Waorani people had been kicked off their patch by PetroCanada, which wanted to drill. They were settled in shacks along the oil communication road, where they were supplied with the same rations as the oil-workers: "Powdered drinks, sugar and tinned tuna... They have now become a community of refugees, living on the fringes of the oil-camps," Survival International alleged.

In July 1987, the indigenous people had struck back. Mgr Alejandro Labaca, Bishop of Coca, and Sister Inés Arango travelled beyond the Río Napo to speak to a group of uncontacted Waorani, or Huaorani, Indians. Mgr Labaca knew that the oil companies would be coming, and wished to make the first contact himself in order to try and protect the Waorani's interests. The oil companies cooperated to the extent of providing a helicopter. Mgr Labaca left instructions that no reprisals should be taken if he and Arango were harmed. They were, being transfixed by 21 spears, each 12ft long. Looking across the Río Napo, I reflected that it had happened less than 50 miles away.

The killing of Labaca and Arango did not prevent the Church from trying to protect the rights of the tribes, and in 1988 the Bishops' Conference actually signed a treaty with the Government which, it hoped, would prevent further incursions. Meanwhile an area of just under 10,000 sq km across the river from Coca had already been designated a national park in 1979. This was the Yasuni National Park.

In fact, so far as I could see, the attitude of Ecuadorians who did want to exploit the *selva* was not necessarily anti-Indian. Rather, it was a rejection of the concept of their separateness. This attitude was best summed up in 1972 by Guillermo Rodríguez Lara, the then military ruler of Ecuador. "There is no more Indian problem," he argued. "We all become white men when we accept the goals of the national culture." To the ears of a modern Western liberal like me, this is racist. But it was not meant to be. I heard something similar from Radu, the Romanian oil engineer, when I returned to Quito. We were sitting outside a bar on the Avenida Amazonas in the city centre. He had been talking about the coming development of the oil industry in the Southern Oriente. I asked him, didn't it mean that the Shuar would go the way of the Waorani? Live in shacks? Get our diseases? Eat tinned tuna?

"Look," he said, "right now these people in the jungle wake up, work, eat, go to bed, breed. That's all. They know nothing of nothing. There are no books, no music, no medicine, no art. There is no reason for them to be alive except to keep themselves that way. What kind of life is that? Think what we can bring them. You will see. It will be good for these people."

As he spoke, something moved behind his chair. It was one of the street kids that scratched a living along the Amazonas, selling flowers and cleaning shoes. Further behind, nearer the kerb, a man with twisted legs dragged himself slowly on his belly towards the Colón.

*

I liked Sacha when I first saw it. That was in late afternoon. We had paid off the taxi in Shushufindi, taken a bus to Proyecto, and then boarded another bus for the two-hour journey to Coca. This was a bus in the local style. It had a Japanese van chassis with a wooden open-sided structure on the back, immensely strong, roofed over, with a luggage rack up top. There was a platform behind for the guard/conductor to ride on. The old and infirm travelled in the cab at the front, while the rest sat on benches in the wooden frame behind. The benches were under cover, but they were not comfortable, and it was hot. So when a bus finally reached Proyecto sometime after three, Alfredo, Andy and I scrambled onto the roof with our bags.

The first time that the bus met something coming the other way, it pulled over to the side of the narrow grit road to avoid it. The nearside wheels scrabbled sideways, and I thought we would tip over, but this strange vehicle was more stable than it seemed. It was quick, too, and the slipstream on the roof was cool. Too cool, in fact, but every now and then we would pull up to let someone off into the undergrowth at the roadside, where his shack nestled amongst the trees and long grasses, the only decoration on the wood or corrugated iron being the political slogans that were splashed across every vertical surface. As the bus slowed, warm air would touch the face gently; then we would be off through the jungle again at 35 or 40 miles an hour, the coachwork swaying as the bus cantered along the narrow dirt carriageway.

Just before five, we passed through Sacha. Another frontier town; low wooden sheds strung out for a mile and a half on either side of the widened road, pickup trucks circling slowly in front of shops, men in hats. School was out, and there were shoals of teenage girls, smartly uniformed in grey skirts and vermillion blazers, unexpected, as if someone had shipped an English grammar school down the Río Napo. The girls chattered, pinched each other, giggled, waved and nudged at the sight of foreigners perched atop a local bus. Their hair was long, glossy, clean and immaculately combed and their uniforms quite perfect, right down to the long white socks. And the sun was shining, the late-afternoon glow that I liked so much, the world seen through a warm-up filter. Yes, I liked Sacha.

But the next day it looked different. It was about two this time, but it was colder and there had been a little rain on the way from Coca; on top of the bus again, we huddled in waterproofs. Someone was turfed off the bus just outside Coca. Papers not in order. Snuck across the border from Colombia. "How long have you lived here, then?" I heard a policeman asking him. "Two thousand years," came the pained reply. By the time we reached Sacha the rain had stopped, but it was over-cast and humid, and my face felt dirty. We ate – not well; the lunch of the day at a cheap restaurant, beef stew with rice pre-ceded by *yaguarlocro*. The latter is a soup of dumplings floating in fat. I ate raw intestine of camel in Africa but I couldn't eat this. I pushed it aside, feeling a bit sick. The previous night we had drunk too much cheap sweet Colombian rum in our hotel room in Coca. In the morning I had taken a shower in our hotel bathroom. It was dirty, and had used toilet-paper piled up high in the bin in the corner. No-one had emptied it. It stank.

I tried the stew. The air felt thicker, damper.

"You wanted to see a dirty oil well," said Alfredo. "An ugly one."

I nodded.

"We'll find one."

A little outside the town, on the main road to Coca, there was an oil installation. It was some way back from the road, but you could see the tall steel pipes through which the gas was being flared off, the bright orange flames clear against the grey sky, threads of black smoke curling upwards from their heat. We turned down a partially-surfaced track nearby, and walked for a mile until we reached a clearing. There was a steel oil tap there. A few yards away was something we had seen before in the jungle; what might once have been a small lagoon, about 50ft wide and 400ft long. It was now filled with solid oil-waste that had crystallized in the sunlight. We threw stones on the surface, but they didn't sink. The clearing smelled like a dock-yard. Not far away a line of eight or nine pipes swung through a gash in the jungle.

Texaco had been the company mainly responsible for oil exploration in the Northern Oriente. Other companies had joined them now, but it was still their symbol that seemed to appear everywhere in the Oriente and they were, with Conoco, the first to bid for the new Shushufindi blocks.

In Britain I contacted them through their London press office. Through 'phone and letter, I asked: were they responsible for this? If not, what do they think would be the technical reason for it? Were they interested in the Southern Oriente? And did they have any fund for contributing to the development of the area in which they are working? I received no reply, apart from a tentative query, relayed from America, as to who I was.

We walked back towards the main road. Where there was tarmac on the track, it was liberally covered with sticky oil waste, giving off a tarry odour in the humid, overcast afternoon. Towards us came a settler family, a man and his teenage sons. Perhaps they were from the highlands, and had swapped shawls and bowler hats for the tee-shirts and flip-flops they were wearing now. They passed us without comment, their faces quite expressionless, their flip-flops sticking on the tacky tarmac. I thought of hot waterfalls plunging into a clear, pebbled pool and multicoloured butterflies and a young mother with a little boy; his stomach was swollen, but she was smiling at him, and rocking him back and forth, very gently.

Unknown to me, others were asking questions too. Two years later, in 1993, a group of Ecuadorians from the Oriente sued Texaco, alleging that the pollution from the company's operations had damaged not only the environment but the health of people in the region. The company had, it was said, discharged huge amounts of toxic and carcinogenic waste into open, unlined pits like the one I have described. It was also alleged to have burned off oil spills, creating heavy smoke and soot. Nine years later the US court decided not to hear the case on the grounds that it was more correctly brought in Ecuador. In 2003 it was, although

Texaco had by then been bought by Chevron. In 2011 the latter was ordered to pay $8.6 billion in damages and clean-up costs, and to make a public apology – or, if it did not do the latter, to pay $18 billion, a sum that eventually became a $19 billion judgment. Chevron has not admitted liability; it has appealed, and has also filed racketeering charges against the plaintiff's legal team. In September 2013 President Correa called for a worldwide boycott of Chevron.

The Nine
Horizons

We were late leaving Delhi. The apron was empty, baking in the heat. The day before we had hired a *tuk-tuk*, one of those gimcrack three-wheelers in which the driver sat ahead and the passengers on a narrow bench behind. A small two-stroke engine popped and farted below us as we drove to Lutyens's huge capital, the dome shivering in the heat, the reddish stone hot to the touch. It had been about 47 deg C and the mid-morning sky had been hazy and ill-defined.

I gazed out over the wing. A small, elderly Russian transport taxied by, complete with gun turret under the tail; it had seen better days. One of a small armada that set out from the former Soviet bloc in those years (it was 1992), packed with enormous women in old-fashioned headscarves with things to sell and things to buy; a tramp-steamer of the skies, the air around its exhausts distorted and liquid.

I began a conversation with a well-dressed man in the seat beside me. We had the same destination. I would be a development volunteer. He was an Indian diplomat. He had just finished three years in Kuwait.

"How was that?" I asked him.

He thought for a moment. "Imagine a supermarket in the desert," he said.

A companionable silence followed. I picked up one of the newspapers that the cabin crew had draped across the armrests, expecting *The Times of India*. But it was their own national newspaper, *Kuensel*. A banner headline ran across the front page: GUPS CALL FOR ACTION ON NGOLOP PROBLEM.

I wondered if the Indian diplomat could tell me what a *gup* was, or indeed a *ngolop*; but he was dozing. In fact, a gup is a village headman or representative. As to the *ngolops*, I would find out soon enough.

A cabin attendant passed by, looking right and left to check belts. She was tall—unusually so—and had a broad Asiatic face with very high cheekbones and golden-brown skin, and a curious lack of expression. Her thick black hair was cut in a bob. She wore a lightweight waist-length silk jacket over what looked like a sleeveless wrap. The wrap, called a *kira*, ran from her chest to her ankles, and formed a sort of tube, leaving little obvious room for movement; it was secured with attractive gold fasteners on her shoulders. Below the wrap was a smart white blouse.

We climbed away from Delhi and across the arid North Indian plain. Lucknow slid below us and we turned gently east. After an hour or so, bright white clouds started to line the horizon to the left; as we neared them, they took firmer shape, for they weren't clouds. We kept them to starboard a while, then drifted slowly across them, and I saw white points and cascades of rock and deep grey-green defiles. The mountains were shrouded here and there by a little cloud—thin as yet, for the monsoon was barely beginning.

Before long, the peaks came closer as we sank into a valley. Later, pilot friends would tell me how, in the monsoon months, they would cruise above the clouds, looking for a hole that was large enough for them to nip through, take a look around, and nip out again in a hurry if there was anything in the way. If there wasn't, they would guess which valley they were in, and guide the four-engined jet through it into the right one so that they could find the airstrip, ready to yank the stick back and pop porpoise-like above the clouds again if they ran out of space, or got lost. (Once above the clouds, landmarks such as Kanchenjunga and the Jomolhari range, and the Tibetan plain behind it, would soon tell them where they were.)

The approach itself was difficult. As we began it, the valley slopes moved up towards the plane's belly. A structure strange to me but clearly a temple of some kind slid below us, wisps of cloud reflecting the sunlight. The peaks were above us now, although we were barely 60 miles away from the blistering Bengal plain. The temple disappeared behind us and we catapulted over the edge of the mountain on which it stood, then dropped like a stone; my stomach flew upward. Later, I would arrive one windy winter's day when the plane would drop into an air-pocket, so shocking us that my neighbour, an urbane and charming acquaintance of royal blood, shrieked and dug her fingers so deep into my arm that it was bruised for a week. Today was smoother. We glided into a deep, rich valley ablaze with agriculture, and as the plane flared and settled, we drifted past a mighty building, half-temple, half-castle, a magnificent riot of white walls, hardwood windows, shingled roof and gilded gargoyles.

We filed down the steps and into the sudden calm of the strange spring morning. There was a small road a few hundred yards away, but nothing moved on it. On either side, the valley was lined with steep slopes, partially forested; the soil between the trees looked light and sandy. It was warm, but much cooler than Delhi, and there was a light breeze. At the far end of the runway, the temple/castle, Paro Dzong, dominated the narrow valley. Nearer at hand was a low wooden terminal. In it we queued before a man wearing what looked like a cross between a dressing-gown and a full-body kilt; the top was loose, voluminous, and I had heard that one could carry six bottles of beer within, kept in place by one's belt. The garment was the *gho*, the male equivalent of a *kira*, and was worn at all times, by law, when more than 300 metres from one's house. Across his shoulder was a *cumney*; this was a cross between a shawl and a scarf and was white – unless you were a *dasho*, which loosely speaking meant a knight of the realm; then it was red. A member of the national assembly wore a purple *cumney*. The King and his spiritual counterpart, the Jhe Khenpo, wore saffron ones.

A stamp was thrust onto a blank page; a large, round, purplish-blue stamp, with Tibetan script around the outside, a row of auspicious symbols such as conch shells, and finally, the words GRATIS VISA. SEEN AT PARO. I went out to join the tourists, smug in the knowledge that whereas they paid up to $200 a day for the privilege of visiting the country, I had won that most elusive prize: a resident's permit for the Kingdom of Bhutan.

*

One of the world's smallest capitals, Thimphu had a population of 31,000 then; today, I believe, it is three times that, but in 1992 it had the air of a small country town, the sort you drive through now and then in England when the motorway is blocked and the police divert you. The difference was its dramatic location, in a very narrow valley at 7,500ft; from its edges, steep slopes rose to peaks twice that height, their summits shrouded in the mist and rain of the monsoon season that was just beginning. The lost valley.

I soon explored Thimphu. In truth, there was not much of it then. There was a long main street that started at the top of a hill, and ran for about a mile and a half. It was punctuated by three little traffic islands. There were no traffic-lights; instead, at these three junctions, handsome little wooden pagodas sprouted from the concrete, complete with the appropriate traditional decoration. In each one, at busy times, there stood a smartly-dressed policeman in a blue, Western-style uniform, directing the traffic with stylised gestures, the balletic grace of which was enhanced by immaculate white gloves. In the early hours of the morning a year or so later, two friends and I emerged from a private bar a hundred yards or so from the central island, well the worse for wear. The street was deserted. My friends made straight for the nearby island and began to walk clockwise about it as if it were a religious structure, chanting *Om mani padme hum* – Behold the Jewel in the Lotus. I then leapt into the pagoda and started to direct imaginary traffic with extravagant hand-gestures. After a minute or so we became aware of a white-gloved policeman standing on the corner, his face a mask in the moonlight. We fled.

The main street was lined with low wooden shops, each with a front partially open to the street. They seemed, for the most part, to sell much the same thing; plastic implements, packets of tea, rather hard soap, chilies, and, for some reason, dried fish – always dried fish, although I never saw anyone buy any. However, Shop No. 9 had beer, while Shop No. 6 was good for potatoes. Here and there were different types of shop; a butcher for instance. And there was a small but very well-kept public library halfway up the street, with an excellent selection of old

English-language paperback novels. It was run by a charming young woman who appeared genuinely embarrassed when I returned some books a week late, and she had to make me pay a few pence in fines.

Nearly opposite was the national bank, which was helpful but not easy to use. One entered from the small car park to find oneself in a dark banking hall with wooden floors; as in India, guards lurked in the gloom, nursing ancient rifles. The banking counters took the form of grilles with tiny apertures, like old-fashioned ticket-offices; behind, one could see shirt-sleeved Indian clerks and their *gho*-clad Bhutanese colleagues writing with pens in huge ledgers. In 1992 there were no computers of any sort in the building at all, so far as I was aware. Withdrawing money involved fighting one's way to the head of one queue, presenting one's papers, taking a brass counter and then joining the crowd jostling and heaving around the window on the other side, waiting to hear the number on your counter called out so that you collect a pile of rupees (if travelling) or *ngultrum*, the local currency. This would happen when the clerk on the first desk got around to bringing the record of his transactions across, usually every 15 or 20 minutes. The bank staff were pleasant, but it was chaos.

There were few other shopping facilities in Bhutan. There were one or two shops where one buy could cassettes of Hindi film music, which was popular, or blank tapes, again Indian; these were mostly good, and not expensive. You could also buy some non-Bhutanese clothes and there were shoes too, but the selection was limited and expensive. A few shops stocked Indian magazines and newspapers, including *filmi* magazines that reported the doings of Bollywood; these were often in English. Starved of glamour, I bought a few myself. At the time, television was forbidden in Bhutan, but videos were everywhere and Hindi Bollywood movies all the rage. (The video shop sold *filmi* magazines. One day I saw two monks staring through the window at the cover of a magazine, the headline on which screamed EXCLUSIVE FIRST PIX JAMES DEAN SEVERED HEAD.)

When it came to restaurants, Thimphu was better supplied. The local ones served *emma datse*, the national dish, made of cheese and burning-hot chilies; I never came to terms with this, but there would also be *dhal bhat* and perhaps *momos*. The latter were little dumplings filled with meat, usually pork (occasionally yak, although I only encountered this once, in Sikkim). Or *paksha-paa*, which was pork (both lean and fat – the Bhutanese made little distinction), with the inevitable hot chilies, served on a large pile of savoury red mountain rice. The pigs had eaten well. Marijuana grows wild over much of Bhutan; Bhutanese people strongly disapproved of its consumption by humans, but used it as fodder. Some schools kept a pig, and small boys and girls in *ghos* and *kiras* trotted cheerfully towards the pigpen with armfuls of weed. The pork was excellent.

Western food was also served in a surprising number of places. There were a lot of short-term foreign consultants in Thimphu, and many were not there long enough to get into cooking. The best restaurant, 89, was a little expensive for volunteers but served good food, including excellent chips; I was told that some Irish volunteers, horrified by the soggy chips, had marched into the kitchen and showed the staff how to make decent ones. In 89 you could have a good yak steak in season – that was when the yaks came down to winter pasture just above the town. Yak was a little gamier and tougher than beef, but pleasant enough. On winter weekends I always enjoyed a long mountain walk, or bicycle ride, in the bright, crisp sun, followed by an evening meal of yak and chips at

89. By the time I left, there were several rivals, but none were quite as good.

I often took my evening meals in Benez. This was a small restaurant-cum-bar next to the guest house, on a side-street; it had perhaps eight tables for four, bare and unadorned, but with a small but rather cosy little bar at the back of the room. It was run by Dasho. Dasho really was a *dasho*, or knight; it is an honorific borne by provincial governors and others those who serve the King at high level. Dasho had been a very senior Government official, but he was an ethnic Nepali, and when the political situation worsened in the late 1980s (of which more later), he had had to leave his post. So he opened a pub instead. However, he was friendly and cheerful, and I never heard him complain. A short, bullet-headed, bald man in his 50s, he ran Benez (even he did not know where the name came from) with his wife, who sat behind the comfortable little bar in a friendly fug of cigarette smoke.

Benez had plenty of booze. There was bottled beer of different types. The best was Kalyani Black Label from India. Dasho normally had plenty but if he hadn't, there was always a Sikkimese beer with a green label called Dansberg; it was not as good, but it served. Rarely, one might have to resort to Golden Eagle (or weasel's piss, as a friend once called it). This had a disgusting soapy taste, but for some reason the Bhutanese liked it. If you couldn't face weasel's piss, there was also He-Man 9000, Sikkim's answer to Special Brew. I could not take either weasel's piss or He-Man so I would sometimes be forced to drink spirits. These do not agree with me, but I would enjoy a Dragon Rum sometimes. This was a refreshing local rum which came into its own in winter, and it was very cheap, I think the equivalent of about 10 pence a shot. Or one could have Bhutan Mist. This was a truly excellent Scotch distilled locally (the Scots had helped,

I think). The local spirits all seemed to come from something called the Army Welfare Project in the southern town of Gey-legphug.

Dasho was very hospitable and informal; one might forget he was a Dasho, were it not for the red *cumney* that he put on before getting into his white Premier Padmini to visit some Government office or other. (I cannot remember him wearing a ceremonial sword, however; perhaps only serving Dashos wore those.) From time to time he would sit and chat. I cannot remember him ever talking politics, and I never asked him to.

But I do remember one conversation we had during the monsoon, not long after I had arrived in Thimphu. It had been a damp, overcast day, and now the rain was sheeting down the windows; I had run here from my flat just behind, my evening reading, a tatty found copy of *The Master and Margarita*, held close to my shirt. Benez was quiet, one or two people sitting at the back table; Dasho's wife sat peaceably behind the bar on her high stool, her cigarette-smoke curling into the soft light above her. Dasho sat opposite me, nursing a Dragon Rum. For some reason we fell to discussing local beliefs. Quite suddenly and calmly, he said that he had once seen a dragon.

I blinked. There was no hint of a smile on his face. "When was this?"

"I was doing my military service. In the 1960s."

"Where?"

"Oh, in the mountains. It was at dusk. Dragons fly at dusk."

"What did it look like?"

"Strange colours."

No Bhutanese wishes to see a dragon; they are bad luck, and I sensed that Dasho did not much want to be pressed on the subject. In any case, at that moment my food arrived, and he excused himself; he never raised the subject again. Dasho was a professional man and widely-travelled; he was either telling the truth or testing my credulity, and to this day I do not know which.

*

Aside from the centre, there was little to see in Thimphu. Even the majestic Dzong, and the majority of the government offices, were not in the town itself but a mile or two to the north. In fact, Thimphu was a bit claustrophobic. So far I had hardly had a chance to leave it.

I wanted a bike. This was partly for exercise, but also because I like bikes and wanted to explore the area. One could buy bikes in Phuntsholing, the southern border town at the foot of the mountains where they met the Bengal plain. But they were similar to English machines of the 1930s, being very upright and very heavy, with rod brakes and a single gear. I wanted something a bit more modern, or a gearbike, as the Indians called them. I mentioned this to another volunteer, Ken, who said a friend was thinking of doing the same, and he would mention it to him.

I forgot about it until two months later, in September. It was, for once, dry and bright; one of those rare days during the monsoon when it stopped pissing down, the concrete walls stopped turning green with fungus for a while, and the clouds drew back off the wooded hills round the valley, revealing the mass of prayer-flags clustered below the radio-mast on the hill to the west. I had been walking around Thimphu. I was passing Benez in the early afternoon when a horn hooted behind me. I turned to see Ken and a friend in a blue Land-Cruiser. "We got something for you," said Ken. In the boot was a very smart red-and-white five-speed racing bicycle. The friend, Padraig, had indeed gone to Siliguri in West Bengal to get his Indian gear-bike, and, hearing that someone else wanted one, he had kindly bought an extra one. It had cost about £38 (about $55) and was called a Hero Hawk.

I loved it, but it was heavy and needed tender loving care. The first fault I found was that the control cable for the derailleur was too short and would change the gears to low ratio, but would not allow the opposite movement. The cones that held the ball-bearings into the axles were loose, too, and one of the brake hoods moved around. A borrowed spanner and screwdriver proved enough to fix most of this, and I chopped up an old brake cable cover for the gears. The valves, like pre-war British ones, had rubber in them. They would not mate with a modern pump, and the Indian adaptors could not cope. Eventually I got a plunger-pump from Siliguri. This consisted of a stainless-steel cylinder with feet that folded out at the bottom; the long plunger was topped by an elegant polished wooden handle. These were much used by rickshaw drivers in India, and were very effective. Lights were another problem. Bhutanese policemen confiscated bikes without lights at night. Someone who was going to Phuntsholing kindly brought back an Indian dynamo set. This lit up the street like a Roman candle but produced far too much power, so that as soon as one got to a certain speed the six-volt front bulb blew, leaving one careering down the main road from the Memorial Chorten in total darkness, wondering how far away the drainage ditch was.

Ken had a bike too. He left Bhutan on it that November. He had been helping in a Phuntsholing factory making plastic piping, but competition from India was fierce, and orders few. Moreover he had lived on the border through the worst of the civil disturbances that marked those years, and had had an eight o'clock curfew; there was little to do in Phuntsholing anyway. But he stayed for most of the two years, and then decided to go home his way, cashing in his air ticket, and hanging a saltire on his bike, on the crossbar of which he had written BHUTAN-SCOTLAND. With another friend, I accompanied him for the first 20 miles one soft Sunday monsoon morning and we waved goodbye, the saltire waving bravely from his rear carrier as he disappeared into the distance. He covered much of the subcontinent before Iranian visa difficulties forced him to give up the following spring.

A young Danish friend was even more ambitious. He bought two sturdy ponies and announced that he was trekking back to Denmark. In the summer of 1993 he set off from Thimphu, and crossed the Bengal plain to the borders of Nepal; but a robbery, and sickness in the ponies, forced him to give up in Kathmandu.

*

The bike let me see something of the countryside. Bhutan is one of the most beautiful countries on earth, but there is little view from the Thimphu valley. The surroundings are wooded hills; no snow-peaks can be seen. For that, one had to climb 3,000ft to the 10,500ft pass of Dochula, a long and steep journey. Even there, there was nothing to see in the wet season, for the whole country would be shrouded in mist. Alternatively, one could climb on foot up the high mountains flanking the Thimphu valley, reaching a plateau at about 14,000 ft from which there were views of the high Himalayas that surrounded us. But I did not know that then; besides, I did not know the footpaths, and had the brains not to wander around strange mountains on my own. There were bears and boars and mudslides, and tree-roots that could twist your ankle and leave you stranded on a path that no-one might use for days to come.

Still, I could ride to the head of the Thimphu valley, through woods and along steep roads adorned with *chortens*, sacred monuments that contained Buddhist relics. After a few miles one reached the point where the last cart-track ran out. Here there was a traditional covered bridge across the rushing blue-white river, the Thimphu Chu, and the beginning of the yak-and-donkey path that led up a narrow gorge to Tibet, two or three days' walk to the north. Now and then lines of men with pack-ponies would appear at the foot of the valley, laden with simple goods – tea urns, green plimsolls – that they had traded with the Chinese guards on the frontier.

Going south from Thimphu instead led one eventually to the Confluence, where two rivers met; one either turned right for Paro or went straight on towards Phuntsholing and the Bengal plain. However, 20 miles or so out of Thimphu there was an earlier turn to the right, a tarmac road which ran along the Gidakom Valley; narrower than the Thimphu Valley at the latter's widest, but wide enough for agriculture, a couple of villages and a small lumber yard. The villages also contained the Leprosy Mission, then run by Danes. In the 10 years of its existence it had made such good progress against the disease that it was being run down. The road petered out after about 10 miles, and a track continued to a far-distant lake in the mountains. I liked riding through the Gidakom Valley; when the sun shone, the buildings shone white-and-brown, and when the chili harvest came, the crop was left drying on the rooves, bright red against the white houses and the deep blue sky. Sometimes one whooshed through a ford and then across the crops that covered the road; they were put there so that cattle-hooves and vehicles would thresh them.

Riding along the main road to the Confluence, I would sometimes pass what looked like public toilets in the middle of nowhere. They were corrugated-iron sheds divided into three cubicles, each one about eight foot wide and about the same depth. Often one would see one of the Indian road labourers hanging around near them, often Bengalis wearing their characteristic *dhotis*. These were their homes, and as far as I could see, the entire family squeezed into these and managed as best they could. I do not know where they got their food; perhaps it was brought up from the plain by their employers, but more probably they had to buy it on the local market like everyone else. I believe they were paid about 15 rupees a day – about 30 pence. In Bhutan, as in any subsistence agrarian economy, there was little labour to spare, and these Indians were essential for road maintenance. The sight of one of these families going slowly and joylessly about their business by the side of the road in the monsoon murk put one's own troubles into perspective.

*

In 1992 the monsoon ran an extra month, right to the end of October. But bad things, too, come to an end.

One Saturday afternoon at the end of the month, I set out on my bicycle, intending to ride up the road towards Dochula. The weather was good, and just after one in the afternoon I rode down the main road to India as far as the majestic Simtokha Dzong, the beautifully-proportioned 14th-century castle about five miles south of the capital. It was here that the Thimphu valley widened out, and Simtokha Dzong commanded a view of it. It was now an ecclesiastical school. When one passed its elegant form, one knew that one had left or entered the area of the capital.

Past the Dzong, I swung round to the left, into a side-turning. This was not quite wide enough for two ordinary cars. In fact, it was the lateral road which connected West and East Bhutan. The most important city of the East, Tashigang, was two long days' drive along this road. First it snaked its way some 12 or 15 miles up to Dochula, the 10,500ft pass that led out of the Western valleys.

I did not think to reach Dochula. But I suppose I just never stopped. I could feel the warm sunlight on my back, but it was friendly, not oppressive. Looking up, I could see ridges of pine trees against the clear sky, and the road was dusted with pine needles. There was a warm, gentle scent. The road ahead wound upwards so steeply that the next two or three bends were stacked almost vertically above my head, the battlements of the concrete retaining walls clearly visible. There was no traffic, aside from the odd jeep-taxi, and the air felt soft and clear. Below me a valley started to deepen, dotted here and there with isolated farmsteads. Sometime in the late afternoon, I struggled up a last short slope to find the road dividing around a long prayer-wall; there were prayer-flags everywhere, and I realized that this was a place of note. I freewheeled to the left of the prayer-wall and onto a small meadow tufted with weeds. I was exhausted, and it was a moment before I lifted my eyes to the horizon, and saw a sight of such beauty that it was almost beyond the human eye. Below me, looking east, the hills tumbled one upon the other into the far, deep valley of Wangdi and Punakha, 6,000ft below. Beyond that, the ramparts rose again, rows of mountains speckled with fields, meadows and patches of forests, trailing off into a distant blue sky. Then I looked left, and realized that I was looking north into the frontiers of Tibet; distant white pinnacles were shrouded with wisps of cloud against a deepening blue, and nearer at hand was a great snowpeak with a strange, flattened, four-corner summit: Masangang. I was to see it from closer to, some months later, and think it one of the finest in the Himalayas.

I stayed there for perhaps an hour, until the shadows rising from up the valley warned me that there was only an hour or so of daylight left. Already a stiffening breeze was chilling me slightly through my shirt, and soon it would be cold. Reluctantly I started down the hill for home. Instead of the two or two-and-a-half-hour climb, I had a 40-minute run down the mountain, twisting around steep, cambered corners slippery with pine-needles and cow-dung. The light faded quickly. Every now and then the shadowy shape of a jeep or minibus would appear suddenly around a bend, causing me to heave on the cheap pressed-steel brakes; these barely worked, and I would sometimes cut past with inches to spare. Then a long straight appeared ahead, and I shot down it at perhaps 40 miles an hour towards the shapely shadow of Simtokha Dzong, looming above the road against the last of the light. The paddy-fields of the Thimphu Valley drifted into view, and then, as I rounded the corner, there was Thimphu, looking more than ever like a woodcut of Middle Earth with the first lights glimmering and the white and gold curves of the main monument, the Memorial Chorten, clearly visible. I shuddered to a halt as I reached the main road, and I think I was laughing.

*

The expatriates grew more welcoming, too. One night, I was invited me to an evening of Scottish dancing. I knew nothing of Scottish dancing, I protested. My hosts replied that this was my chance to find out. The ordeal that lay ahead would take place at their spacious flat, not far from my own. It was led by a Scottish vet, who was based some way south of Thimphu, and was one of those foreigners who were almost universally respected by both the Bhutanese and foreigners; he had already been in the country for some years when I arrived, and was to remain there for several years after I left. When it came to Scottish dancing, he was serious, and something of a parade-ground atmosphere developed as we struggled to put our feet in the right place at the right time. He was accompanied by his tall, graceful daughter, who seemed to be as dedicated as he was, and I developed an irrational fear of stepping on her bare feet. The hosts had thoughtfully provided a very large crate of Indian beer for the evening and I started to sit out the odd dance beside it; as a result, my coordination deteriorated further, and I sat out more dances. By the end of the evening I realized that I was not going to be the toast of Thimphu society through my dancing skills, but no-one seemed to mind that much, even the Scottish vet – who, as I was later to find, was a nice man with a friendly family. I left the flat, more than slightly drunk, to see a great harvest moon hovering over the town, and lighting the frosty pavements like a lamp. Who'd have thought, I asked myself, that I'd be Scottish dancing in a place where men wear *ghos* and there are 10,000 monks in red and saffron.

*

Bit by bit, I was also absorbing the Bhutanese way of work.

It was deeply hierarchical. Confronted by a Minister, a lower member of staff – even quite a senior one in his own right – would make the appropriate gestures with his *cumney*, the white scarf across the shoulder. I have already mentioned that these had different colours for certain rankings; white for an ordinary individual, blue for a member of the National Assembly, red for a *dasho*, and saffron for the King himself and for the Jhe Kenpo, the supreme religious figure, who was in theory a parallel Head of State. There was another as well – that of the *dzongrub*, or deputy provincial governor; his cumney was white, but edged with a pattern. All this enabled people to know where they were in the food-chain. Although I sometimes heard some of the more Westernised Bhutanese grumble about one or two of the restrictions they faced in their country, I rarely heard complaints about this; perhaps they felt that as long as everyone knew their place, everyone *had* a place, and this was no bad thing in a time of change. I would have found these formalities hard to perform, but by wearing Western clothes, I kept out of the Bhutanese power-structure, and was not expected to.

People's beliefs also dictated office behaviour to some extent. A pregnancy went unremarked. I found this curious at first, as the Bhutanese are not prudish, and do divorce and change partners, at least up to a point. In fact it was not prudery; to mention a pregnancy was to attract the attention of the evil eye. Another puzzling habit was the burning of papers. Between the huts occupied by the ministries and departments were small, open-sided concrete bins, about two feet square. These were usually either filled with paper, or smouldering gently. The Tibetan-derived Dzongkha script is sacred, and must not be thrown away; it must be burned (it then ascends to Heaven). So any memo, duty roster, canteen menu or other routine item was dealt with in this way.

Fortunately Dzongkha was not used for everything. The script had about 80 basic characters, with perhaps three common mutations for each, and the grammar and orthography were challenging. Typewriters for the script existed, but if someone was well-educated enough to understand Dzongkha, they also read English. (The only exceptions were the monks, who generally spoke Dzongkha alone.) After suggesting, several times, that we ought perhaps to be producing material in

Dzongkha as well as English, I was quietly but frankly told that Nepali would be at least as much use and English even better. I have since wondered: would it have been sacrilegious to delete a file written in Dzongkha? Would one have had to transfer it to floppy, and burn that? (Ordinary rubbish, however, was disposed of with less care. Bhutanese people worried little about rubbish. The town government did, and big green steel cylinders had recently started to sprout all over Thimphu decorated with the legend USE ME. For this reason, a rubbish bin was known in Bhutan as a useme.)

There was a wider ambivalence amongst the Bhutanese about development. It seemed, to many, to challenge their unique culture and polity, and send them the way of the other independent Himalayan Buddhist kingdoms (they were thinking chiefly of Sikkim). But it would also make them better-placed to resist the cultural assault from the Bengal plain—which many regarded as a greater menace.

It would be easy to see Bhutan as quaint, charming; Shangri-La – but in Bhutan, as everywhere, you patronise at your peril. Bhutan had just passed through a year in which the Southern problem was as bad as it would ever be.

People of ethnic Nepali origin had long settled the southern flanks of the Eastern Himalayas, where Bhutan tumbled down to the plain. In the early years of the 20th century, the building of the railway through Assam brought more of them to the region, to work on its construction; when it was done, more settled on the fertile, underpopulated southern slopes, raising crops such as cardamom. By the late 1980s they constituted a large part of the country's population, to an extent that could, it was felt, call into question Bhutan's existing identity. The Bhutanese reacted with a series of measures, including the compulsory wearing of national dress and a strict nationality law. Tens of thousands of ethnic Nepalis, not all of them resident in the south, lost their citizenship, or felt discriminated against to the extent that they felt they should leave. In the year or two before I arrived, it was not unusual for a colleague or acquaintance to simply pass out of view. Months later one would hear that they had been seen in Kakarbhitta, the small town just inside Nepal where the ethnic Nepalis were sheltered in refugee camps (they were not Nepali citizens either). Few suffered any worse fate than this, but there was some violence, and an insurgency movement in the south (these were the *ngolops* I had seen in the newspaper headline). This was why Ken had faced an 8pm curfew in the southern border town of Phuntsholing; it was still in force when I first visited the town, and the tension was palpable.

In fact, by 1992, the very worst was over. But we had no way of knowing this then. The teaching volunteers in particular found the situation difficult; they had seen many of their pupils forced to leave the country before their education could be completed. Some went to visit the camps in Nepal to see them. The Government must have known this; Bhutan was not a police state, but it was inconceivable that they did not have information from the camps. Other volunteers served out their time in Bhutan, and then went to work as volunteers in the camps for some months. I met one, a good friend, in Kathmandu in December 1993; she had been working on a poor diet with little support and looked thin and ill.

In later months I got to know several younger Bhutanese in their 20s who were members of the Royal Family; although not of the King's immediate family, they knew him and were profoundly loyal. They were warm, able men who enjoyed a few beers but also worked hard in the Thimphu ministries, and were generally respected by other civil servants. (The King, who lived simply and worked hard, took a dim view of quasi-Royal freeloaders.) They always encouraged me, but we had completely opposite views on the Southern problem. Once or twice I was asked what I thought about it, and I replied that I was not about to tell the Bhutanese how to run their country; but that I believed in human rights, and I did not like it. I said that they must not press me on the subject; they accepted this, and we talked of other matters.

One point they made to me stood out. A country should be governed for the good of its people, to be sure; but individuals as such had no inherent rights. "You are a Westerner, and you believe that they do," one of them said to me one night. "What you guys don't understand is that not everyone accepts that. Why should we?" Actually I *did* understand that. Marxists make the same point. My counter-argument was that individuals must have inalienable rights – there was no other ethical basis for society. However, if you are brought up in the Buddhist intellectual tradition, then there may be; the Buddhist conception of the individual is different, and arguably makes only collective rights possible.

In any case, what to a Westerner was a debate about human rights was to a Bhutanese an argument about their national survival. I realised this more fully when I travelled to Sikkim with a friend at the end of 1993. Gangtok was cheerful and lively – in fact, I liked it; but every face seemed to be Nepali or Bengali. The Bhutanese had told me that the indigenous people of Sikkim now accounted for just 15% of the population. Our visit was far too brief for us to know if this was true. But from what little we saw, the Himalayan kingdom that had existed there as recently as the 1970s had left little trace. It was easy to understand the rising tide of panic in Bhutan, if harder to accept the civil-rights violations it had engendered. In any case, as someone who loved Bhutan but had no stake in its future, I did not feel I had anything useful to say about all this, and perhaps I still don't.

*

All of which made one wonder: what kind of man, really, was the King?

Still in his 30s, he seemed younger; an impressive figure, he always looked fit and well. I would see him at times as he emerged from the Planning Ministry opposite; one always knew he was there from the blue Land-Cruiser that stood in front of that hut, attended by two or three immaculately-uniformed police officers. Then, after a long meeting, the King would emerge, climb briskly into the front passenger seat of the Land-Cruiser (which was far from new) and be driven away. As the car disappeared down past the canteen, he seemed to stretch, and to sigh with relief; and – this surprised me – he would light a long thin cheroot with evident enjoyment. For cultural reasons, smoking is frowned upon in Bhutan. One assumes he observed his own strict ban on smoking in the Dzong, where his office was.

The cigars were a rare indulgence; the King was moderate, if not austere, in his personal habits. He expected his family, too, to exercise restraint. Like his father, perhaps more so, he worked. Few recent monarchs can have been so deeply involved in their country's future.

He had conceived the idea of "Gross National Happiness". In more recent years, this has been marketed to the rest of the world and has been received with almost messianic enthusiasm by those with a weakness for the mystical. Perhaps it should not be. Tshering Tobgay, who I knew as a young man in Bhutan and who many years later, in 2013, was elected Prime Minister, has recently warned that the concept is overused and should not be allowed to mask problems with corruption and inequality.

In its origins, however, Bhutanese development policy was quite practical. The principle was an economy designed to afford its people an overall quality of life. Thus Bhutan's food policy was aimed not at self-sufficiency, but at self-reliance. Bhutan could provide 100% of its food, but the idea was to produce just 70%. The balance would be imported with a cash surplus earned through export of food products. Thus farmers would have a cash income with which to buy tools and domestic implements instead of making such items as well as working in the fields. There was wisdom in this. Those who advise developing countries to stick with pure subsistence farming should be made to try it themselves for a while.

Tied in with this policy was an integral concern for environmental conservation, and in 1993 the National Environment Commission began operation. One of its functions was to enforce environmental audits of every new development project. It also wrote a national environment policy. The King had inspired all this and much else besides, toiling into the night in his simply-furnished residence in the Thimphu valley.

This may give the impression of benevolent despotism, but the truth was more complex. On the one hand, the King presided over the troubling events in the south; yet years later he would lead Bhutan to democracy, and, having done so, would abdicate. For the moment, however, the King was actively involved in all aspects of government. He had come to the throne in 1974 at the age of just 17, and had succeeded the great reforming Third King of Bhutan, who had taken the first steps to open the country to the outside world, and had introduced the first modern health and education services.

The closest I ever got to the King was one spring day in

1994. I was on my way to Helvetas, the Swiss aid organization, which worked from a large, pleasant house not far from the river. It was also very close to the crematorium – only a problem, according to the Helvetas representative, when the wind was blowing in a certain direction. For some reason I did not take my bike that day, but took a short-cut on foot past the front door of the Dzong. This was all right provided you were properly dressed, and I was, complete with my all-purpose sports jacket, and a rather greasy old silk tie. As I approached the front door I noticed a Land Cruiser parked in front; a small knot of people came down the steps towards it. "That's funny," I thought, "that bloke's wearing a saffron *cumney*. Only the King and the Jhe Khenpo can wear..." Then I stopped and stood stock-still, looking down at the tarmac, for one was forbidden to look the King in the face. But I had time to catch a glance from the King as I did so. I don't know if he recognized me, but as I drank with one or two of his nephews and parked my bike below (far below) his office window, perhaps he did know who I was. I thought I saw a slight smile pass across his face. Then he got into his car and pulled away, leaving a wisp or two of exhaust on the warm spring air.

*

I enjoyed my own work well enough, and I hope I made a contribution. We were establishing a communications unit for the Department of Agriculture. There were six or seven of us; my Bhutanese counterpart, Samdrup, and I, and a number of Bhutanese colleagues, plus an English consultant who had spent a few months with us earlier on. The Department had a newsletter and together Samdrup and I turned it into a cheerful little tabloid, complete with a crossword on the back. Gripping

features included *Mastitis - the menace in your shed*, liberally illustrated with cross-sections of diseased udders; and my
personal favourite, written by a colleague and headlined *Dead
Frogs*. It concerned a method dreamed up by the International
Rice Research Institute in the Philippines. "If you have problems with the rice bug in paddy during the ripening stage, simply tie and peg a dead frog (arms outstretched) in the middle
of a field," he advised. This attracted the bugs, which could then
be zapped with a localised application of insecticide, instead
of spraying the whole field. "Three to four such frogs could be
required for half an acre... You do not need to kill a frog – dead
frogs are abundant... Who knows – perhaps, just because of a
dead frog, the level in the grain-boxes could go higher, taking
us nearer our goal of self-sufficiency!"

There were deeper matters. In the hut opposite us was the
National Environment Commission. In 1993, with the support
of the Swiss, it commissioned a number of background papers
for Bhutan's national environment policy, then under development. I was asked to edit the papers, and was fascinated. The
NEC's authors had not avoided controversy. One, for example,
was titled *Environmental control – a new form of repression?* It
was not anti-conservation, but it dissected the various ways
in which ordinary people might be tyrannised in the name of
environmental correctness, and it was chilling. Several papers
challenged orthodox Bhutanese opinion and even government
policy. One was written by a senior staff member of its own
Planning Commission. The paper, *The Nomad's Gamble* by
Karma Ura, set out the case for allowing pastoralists to police
the use of pasture themselves. Government policy, and the law,
was that pasture-usage, for environmental reasons, was under
State control. Karma argued that pastoralists had centuries-
old mechanisms for this; that they were finely-balanced, and

that official interference would unbalance them and would end with exactly the degradation that was feared. He did not have to point out the economic significance of this in Bhutan, the rural economy of which was heavily dependent on livestock and livestock products.

Karma described how the yak-herders of a remote high-altitude area near Haa would meet once a year and shake dice; those with the highest score would get the first choice of summer pasture. These areas of pasture were strictly defined. So was their carrying capacity, and any herder who grazed too many beasts on the land would face trouble with his peers. More to the point, if he allowed his herd to become too large, he would be in trouble when he had to shift it to a poorer pasture; so he didn't. Of course someone might throw low numbers several years running, so those who lost out on summer pasture got the pick of the winter grazing. Karma found a similar informal system in operation amongst cattle-herders in central Bhutan. He was not the only person to raise the point, but his position in the Planning Commission, and the elegance with which he had put his argument, may have proved decisive.

The paper needed little editing. Karma Ura was a fine writer. He was also in a prestigious position at the Planning Commission. Yet he had done his research himself, on foot, over the King's Birthday holiday the previous November, taking a stout stick and walking to the highest reaches of the mountains of Haa.

Karma Ura is now the author of several books and papers. When I knew him, he was producing the first English translation of Bhutan's important 19th-century epic, *The Lo-Sey of Pemai Tshewang Tashi*.

This purports to be an account of riding to battle in one of Bhutan's many civil wars written by a participant, Tshewang Tashi, a chamberlain to the ruler of Wangdi Dzong. I say purports, because the author describes, at the end, his own suicide; this is perhaps a more difficult philosophical problem for the Western mind than it is for the Bhutanese. However, it is not fiction. Karma thought the battle at Trongsa Dzong described in the epic had taken place in 1875 or 1876; indeed, many real figures had been involved in that conflict. They included, peripherally, Paro strongman Ugyen Wangchuk – who much later, in 1907, became Bhutan's first modern King. The *Lo-Sey* is a reminder of the ghastly chaos that his dynasty brought to an end. It seems Tshewang Tashi himself had also been real enough, and had led an expeditionary force from Wangdi to Trongsa, where he was defeated. Trapped on the spectacular cliff of Thomangdrak opposite Trongsa Dzong, he took his own life rather than allow the enemy to claim it for themselves. Whether he actually wrote the *Lo-Sey*, either before or after his death, is a question best left to Karma.

It is a work of life and vigour. Here, Tshewang Tashi breaks for the night while leading his force to Pelela, the very high pass that divides western from central Bhutan, and must still be crossed when travelling from Wangdi to Trongsa; in fact he followed roughly the same route as the modern road. While sleeping on the approach to Pelela, he has a nightmare:

I saw corpses and flesh strewn on the ground
I saw offerings of blood erupt into the sky
I saw the radiant sun sink to the west
I saw the moon seized by an eclipse
I saw the stars dim and disappear in the sky
I saw flowers nipped by the frost.

Yet much of the *Lo-Sey* is elegiac, as Tshewang Tashi wishes that he was going home to the beautiful hamlet of his birth instead of to what he is certain will be his fate. Thus, the following morning, struggling across Pelela, he records:

The mountain rises higher and higher
I wish it was not Pelela of the nine horizons
But the birthplace of I, Tshewang Tashi

The epic cannot have been easy to translate, for there were many cultural concepts not easily put in English. Nonetheless it is worth reading, with its yearning, its appreciation of light and shade and its evocation of the slow, sinister, approach of death; in the final verses, the blood seems almost to seep from the ground although the battle has not yet begun. Karma has since published his translation; it is available in the West.[1] When I first saw it, the difficulties he must have had translating out of Dzongka were obvious, although I scarcely knew the language at all. But it was a sharp reminder that Dzongka, although spoken by only a few hundred thousand people, was not an obscure local dialect but the vehicle of centuries of cultural and religious expression.

A few weeks before I left Bhutan, Karma rang me and asked me to meet him in town. He arrived bearing the first draft of his translation of the *Lo-Sey*. "I have the translation. You have the voice," he said. This was true. I have an unusually deep voice, with an added edge at the time as I was still a heavy smoker. Karma wanted me to record a recitation for Bhutan national radio.

I agreed at once although I am not sure if Karma was happy with the result, and I do not know if it was ever broadcast,

---

1 *The Ballad of Pemi Tshewang Tashi: A Wind Borne Feather.*
Karma Ura/Helvetas, 1996.

or indeed still exists. We spent several sessions of an hour or two each in a studio in the radio station above the golf course. Karma was after, not so much a recitation, as a performance; I am not an actor but I did my best, and he conducted me as one might an orchestra, waving his copy of the script in the air with increasing urgency as I came to the spot where Tshewang Tashi describes preparing for his gory death – which, it seemed, did not prevent him writing about it afterwards.

But then, as Karma put it in his introduction:

The prospect of his flesh, blood and bones being strewn and spattered at the base of the cliff was made less unpleasant by his faith and hope that he would be speedily and swiftly reborn once again in his happy hamlet. [But] he could be reintroduced in this world only by placing himself in a new pattern of human relationship – say for example by being reborn as his sister's son. Thus, in a curious and rapid turn of events, he could become his own nephew.

I don't think Karma found anything so strange about this and neither did I at the time.

*

Of course, there was a Bhutan beyond Thimphu; in fact, most volunteers worked some way from the capital. They were mainly teachers. (Bhutanese schools taught in English, although the children did learn Dzongkha.) For the first year, the volunteers stayed in one village and taught. This first year could be an inspiring experience, but the volunteers were very much on their own and strength of character was essential. It is an experience that has been described very well in a book by Canadian volunteer Jamie Zeppa, who taught in an isolated community in the east of Bhutan.[2] Jamie went on to Sherubtse College, teaching the young people who would become Bhutan's civil-service elite. This was unusual; more often, the teachers (who were mostly but not all women) became resource teachers for their *Dzongkhag*, or province, and travelled much of the time, supporting and advising their Bhutanese colleagues. None of the *Dzongkhags* were easy to travel in, but some had a sealed road running through them, and the teacher could use a Bajaj (an Indian Vespa) for at least some of their journeys. Others had virtually no roads at all. These included Lhuntse in the north, and the most notorious of them all, Shemgang, a vast Dzongkhag that stretched from the centre of Bhutan to its southern frontier. It was the least-developed region of Bhutan, as remote as even the very high land close to Tibet. Apart from roads running on its northern and western borders, Shemgang had no sealed roads at all.

The resource teachers could spend as much as seven out of eight weeks walking between villages, coping with drunken porters, isolation and the monsoon rains. Not least of the hazards was the local firewater, *arra*, which was always offered, often first thing in the morning; more than one teacher awoke to find what looked like a tumbler of water placed thoughtfully beside their bed by their host in the village, and gulped it back, giving an explosive start to the day. Etiquette, particularly in the east, demanded that one do everything possible to force *arra* on a guest; cover the tumbler with your hand and the *arra* was poured over it by a giggling host. But at least this set one up for the leeches, of which there were many in the forests under about 5,000ft; these waited in the branches, sensed movement

---

2 *Beyond the sky and the earth* (Macmillan, 1999). Jamie, a talented writer, also later produced a very good novel.

and dropped onto the flesh of the traveller below. Less often, there were Himalayan black bears. Bears have no wish to meet humans, and if they do attack it is normally because they have done so suddenly. So those who walked on their own in the mountains often carried bells attached to their waists to warn animals of their approach. But sometimes bear and teacher did meet without warning, although they never did each other any harm as far as I know.

Besides the physical dangers, there were blows to one's ego. One English ex-headmistress told how she had been helped on with her *kira* by the lady of the house in which she was staying. "Oh, Madam," she said, shocked, "you have hairy legs, like a buffalo." On another occasion she strode into a remote village with another volunteer and, the next morning, attended assembly at the school. The headmaster decided to deliver a lecture to the Bhutanese teachers on the need to make sacrifices for the country's future. No-one, he said, should be afraid to walk for days to the remotest schools. He indicated the two English-women. "They can do it," he said, "and they are *fatty* types."

I was less adventurous. But one spring an American United Nations volunteer and I decided to cross much of the country on the lateral road, using his small motorbike. This journey required a permit and I made several trips into the ornately gloomy wooden interior of the main administrative centre-cum-castle, the Dzong. This involved finding the tiny cubby-hole where the lady in charge of internal visas worked, crouched over a typewriter before a painted background of mandalas, wearing a shiny silk waistcoat over her blouse and *kira*.

One Saturday morning in early May, Tom appeared at my flat with the little trail bike. It was already laden with bags, Tom's modest luggage and the bits and pieces he was taking to other volunteers along the way. I added my own bright-green rucksack, with washing things, a towel, a change of clothes and nothing more. But when we had finished securing this to the back of the bike with bits of elastic, there was far more luggage than bike, and I wondered just how far we were going to get. There was a slight slope down to my door. Tom revved the engine and tried to move away, but the bike stalled. Exasperated, on the third attempt he revved it high and banged in the clutch. The little bike took off as if it had been stung, the front wheel rising high in the air, Tom hanging onto the handlebars in an effort not to slide arse-first into my rucksack. After what seemed an age, he reached the top of the slope and the front wheel bashed down on the surface, sending little spurts of gravel into the still morning air. "OK, get on," said Tom. As he pulled away, I put my foot on the right footpeg. It broke.

But we made it across Dochula (and later Pelela – Pelela of the nine horizons – which was 12,000ft). Tom handled the bike with great skill. A laconic, rather easy-going man, he worked with the Thimphu city government. (Like Jamie he was a good writer, and would later produce an excellent book of short stories, each a deeply observed picture of some aspect of Bhutanese life.[3])

At the end of the first day we swung off the tarmac road onto a wide gravel track. At first, this climbed gently; but it became imperceptibly steeper, and the little fist of the single piston slammed up and down as fast as it would go as we crawled up in first gear, just fast enough to keep a straight line. As we climbed, chasing the last of the afternoon's sunshine up the mountain, we could see the hillsides to the north and east. Just as the last patches of sun slipped away, we struggled round a

---

3 Tom Slocum, *In His Majesty's Civil Service: And Other Contemporary Tales from the Kingdom of Bhutan* (1996). It has recently (2011) been republished in paperback.

last bend to find the village before us. It really was a village, with the houses arranged around a broad central area; many Bhutanese houses stand alone in their paddies, the neighbour just within hailing distance. A few people milled about, mostly the very young or old; it was a busy time in the farming calendar and everyone who could work was in the fields, using the last of the light.

The bush telegraph had warned the volunteer teacher in the village that we were coming, and she stood waiting for us. She helped us unload the bike and we walked together through the twilight fields around the village. Here on top of the mountain, there were plenty of trees, and the fields looked prosperous. Our friend showed us a small pit full of rocks; this, she explained, was where the women of the village came to bathe. The rocks would be heated until they glowed and flung into the water, making clouds of steam. She described lying back in the water and watching the stars swarm across the coal-black sky above the steam.

And she talked about her village, which she swore had been painted by Brueghel the Elder. "You see, everyone is there in the square," she said, "and they work and they work and they have so much to do, and no-one seems aware of anyone else." Years later, standing before the Brueghels in the Palais des Beaux-Arts in Brussels, watching the wheelwrights and the coopers go about their business, I suddenly remembered my friend and her medieval village on top of its mountain.

That night we climbed the outside ladder to eat in the house of the neighbour upstairs. We sat on the floor before the *bukhari*, the wood-burning stove; this was lighted for cooking, and was kept burning, because at 8,000ft the air soon cooled when the sun went down. It was quiet in the room. There was little furniture, for the Bhutanese do not use much, just short low benches with padded tops that can be removed so that the space within can be used for storage. In fact there always seemed something spare and spacious about the Bhutanese room, despite the thick walls and the small windows. Spare but not austere, for the walls were covered with all the symbols of Buddhism, from conch shells to images of the saints; the outside walls would often bear fertility symbols in the shape of a giant penis.

A dog came padding through the next room. The Bhutanese seemed to like dogs, and, as Buddhists, were in general respectful of other living things. The dog stretched its forepaws over the raised lip of the doorway; all rooms had these. They are designed to prevent small malevolent spirits entering the room. The dog dragged its hind legs across the lip. Our host handed us tin plates piled high with red rice. I tried to remember the dos and don'ts of the Bhutanese household. Do not whistle; this will attract evil spirits. Do not call someone's name at night; the same spirits will remember it. We finished our rice and drank some *suja*, butter tea. "You may go now," said our host gently, meaning nothing more or less than what he said; and we scrambled down the ladder in the dark and rolled ourselves in our sleeping bags and I fell asleep nearly at once, the sound of the little steel fist buzzing in my ears.

In the morning the villagers kindly asked us in to see their temple, which they were redecorating; in Bhutan, one visits a village temple strictly by invitation. We climbed a stepladder up the side of a small, square building, and found ourselves in a small, square white room. On the wall, there was a half-completed painting of a terrifying deity. The deity was identical to those on thousands of walls in Bhutan and elsewhere in the Buddhist world, often many hundreds of years old. The paintings, like the village itself, were much was they would have been in the Middle Ages. Yet here they were in progress, with what had yet to be painted being neatly sketched out on the white wall in pencil. I was suddenly struck by the fact that identical deities must also once have been half-sketched, half-painted, the artist taking a break, perhaps, for *suja*, or showing his work to a visitor, a few chickens running about in the yard below, a sloshing sound as a housewife threw the slops from her balcony, the cry of a child that has fallen over, the creak of a door in the middle distance; a morning just like today, a thousand years ago.

We travelled on for several days. I especially remember a village south of Trongsa in central Bhutan, where we stayed with another volunteer teacher. The village was halfway up a very deep river valley. The scattered houses and paddies on the far slope were at least three miles away, tiny features on a massive hillside that bulked left and right as far as the eye could see. No road ran down the valley on the other side. The valley was so deep that to have reached the houses opposite on foot would have taken five or six hours, even if one had no trouble crossing the river. Indeed, the landscape was on so vast a scale that, from our friend's garden, one could see three, four, five villages at each glance, all of them distinct communities, and two or three miles at least from its nearest neighbour. I wondered how much each one knew of the other. The Bhutanese are not insular, but they are very self-contained, and I imagined them living quietly over there, unconcerned with the pinprick headlamps they must have seen now and then on the road across the river.

The sides of the valley were very lush. Parts were wooded, especially higher up; others were covered in scrub, but much of the vast hillside was carved into intricate terraces. It was spring; transplanting was not far away, and the paddies were a vibrant green. The houses between the paddies were bright white with new paint and seemed to sparkle in the sunshine. Here, high above the Mangde Chu, the steep rushing river that roared out from the high snowpeaks a few miles to the north, I knew I was in a living, breathing landscape, its fabulous beauty enhanced rather than spoiled by a rural economy that was at one with its environment, not struggling with it. It was a memory that would return to me again and again in later years in the Middle East, where man seemed to have taken on his surroundings and fought them to a bloody standstill.

That evening our friend, pottering in the house as the sun went down, sent us to the local shop for weasel's piss. The shop functioned as a bar as well of course, so we had a couple of nips each of Dragon Rum. In the house we drank some of the weasel's piss. Then we went to a party given by friends of our friend's (actually the whole village was friends with her; after all, it wasn't very big). Twice we went out to get more weasel's piss but then we found we had drunk every bottle in the village, so we switched back to Dragon Rum. I can remember sitting on a log outside with the teacher in the warm spring air. Later we had an argument. I cannot remember what it was about. Both she and I had hot tempers and we were still screaming at each other when we got back to the house in the early hours of the morning. We had come along the road, and had to negotiate the steep slope down into the yard; it was pitch-dark, and she grabbed my arm. I think she was trying to help me find my way. Or perhaps she was trying to throw me in the mud. In any case the two of us collapsed in a heap at the foot of the slope, rolling on top of each other. Somehow we all got up the ladder without breaking our necks and she disappeared to bed, slamming the door behind her.

Early the next morning we loaded up. We had been here two days and the bike seemed unfamiliar. Together we strained to push it up to the road. Tom checked the luggage straps and climbed on. He pumped the kick-starter a few times and then the engine chuckled into life with a whiff of undigested petrol. "OK, get on," he said wearily. He had drunk less than I the night before but he looked tired. Our friend stood beside us, *kira* and blouse still immaculate. She looked sad, or perhaps she was just hung over. "Please be very careful on the way," she said. She kissed us each gently on the cheek, and stood for a moment as we pulled away. The wind cut through the Dragon Rum fumes and I felt a little better. I glanced back, to see her turning away down the slope.

Six months later I travelled to Bumthang in Central Bhutan for a conference. There was no bike this time, just a big comfortable Land-Cruiser. It was autumn by now, a bright day, the oaks on the passes a brilliant orange. On the way back to Thimphu we stopped for lunch in Trongsa, in a hotel where foreigners often stayed or ate; it was run by a Tibetan woman whose warmth and kindness to volunteers were legendary. As we left I saw our friend. She was standing with another woman by the side of the road; I think they were looking for a lift. We talked for a few minutes, then it was time to go. On a sudden impulse I dug into my luggage and found a pot of local honey that I had bought the day before. I ran back to her and handed it to her. We laughed and kissed each other goodbye and then I got back into the car and we drove away, leaving her standing outside the hotel. A few weeks later I left Bhutan forever and I never saw her again.

*

I loved to walk in the mountains around Thimphu. As I have said, it was not always wise to do so alone; there was no mountain rescue service, and bears lived in the forests on the lower slopes. My usual partner in crime, Piet, was a Dutch consultant in his mid-40s with a frightening ability to walk and cycle long distances in places that were inaccessible, dangerous or just plain odd. (Twenty years later, he still does. Currently back in Bhutan, he has quite recently cycled across – and beautifully photographed – Mongolia, China and Ladakh.) Piet, his American wife Melissa and their friend Linda, herself a former volunteer, were endlessly hospitable. Long walks often ended with a beer on their veranda overlooking Thimphu, the lights of the town coming on as the shadows spread up the mountainsides from the valley floor.

Passing through Kathmandu, I bought a new pair of trekking boots from a shop run by a monk. ("I know a shop where you can get good boots," a friend had had said. "You'll like this place. It's run by a monk." The monk smiled and bargained hard.) Usually with Piet, sometimes with Tom, and often with other friends, we would set out on a Saturday morning at maybe nine, and by lunchtime we could enjoy our sandwiches at 14,000ft above the monastery of Phajoding, its golden rooves glittering in the sun, and Thimphu spread out like a map 7,000ft below us. Now and again we would press on further and higher, to a moorland where, in summer, there would be herds of yak hundreds strong, and the horizon was flecked with snowpeaks: Bhutan's highest mountains, Jomolhari, Jichu Drakey and Tsheringgang. In the far distance, on the borders of Nepal, West Bengal and Sikkim, one could just make out the long form of Kanchenjunga. (In December 1992 I went to Darjeeling, and got up far too early one morning to watch the snowfields on the mountain catch fire as the first rays of the sun slid over Tiger Hill to its east and the first light crept slowly into the deep valley below.)

To walk out of the Thimphu valley was to walk into a different world, with its high plateaux, moorlands, grouse-like birds, distant snowpeaks, huge herds of yak, and strong winds that whipped past you then dropped suddenly in the calm of a bright, warm winter's afternoon.

On the high moorland at 14,000ft, a few hours' walk above the town, rose a round green hill with a curious regularity of shape. It was used for sky burial. In the Himalayas, herders and others at very high altitudes practice this for harshly practical reasons. In the winter, the ground may be too hard to break. Moreover, there will be little fuel with which to cremate a body, as they would down in the valley. So the body is laid out on top of a hill used for that purpose, and the bones broken with an axe. The funeral party will then light a small fire, which will attract the lammergeyers, mighty condor-like carrion birds with a wingspan many feet across. These would normally be circling on currents far to the south, nearer to Paro; but would perceive the fire from up to 60 or 70 miles away. They would then soar in to perform the task for which they had been summoned. I would shiver slightly when passing that hill, and quicken my stride for the scarp a mile or two away where rhododendron-bushes overlooked Thimphu town and the known world, 7,000ft below.

Towards the end of January, eight months or so after I had arrived, I made a much longer walk than usual. I had by now explored much of the west side of the valley, but the east was unknown to me. The mountains rose just as steeply, but to the north-east there was a pass through which one could get through to the Punakha valley. This was the pass of Sinchula, after which the original treaty between Bhutan and the British had been named. (The name of every pass ended in –la. This is an all-purpose word in Dzongkha meaning yes, go through, after you, I concede; and is often added on to the end of sentences as a courtesy, even when speaking in English. It also means a pass.)

Once, Punakha had been the capital, and the route to the outside world had led through to Haa via Sinchula. The narrow footpath had thus been one of Bhutan's major highways until the mid-1960s. Then the road had been built through the more southerly pass of Dochula. Whereas the road route to Punakha was 50 or 60 miles, the journey over Sinchula was barely 20; but it was higher and steeper, and a road would not have been feasible. The pass was now little frequented, and although some Bhutanese yak-herders still used it, few Westerners knew where it was.

One of those who did was a teaching volunteer who lived in a village in the Punakha valley, some way north of the town itself. The plan was to cross Sinchula as fast as possible, starting early on Saturday morning, and spend the night at her small house in the village in the Punakha valley. We thought we should make it by nightfall. The next morning, we would be picked up by a friend's kindly driver. It was not the best time of year for this. In winter, the weather was either kind or very unkind, and the days were short. But the volunteer was soon to move to Punakha for her second year, and it was the last chance. I decided I could not miss this; the very word Sinchula was romantic.

A number of us started early on a Saturday. There was the odd splash of blue sky, but for the most part it was white and grey, and the air felt damp. It was fairly cold. We made rapid progress for the first hour or two, and then found ourselves blocked by a thick forest of bamboo; the track to the pass was nowhere to be seen, and the ground was marshy underfoot. The weather was deteriorating. We spent perhaps two hours searching for the track; eventually someone found it, and we started to ascend the pass. By now, there was a race against time. The summit was not far away, and anyway, it was only about 11,000ft. The problem was on the other side, where the greater part of the route lay, often over an indifferent surface; worse, the Punakha valley was far lower than Thimphu, and we would have to descend some 7,000ft from the summit.

Eventually, the distinctive *chorten* that marked Sinchula – once the most important pass in Bhutan – appeared above us. Turning round, I saw what remains in my memory as one of the most striking images of my time in Bhutan. The track wound up to the pass in a succession of hairpins, so that some of the walkers behind and below me lay to my right, and others to the left, all at varying heights. It was, as I commented in a letter, "like a scene from a documentary of the 1930s, of the Long March perhaps... The weather worsening, the grey-white sky barely above us, all colour gone, a scene of high contrast. The walkers are black figures on a brown and white landscape, flecks of snow swirling around them. Above us, the prayer-flags by the *chorten* flap and tear in the rising wind."

We broke briefly for food, and ploughed on. The track was narrow and we had to go in single file. It ran for mile after mile through woods, descending gradually; now and then it would debouch into a yak-meadow, from which our exit had to be picked with care, lest we make for Tibet. We didn't stop. There wasn't time. At about four, we descended a steeper-than-usual stretch to find a wide, rushing stream; we were now in the Punakha valley. After another hour, we started to pass farmhouses. This meant there would be somewhere to take shelter if we must; and we discussed it, for the light was now fading.

The farmhouses themselves were beautiful. Punakha was a rich valley, and the white lower walls of the houses were adorned with snarling blue demons, yellow and orange gods, the usual conch shells and the usual fertility symbols, the flying pink penises. Here and there the houses were surrounded by neat enclosures, and some had clusters of tall straight poplars. We picked our way across the skillfully-made bunds between the rice paddies.

As we strode on between the fields, the quality of the light started to change; the clouds were now grey and thin, and the redness of the sunset tinted the dusk. The outlines of the houses became less distinct. It was past half-past five, and it would soon be dark. I was surprised that we saw hardly a human being, or even a dog. The red-grey countryside seemed completely empty, and rather sinister.

We had been walking for about 11 hours when we entered a village, and the teacher led the way to a dark house. We climbed carefully up the outside staircase in the gloom. She found a blue iron East German kerosene lamp, and screwed out the wick. In the darkness of the house, the feeble yellow light shone on exhausted faces. We unrolled our sleeping-bags from our rucksacks, and ate some red rice that the teacher, who had had much practice, prepared in the dark; and we went to sleep.

I slept well, and was one of the last to awake. It was after half-past seven. And the room was flooded with light. I could see the teacher busy preparing food at the head of the outside staircase and asked if I could help. "Later," she said, and indicated the track down which we had come. "There's a tap up there, if you want to wash; about two hundred yards, through the gate and on your left." Few volunteers outside Thimphu had running water or electric light in their houses.

I emerged into a bright blue and green world, and it was intensely beautiful. The weather had cleared completely overnight; moreover we were at half the altitude of Thimphu, and it was gloriously warm. Two of my companions were chatting to one of the teacher's Indian colleagues. With him was a sleek, well-fed golden labrador that gambolled happily, wagging its tail at everyone. A few villagers milled around. There was little for them to do in the fields in January; winter wheat was sometimes grown on the paddies, but it was uneconomic that year. The lush grass and fields shone, even though it was winter; the fresh morning sky was dotted here and there by tiny, fluffy white clouds, and life was good. The Long March had been a good idea, after all.

Later in the morning, we walked down to the roadhead a couple of miles away, to find VSO's driver waiting with the Land Cruiser, and we drove into Punakha for a leisurely brunch. During this, we were approached by a young man of perhaps 20, wearing a gho folded down to his waist and a white T-shirt, a black leather jacket, dark glasses and spiky hair. He was a civil servant, he explained, and needed to get to Thimphu before work the next day; all the bus tickets were sold. Could he come with us? As the car was very full, he sat in the boot at the back, and we set off for home.

The road passed down the Punakha valley, alongside the Mo Chu, a wide, fast river. The weather remained beautiful. As we began the long climb to Dochula, we passed an isolated *lakhang*, or temple, in the paddy-fields below. This was dedicated to Drukpa Kunley, the Divine Madman, a saint from the 17th century not noted for abstention; the Bhutanese regarded him as the guardian of fertility. The *lakhang* was a place of pilgrimage for those longing for a child. I remembered hearing that an expatriate, unable to conceive, had gone there in her best *kira*, and had participated in the usual ceremony in which she was whacked over the head with a giant penis whereupon, she told friends, she had felt something lurch in her stomach.

She gave birth nine months later.

I watched the *lakhang* recede as we climbed into the forest. The young Bhutanese stretched and adjusted his position; he was surrounded by the teacher's gas-bottles and I was glad he did not smoke.

"You have had the weekend in Punakha? To get warm perhaps?"

"Oh, we walked!" we said proudly. "Right across Sinchula."

"Oh," he said. He thought for a moment. "Yes, I have done that. Seven, eight times. When I was seven, eight years old."

He explained. From Thimphu, he was the middle child of seven, and, as was the custom in such cases, his father had given him to the monk-body in order to accumulate karma for the family. He had been miserable from the beginning, and had escaped from the monk-body's winter residence in Punakha Dzong and walked across Sinchula to his family. His father brought him back. And back. And back. And eventually admitted defeat, allowing the boy to return home and to go to school in the normal way. I tried to imagine a small, intense figure in a red robe, his head shaven, plastic flip-flops on his feet, striding through the forest and over Sinchula in the biting wind of winter.

A month or two later we walked very high, to the base camp for Jomolhari, returning down the steep valley of the Paro Chu, the river that flows from the mountain. Jomolhari lies on the border between Bhutan and Tibet. It is over 24,000ft (about 7,300 m); the base camp itself was about 13,500ft (4,100 m). We came close to the snowpeaks, the distant summits of which stream slim plumes of snow against a deep blue sky. To glimpse that remote, icy world, even from far below, was to feel strangely lonely thereafter, as if one had glimpsed one's ultimate destiny and been forced, for now, to turn away.

When we were there it snowed. The next day, we were on a high path looking out over row after row of snowy ridges, gleaming in the morning sun, with no trace of man. We had reached a shallow valley of scree; snow still lay on much of it, and we found the tracks of a snow leopard. They were very fresh, and I am quite sure the damn thing was looking at us, although we could see nothing. Snow leopards live over most of the Himalayas, including the northern ridges in Kazakhstan and elsewhere in the former Soviet Union. But they are few in number, and although it was well-known that they lived in Bhutan (they can attack yak), I knew no-one who had seen one. We were not to be lucky that day.

The scree valley eventually turned up a steep, very long, slope between two high ridges. Halfway up we stopped to eat some chocolate, and to admire the sinister immensity of the desolate slope. Tiny pink flowers grew amongst the stones, a strange survival in this place. As we began the last 500ft to the summit, we crossed a patch of snow and here, and I noticed more tracks, looked away, and then looked back, for these tracks were not the same. The others were sceptical, and I am myself not quite sure of what I saw that day; but the shape of the prints seemed to correspond very roughly to those in the famous pictures taken by Eric Shipton in Nepal in 1951, and reported by others. Melting of snow does distort and enlarge a paw-print, and there is no doubt that some sightings could be ascribed to the prints of a snow leopard or Himalayan black bear that are some hours old. But the proximity of these prints to the earlier ones of a snow leopard was intriguing.

Later that year, passing through Kathmandu, I bought a slim paperback, *Yeti – fact or fiction?* by Majpuria and Kumar. The authors, one of whom was a professor at Tribhuvan University in Kathmandu, quoted the theory of a Professor Proshnev who, after researching the Yeti phenomenon in Kyrgyzstan in the 1950s, suggested that there was a symbiotic relationship between the Yeti and the snow leopard and that they flushed out each other's prey; as supporting evidence, he pointed out that the snow leopard, unlike other leopards, does not attack man. Perhaps what we had stumbled on, on the slopes of Ngele-La that cold morning, was two friends on a hunting expedition.

Theories about the Yeti's real size and shape vary, and there is a widespread belief in the mountains that there are several types of creature, some dangerous to man, others not. Although most of the publicised sightings originate from Nepal, in particular the area around the Khumbu Valley, the Yeti is as widespread as the snow leopard, and Majpuria and Kumar theorised about a 'Yeti belt' extending into Mongolia and northeast Siberia and down through Alaska into British Columbia.

The World Wildlife Fund's country director in Bhutan was Nepali, and was himself from the 'Yeti country' of Eastern Nepal. Before I left Bhutan I met him on business, and I took the opportunity to ask him if he believed in the beast himself. He laughed and shook his head. "By the way," he went on, "I suppose I should tell you about our Yeti Project." He was providing low-level funding for a couple of locals in Eastern Bhutan to follow-up Yeti sightings. On another occasion I was able to see several plaster-casts of alleged Yeti footprints, which were kept in the office of the Director-General of Forestry in Thimphu. Most Bhutanese people did believe in the Yeti. Amongst educated people, it seemed, there was a certain schizophrenia; no-one wanted to admit to themselves that they believed it, but no-one could quite lay it aside.

I remember that walk not just for those strange tracks, but for the fact that we walked with guides – almost the only time I did so – and they brought yak. Yak are similar in appearance to shaggy Highland cattle, to which they are related. They are stocky and very strong, with long, spiky horns and long, thick coats. They are immensely capable in difficult terrain and can put up with intense cold and very high altitudes. But they cannot safely be brought down to the plain; below about 8,000ft they suffer increasing environmental stress, and are vulnerable to diseases such as liver fluke. The Bhutanese breed fine yak, having continued to trade stock with Tibet, mostly in the east around Tashiyangtse. Indeed, the wealth of many ancient monasteries was tied up in great herds of yak that could run into thousands, and which roamed the high plateaux; a spectacular sight, but one not seen at lower altitudes.

Yak are strong pack animals, but they are also bad-tempered and nervous. They can certainly injure people. Bhutanese yak-drivers will establish which animal is dominant in a group, and will mark it with tufts of red cloth or wool; if this beast can be kept going in the right direction, its peers will follow it. An alternative is to eschew yak in favour of *dzos*. A *dzo* is a cross between a yak and a cow; it is just as strong and is easier to control, but it is sterile.

One afternoon near the end of the trek, we sat on rocks by a river and watched the yak. They were feeling the heat; it cannot have been much more than 55oF, but that was enough for them. We had brought them very low. They waded together, very slowly, into the river, and stood there panting, the water up to their chests, their long hair dragging in the current. The river at that spot was a quite extraordinary cobalt blue. I can remember watching it for a long time and wishing that I could stay there forever.

We walked and we walked and we walked, and from October to June the weather was, for the most part, with us. Even in winter, although the early mornings were very cold, the sun soon warmed the back of your neck, and the light was clear. There were few clouds. But it was as well to be home before sundown; the temperature dropped quickly then. On one occasion, we were caught by a rare snowstorm. It was a lesson we did not forget. But March and April brought the spring, The trees in the Thimphu valley burst into white and pink blossom. They were often surrounded by prayer-flags against a background of brightly-decorated traditional houses, set amid greening paddies under a deep blue sky. Soon the rhododendrons began, appearing first just above Thimphu and then moving higher, so that they could still be seen in June if one cared to climb a few thousand feet. It was worth it. They were astounding. But by this time the clouds were starting to build up in the afternoons, and in July the monsoon broke. We continued to walk, for it rarely rained before midday. Now and then it didn't at all. But usually a monsoon walk was a wet business, with muddy boots and wet cagoules dropped in heaps at the end of the day.

A monsoon walk had its gifts. By the time the cloud started to build at midday, one was above it, and could look down and watch it boiling up out of the Thimphu valley, smothering the small capital below. One afternoon we reached the ridge above Phajoding to find that there was little to see. Cloud had closed in below us and we were looking down on its topside, but now and again we could see the mountains across the valley. There was a higher layer of cloud above us, and it was raining slightly. We sat and ate lunch, huddled in cagoules, and the weather closed in around us so that after a few minutes we could see barely 20 yards; beyond that, in all directions, all was white. Then a patch of grey appeared in the clouds below us, and widened slowly. Eventually, the little city of Thimphu could be seen, neatly framed by the hole in the cloud. Everything else remained white. So there was a city, floating like the centre of an unfinished canvas. It remained there for several minutes before the sky reclaimed it and we were left, marooned, above a sea of white.

*

I was happy with very little then. Apart from my clothes and my boots, the only possessions I had in Bhutan that I owned were my Indian bicycle and a cheap stereo cassette-deck. Together they had cost me perhaps £75. Both kept going wrong. I spent much of my time tinkering. When I was not tinkering, I was reading something from the well-stocked public library. Or sitting in Benez, either chatting to someone or reading quietly. My whole life was in Thimphu, for I owned little in England, and had no money in the bank. (Indeed, when I had left, I had been some £125 in debt, but my friend, who was an accountant, told me I was entitled to a tax rebate that would pay this off. Three weeks after I arrived in Bhutan I received a cheerful note from London. "I have recovered the sum of £130 from the Sons of Satan and have given it to those leeches you bank with," it said.) My only income was my salary from the Department of Agriculture; about £60 ($100) a month, it was just enough. As I was 35 when I arrived in Bhutan, and most of my contemporaries had bought houses and started families, all this should have worried me. It didn't.

My work at the Department of Agriculture had gone well, and I had extended my two-year posting for six months. I liked my Bhutanese colleagues a great deal, and was proud of the communications unit we had founded for the Department, the newsletters and booklets we had produced, the little darkroom I had set up with Indian equipment, and our desktop publishing (quite new even in the West then). I also admired Bhutan's balanced and careful approach to development. I still do.

But I could not stay in Bhutan forever. The Government did not like foreigners to hang around when their job was done, and with good reason; it was becoming clear that my colleagues could soon do the work themselves, and of course they would want to. I had already been interviewed for a new job in the Middle East. In December 1994 I disposed of my few belongings. My cassette-player was badly worn, so I gave it to a Bhutanese friend who I knew could fix it. I left a box of tapes in the office. I gave the bike to a fellow-volunteer. I returned my books to the library; those that were mine, I gave away. I threw all the *filmi* magazines into the useme a few yards or so from my flat. (When I went into Benez half an hour later, I found the customers happily reading them.) At last I had no more than I could carry on my back. That was how I came to Bhutan. Now I left with less.

Two days before departure, I closed my little flat and took my rucksack up the hill to the big house where Piet, Melissa and Linda lived. The day before I left, Piet organized a leaving party. Being Piet, he organized it in a yak-meadow at 11,000 ft. We walked for four hours to get there, in a snowstorm. We huddled round a fire and drank lots of beer and rum. Then a Japanese friend drove me back to Thimphu as darkness fell on my last day in paradise.

An American friend, Ed, was flying the plane the next day. So he asked me to join him on the flight deck. The tall stewardess strapped me into the jump-seat, and I looked out through the clear, bright air at the peaks of Jomolhari, Jichu Drakey and Tsheringgang as they slipped behind us, revealing the brown shadow of the Tibetan pleateau behind them. We crossed North Bengal, with Darjeeling and Kalimpong slipping away in their turn; passed the towering walls of Kanchenjunga; and then there was another mountain to starboard, its summit streaming snow. "Take a look, huh," said Ed. "Most people won't get that close to Everest."

At Kathmandu I walked away across the tarmac wearing a huge cowboy hat a friend had given me. Ed leaned out of the window. "You take it easy," he called. "You take care of yourself, OK?" And several other people seemed to be yelling and clapping and cheering, but I could barely hear them for the noise of a door and the crash of steel bolts as they slammed into place forever.

Master of the Tiger

I arrived in Aleppo late on a November evening in 1994, having been assured that my visa awaited me at the airport, and that I would be met. In the ramshackle arrivals hall, a bemused frontier guard did not believe that I was expected, despite a large envelope with my name on it being pinned to the wall behind his head. It was raining. The driver who had come to meet me had missed me. Finding no-one, I hailed a taxi, a bright yellow Mercedes that was 40 years old. I knew a little Arabic, and directed the driver to the only hotel I knew of in Aleppo, the Baron. The hotel gave me a room, albeit with caution; Syria was locked down tight, I had not booked, and strangers were more welcome when you knew their business. I was given a very basic room that needed work, but it was clean and the bed was comfortable enough. I had had a long journey. I slept.

In the morning they drove me out to the research centre where I was to be interviewed, 20 miles to the south on the main Damascus highway. I gazed at the flat countryside, grey in the rain, scattered with half-completed houses and cement works. I had come from Bhutan in the eastern Himalayas, where I had been for over two years, and which I would soon have to leave. I thought of the Thimphu valley, surrounded by high hills that sparkled in the sun below a bright autumn sky, the warmth of the sun, the surrounding snowpeaks, the great herds of yaks on the uplands, and the quiet river where I had recently seen an otter.

*

When I returned to Aleppo to take up my post in March 1995, it was spring, and life looked much better.

I settled right in the middle of the city. Although nearly 40, I was single and had no wish to immure myself in a comfortable but soulless flat in the University quarter, where most of my colleagues from the research centre, and the few other foreigners in the city, lived. I asked my employer's accommodation officer if he could find me somewhere in the city centre. He was taken aback; no-one did that. I suspect the authorities liked outsiders grouped in one place, where they would not get too involved in the life of the city. But after a week or two he found a flat in in the romantically-named Kahlil Gibran Street, just off the main square.

It was never really a comfortable flat, no-one I knew lived nearby, and parking was hell. Yet in a way I liked it well enough. There was a tiny balcony on which I could sit through the oppressively hot summer evenings, with a view of the art shop opposite, run by an artist whose precise, slightly kitsch work was displayed in the window. Below me was a printing firm that used old-fashioned letterpress machines; at busy times they worked through the night, and my bedroom shook from the thumping machinery below. Across the hall was a medical laboratory; they closed for several hours in the afternoon, and now and then I would come home at three o'clock to find a patient or two waiting in the hall for them to open at five. One sticky summer afternoon I found an old couple, in traditional dress, clearly rural, the husband ill, the wife frightened, lying back against my door. The wife apologised for blocking my doorway. I took a litre bottle of cold water out to them and she thanked me so profusely that it humbled me; her hands flew back and forth as she called upon God to remember my kindness.

In the early spring of 1997 I moved to a far better-appointed flat in a French-built, mandate-era building in Azizieh, the Christian quarter, half a mile or so to the north, just behind the Latin Church. This was better, though I never grew to like its *mazout* stoves. *Mazout* was low-grade, dirty diesel; one filled a tank above the stove in the living-room or bedroom, and it dripped slowly through to the furnace, the glass door of which gave off a flicker of light and the illusion of a hearth. The fumes from the *mazout* brooded in the winter sky above Aleppo and there was a constant whiff of diesel, the end of which was a welcome sign of spring.

From the beginning, I walked. There is no other way to see a city and sense its rhythms.

The first thing one noticed, oddly, was that Aleppo was a living motor museum. The import duties were high, and the most ghastly heap was worth several thousand dollars provided it had the coveted domestic licence plate. Syrians did not, therefore, scrap their cars; they updated them. One often saw a 30 or 40-year old Volvo or Vauxhall with a modern interior, and the engines and transmissions often bore little relation to the originals. The exceptions were the huge De Sotos and Buicks, mostly from the early or mid-1950s, that had huge "lazy" V8s; I learned to recognise their throaty burble as they drifted down the main drag, Shoukri-al Qouwatly Street.

Each car was a riot of chrome, huge mirrors, fins and sumptuous paintwork that was often clearly original. My heart was stolen by a '55 Buick that passed by one day, a deep dark blue with a white roof, its grille a huge gaping chromium and steel mouth that seemed set to swallow the pedestrians who scuttled across the street before it.

In the early evening I would stroll around Azizieh, enjoying the relaxed atmosphere. The streets were full of beautifully-groomed young men in bright, well-tailored coloured shirts, every bristle of the moustache trimmed to perfection. The women dressed smartly in fashions just a little from yesterday; younger women slipped by in twos and threes in jeans and blouses, big hair clouding their shoulders, wrists and ears hung with gold. But there were others, women with long, severe dresses, headscarves and headbands, and others still cloaked in severe black *abayas*. Sometimes these had horizontal bands for the eyes; but now and then the black veil cloaked the eyes also, so that although the occupant could see you, you could not see them. Once, and just once, I saw a woman so dressed lift her veil briefly; I caught a glimpse of a face that seemed pale and terrified. The veil dropped quickly.

*

As a single man in Aleppo, I could not meet women outside my work. The Syrian and other Arab women at the research centre were kind, funny, and sophisticated; some were professional scientists and were highly accomplished. But a woman's public reputation was fragile, and to have met them privately would have been tantamount to announcing one's engagement. (Life for a single woman was of course even more constricted than it was for me.) There was thus no way of getting to know someone well enough to decide whether to proceed. In general, single men struggled, especially foreigners, for life was organised strongly around the family. Thus the city had many excellent restaurants, but a male group would be confined to the "non-family" room, almost always the least attractive area; otherwise, it was felt, we would ogle and pester women. In this atmosphere, prostitution should have thrived, but I heard of little evidence. But I am sure it was there.

On two occasions, I did visit clubs. The first was a dingy basement to which a friend had procured an invitation; a few men sat and stared at a bored-looking woman who danced without enthusiasm. I left after a few minutes. On the second occasion an Australian friend, a postgraduate student from the centre, called by, and we decided to go out and eat. We had seen what looked like an open-air restaurant behind a high fence not far from the Baron Hotel. We pushed open the gate and found ourselves in an open space with numerous tables, mostly empty, and a large stage at the far end. A waiter explained that it was not a restaurant but a club, but that we were welcome simply to eat. We were served *shish tawouk* (chicken kebab, with cooked tomatoes and unleavened bread) and a salad, a quite ordinary dish but of good quality, and bottles of local beer.

After some time a slim woman in her early 30s approached us and sat down at our table. She spoke only Arabic, but she was Egyptian, and I could understand her up to a point. (The local Aleppian dialect was very difficult.) She was a woman of great charm. I sensed that she might be available herself, but that her real function was to find out what we wanted. I explained that we were there simply to eat but told her that I thought her most attractive – which she was, with a pale face and delicate features and a well-tended head of frizzy black hair. She left us, but gracefully. Then a well-dressed man appeared on the stage, holding a microphone; music came from tinny speakers, and a large number of women processed onto the stage. They varied in size and shape, but most were young. They did not seem Syrian; Arab women can certainly be blonde, especially in the eastern Arab world, but these were very slim and pale and looked Slavic. They danced slowly and listlessly. Something was not right about them and I wondered if they were exhausted or even drugged. I had heard vague rumours of trafficking, but Syria was not a place where you asked too many questions. We finished our meal, which had been pleasant enough, and left; I never returned.

*

But there were other places where single men were welcome. Early on, I started going to a cafe opposite the Citadel to join a colleague's son for tea and a game of backgammon. The waiter brought the backgammon set and a hookah (also known as a *nargileh*, or hubble-bubble, as foreigners called it). The hookah is a sophisticated way to smoke; the heat is provided not by burning tobacco but by a glowing piece of charcoal. Inhalation draws the smoke from this downwards through the tobacco and the resulting smoke passes through a bowl of water to reach the smoker in purified form. The tobacco was usually from Bahrain and was infused with the scent of fruit, usually apple or apricot. Etiquette surrounds the water pipe. It is generally shared, and the mouthpiece is passed back and forth; to pass it with the nozzle pointing at one's companion is the height of rudeness, as it is phallic in shape. Worse, the glowing charcoal is exposed in the upper bowl, a convenient place to light a cigarette – but to do so is to indicate to the hookah-smoker that one has slept with his wife or sister. But a hookah was a pleasant habit, and we whiled away some pleasant afternoon hours with backgammon and the scent of Bahraini tobacco, in the shadow of the great square Citadel, a medieval structure on a site that had, it was said, been sacred or fortified since the third century BC, and upon which Abraham was said to have milked his sheep.

There were also restaurants where gatherings of men were welcome enough. One or two were in restored mercantile houses in the old quarter; the Sissi House and the Jasmine House, in particuar, were extremely beautiful – they were designed at least in part for tourists, but were none the worse for that. But I always liked Al-Andalus, a cheery local hangout on the roof of a four-storey building very close to the Baron. The restaurant was open but protected by awnings, and there was a cool and pleasant breeze on summer's evenings, which could be insufferably hot in July, August and early September. The food was much the same as that served in most of the restaurants in the city centre, and in much of the eastern Arab world; the ubiquitous *shish tawouk*, *tabbouleh* salad, *hummus* and *kibbeh* (the latter being a ball of bulgur and minced lamb).

Aleppo was known for its good food, and had its own takes on these Middle Eastern favourites. The region also had a distinctive seasonal lamb dish, *laham karaz*, prepared with cherries (though I never found this in a restaurant, only in a friend's house). There were also various pastries. Two in particular were said to be unique to Aleppo: *tosca* and *maria*, associated with a well-known local restaurant. They were said to be named after two young women, who, fleeing from the Hungarian Revolution in 1956, found refuge as dancers in Aleppo; one night when they were clearly very homesick, the restaurateur asked them to describe favourites that they missed from home, so that he could recreate them.

When not eating out, I cooked a modest meal at home and spent a while reading, then strolled out for a beer at the Baron Hotel. The Baron, in which I had stayed on my first night, had been built in 1909 by the Mazloumian family, which still ran it; the current Mazloumian, Armen, was always welcoming to me. The hotel had sheltered, amongst others, General de Gaulle, Teddy Roosevelt, Lawrence of Arabia (a portrait of whom hung in the lounge) and Agatha Christie, who passed through frequently with her archaeologist husband, Max Mallowan. But that is all well-known, and has been much written about elsewhere. (The best account I have read of life in the hotel is by the American journalist Charles Glass, who was there in 1987 shortly before being kidnapped in Lebanon.[4])

My Baron was the bar. Sometime around eight I would enter, to be greeted by the cheerful Kurd who ran the bar and was generally known as Charlie.

The bar itself was an old-fashioned place of leather armchairs, and Charlie stood in front of shelves that were set into an alcove that mirrored the high pointed windows in size and shape. On the shelves stood bottles that had probably not been touched for years. A leather panel with slots for shot bottles, long empty, proclaimed: "Underberg. After a good meal". There were scattered advertising slogans from long ago; a large metal poster showed what looked like a Douglas DC4 flying above the clouds, with the slogan "Fly above the weather with Pan American". On the left of the bar, by the window, next to a dim table lamp, stood a foot-high Indian gentleman on a pedestal with AIR INDIA emblazoned on it; one of his hands had come loose from the wire framework that held him together

---

4 *Tribes With Flags: A Dangerous Passage Through the Chaos of the Middle East*, Atlantic Monthly Press, 1991.

and dangled down towards the light-switch.

I liked the bar stool by that window. I wondered who had sat there before me; perhaps the spy Kim Philby, who used to call by when he was based in Beirut, and get wasted at the Baron bar as he drank his way down to his final defection. I doubt if he did it on Shark, the cloudy and worrying local beer, or on the only alternative, a cheap export version of a German beer, which gave me a headache.

No-one so colourful as Philby was there in my day. There was a young Italian who was riding around the world on a Vespa; he got very drunk and tried to fight me. There was a German engineer who got very drunk and tried to fight everyone. There were various contractors, expats, students of Arabic, scientists from the centre and the odd tourist, most from Europe (Americans did come, but they were rare). But if you half-closed your eyes, you could see Allenby or De Gaulle marching down the stairs, pulling on their gloves and barking orders; or Agatha Christie, writing *Murder on the Orient Express* on the veranda – which, I am told, she did.

*

I did not feel oppressed in Syria, but there were constant reminders of the regime. Drivers pulled over quickly to let a black car pass; many subjects were taboo, and the city was strewn with posters of Assad and his two sons, his heir apparent Bashar, and the former heir apparent, Bassel, who had died in a car crash some months before I arrived. Aleppians occasionally referred to these posters as "Father, Son and Holy Ghost". More often, they kept their own counsel. In fact, Aleppo felt very isolated.

But it had not always been so. In our day, few westerners knew of the city before the fighting began in 2011. But an educated Elizabethan would have done. Before I left for Syria, my mother copied out for me a quotation from one of the Three Witches in *Macbeth*:

> *Her husband's to Aleppo gone, master o' the Tiger;*
> *But in a sieve I'll thither sail,*
> *And, like a rat without a tail,*
> *I'll do, I'll do, and I'll do.*

Shakespeare's witch is expressing spite; she wishes to avenge a slight from the sailor's wife. In fact, the verse is likely a reference to the English merchant adventurer Ralph Fitch, who sailed for the Levant in the *Tyger* in 1583.

Fitch, and others, had good reasons to make for Aleppo. For centuries it had been a key city at the western end of the Silk Road, a role it did not entirely lose until the Suez Canal opened in the late 19th century. When it did, however, the city's importance declined precipitously, to be further diminished by the loss of its Anatolian hinterland after Versailles, and then by the transfer of its port, Alexandretta, by the French to Turkey in the 1930s (it is now Iskenderun). The *coup de grace* had been Syria's isolation since then under a succession of authoritarian rulers, the most recent of which was Hafez al-Assad. At times the city seemed to have a rather grumpy concept of itself, as do individuals when they have declined in importance.

Yet there were sudden reminders of the glories of the past. The great souk of Aleppo was one. The souk was a place of pulsating life. It was many miles of vaulted stone passages, lined by the shops of merchants in cloth or copper, jewelry or other goods; an extraordinary community with its own ancient souks and baths. I passed through it often, for at its heart was one of the world's oldest inhabited houses, the former Venetian embassy and later the Consulate of the Low Countries. The house was a strange and intricate place lined with aged books of likely great worth. I had friends living in the house – an Australian researcher, and later a Danish poet whose presence puzzled the security police, the Mukhabarat.

One day, as I walked past the Hamam al-Nahaseen, the baths in the copper souk, I saw a man in what looked like a Western suit, standing slightly lost amid the cheerful din of shouting shopkeepers and clattering mules. On his head was a Kyrgyz cap. It was a sign of an ancient route that had reopened. A century earlier the Hejaz Railway had been built at least in part to carry pilgrims south through Syria to the Haj. Today, with the fall of the Soviet bloc, they had resumed their journey; not by train this time, but in broken-down old buses, financing their journey with whatever goods they could sell along the way. Sometimes these were carpets, and the merchants in the souk had new stocks from Bukhara and suchlike to sell alongside the local products, themselves very fine.

There were newer links with the outside world. Many Syrians had worked in South America, and the groceries sold packets of *maté* for those who had kept the taste; when the World Cup came round in 1998, someone hung out a huge Brazilian flag that dominated the next street to mine. There was an international jazz festival. The British Council organised the odd tour. (A Reduced Shakespeare Company take on *Macbeth*, however, left the locals bemused. One of the actors wore a large codpiece. An elderly Syrian next to me whispered, "Genitalia?" He left at the interval.) A young photographer, Issa Touma, was pioneering a festival of photography. We had mutual friends and I met him on a number of occasions; today, years later, in the chaos of the civil war, he has not given up this dream, and continues to organise an exhibition of sorts, despite the horror around him. Young Syrians did not want to be isolated by politics or by anything else.

Yet Aleppians seemed constrained by distrust, not just of their government or of outsiders, but of each other. One did not discuss religion but was aware of its importance. Aleppo was home to people of many faiths; Christian as well as Muslim, and from many subdivisions of those faiths. Alawite, Druze and Yezidi people were also present, although not in such numbers as elsewhere in Syria; their belief systems are complex and sometimes secret, and their relationship to Islam is not always clear. Other people were Armenian, descendants of those who had fled the terrible events that befell them in the First World War. In their case, the relationship with other Aleppians seemed very cordial; still, one did not discuss such matters. In general, everyone seemed to get along well enough, certainly as individuals, but one sensed tensions and I wondered, as I have in other countries, if there was any real sense of shared identity, and what it was.

*

The centre I worked in, the International Center for Agriculture in the Dry Areas, or ICARDA, was a curious island, with its international staff and the sound of English in the corridors. It was also 30 or 40 minutes' drive south of Aleppo. It was a journey I made every day in my smart Peugeot 405 Break, either alone or with a car-pool partner. It was not a journey I enjoyed. Driving in Syria was dangerous. A scientist had been killed on his commute two years earlier; a few weeks after I arrived, a popular Lebanese research student died on her way home from a field trip. I got used to it, but never grew to like it.

I started a magazine, *Caravan*. It was to be a communications tool for ICARDA. The first issue had an article in it called *When sheep's tails had wheels* – a reference to the local *Awassi* sheep, whose enormous tail stored fat for the winter. A colleague had found an 18th-century account of Aleppo by an English trader that recounted how farmers tied these huge tails to boards, to prevent damage, and now and then put little wheels on them to ease the sheep's movement.

I loved editing *Caravan*. It was all about what, to me, mattered: feeding the world without wrecking it. ICARDA had achieved much in its 20-year existence, helping to develop new varieties of chickpea and lentil and wheat and barley, finding new ways of improving pasture, devising crop and livestock rotations and doing much else. It had had a hard beginning, being founded in Lebanon just as that country's long and miserable civil war was beginning. The Syrian government had invited it to move to Aleppo instead, and had provided the land.[5]

The research centre was on a low hill with a view down the Orontes valley towards Hama. The fields were a bright beautiful green and the scrubby, rocky hills in the countryside were scattered with small bright flowers. To our west lay the coastal mountains of Syria, an extension of the Anti-Lebanon chain; lower, but still over 4,000ft in places. To reach them, one drove south then south-west to Jisr Al-Shughur, then turned south into a long, narrow valley between two spurs of the mountains. Some 20 miles down this valley, a small country road opened to the right and one followed its vertiginous twists and turns, climbing over 3,000ft above the valley floor, which was lush with crops. Driving back into the valley one spring afternoon, I

---

5 As Syria's own civil war developed in 2012, the campus was looted, and the centre was forced to return to Lebanon. However, its work is being continued both there, and by its many friends amongst the scientists in the Arab world and elsewhere.

suddenly realised what it was; it was the final stretch of the Rift Valley, come from Kenya and beyond, and stretching north for some 50-60 miles more before its long journey was brought to an abrupt end by the mountains of Anatolia.

Not long before that point, where the valley had become shallow, a curious ruined church sat just above the valley floor. In the nave was the stump of what had once been a high pillar. This was the basilica of St Simeon Stylites, and the pillar was the one upon which he had perched for 37 years until his death in 459; in the words of Tennyson's rather terrible poem:

In hungers and in thirsts, fevers and cold,
In coughs, aches, stitches, ulcerous throes and cramps,
A sign betwixt the meadow and the cloud,
Patient on this tall pillar I have borne
Rain, wind, frost, heat, hail, damp, and sleet, and snow

Which is I suppose what one expects if one sits on a pillar in all weathers. I visited often, but it was not the sacrifice of St Simeon that drew me to that spot; it was the location above the valley, with its wildflowers and fig trees and the ruined basilica's naked arches of honey-coloured stone against a bright blue spring or autumn sky.

The basilica was not the only remnant of the Byzantine world. Stretching south towards Hama and Homs, scattered across the scrubby hills with their thin soil, were the abandoned cities of Syria; houses, halls, olive-presses and storehouses, wrought of beautifully dressed stone, their rooves missing but otherwise laughing at time. A civilisation as good as ours, but gone. As to why, no-one was sure; some said that the soil had been worked out – others, that the tide of the Arab invasion, driven north by the fire of their new religion, had blocked the people from their Byzantine markets and wrecked their economy. Like so much in Syria, this was political. A message about soil erosion? Or a negative slant on the coming of Islam?

My favourite reminder of antiquity was a steeply-arched second-century bridge across a river in a deep green valley in the Kurdish country to the north of Aleppo, close to the Turkish border. Driving across it took some courage due to its steep apex, narrowness and absence of guardrails, and the uneven cobbles; I did it several times in my official Peugeot, mindful of a space of barely a foot on either side of the car. Yet trucks appeared to cross frequently, sailing merrily to the apex and drifting down the other side at three times the speed I dared do it. The bridge was a favourite spot, as there was a small pool in the river and one could swim there. To reach it one drove for 40 minutes or so north of Aleppo along country roads until one reached a town called 'Azzaz. The town was described in the Lonely Planet guide as "a windy little dump" and indeed it did not impress, the wind catching the discarded plastic bags and tossing them around the unkempt narrow streets. But 'Azzaz is contested now, the scene of some of the heaviest fighting in north-west Syria. I wonder where most of its people are; and I wonder whether the bridge is still there.

The mountains were a border between worlds. To our west, across the mountains, lay the Mediterranean world. To our east lay the great plains that ran eventually into the eastern border of the Fertile Crescent, to the Tigris and the Euphrates, beyond which lay Central Asia – Iran, Afghanistan, and the former Soviet republics to the north. These plains were an ecological zone of their own. A colleague defined them for me as areas where there was sufficient rainfall for pastoralists, but where settled agriculture was not viable in most years although it was sometimes tried – an experiment that sometimes met with brief success, but then failed, having destroyed the native vegetation that might have supported camels or a few sheep. We called these plains the steppe. The traveller and colonial administrator Gertrude Bell, who crossed the region in 1905, had a more romantic name for it, titling her book *Between the desert and the sown*. The steppe was home to the Bedouin, who had shifted from camel to sheep but still ran their own lives and kept clear of each other, lest a dispute over scarce grazing be settled with a 19th-century musket or worse.

I had thought I did not like flat places. The steppe converted me. It was not completely flat; there was just enough relief for long perspectives, and in places one could see for many miles. It was semi-arid and in the hot season, the grass struggled to survive, barely shielding the grey baked earth. But once I went out there in spring; there was grass, there were wildflowers there too, and clouds that billowed across horizons so vast that they freed and fed the soul. I did not need to ask why people made their life there.

*

I left Syria in 1998. I had not really been there long – less than four years – and I had lived there as a foreigner, with a superficial understanding of the country and its people. Since then I have lived in five other countries, and I thought little about my years in Syria until the civil war began in 2011. Even then, it seemed for a while as if Aleppo would escape more or less unscathed.

As we now know, it hasn't. I was finally prompted to write this piece by the shocking deaths, early in 2013, of scores of students as they sat their exams at Aleppo University. Of course, nothing I write can illuminate what is happening now; neither can I suggest any way of bringing this conflict to an end. What I can do, I hope, is to point out that this city is not a place on a map or a name in the news; it is a real city that has hundreds of thousands of people trapped in it, and some of them are getting killed. Even those who have left for the safety of Turkey, Lebanon and Jordan have little to look forward to, as aid agencies struggle to provide them with shelter through the winter.

One day, one way or another, the conflict in Syria will come to an end. Meanwhile I will remember Aleppo and the region as I last saw it; bolts of cloth in an ancient souk, flat rooves studded with domes, men in bright shirts, water-pipes and backgammon, *shish tawouk* and *laham karaz*; great open plains with billowing clouds; farmers with donkeys; lines of olive trees marching to the horizon and the border with Turkey, the hills of Anatolia rising in the distance; an old-fashioned bar with leather armchairs and ancient bottles; the breeze and the scent of spring at the Basilica of St Simeon, the valley floor ablaze with green; an ancient Buick burbling past below my balcony through the warm evening air.

If it's Tuesday, this must be Bishkek

The phone brought me in from the tiny terrace where I had been taking a beer before dinner. It was Saturday; I had been walking in the Forêt de Soignes on the edge of Brussels, trying not to think too hard about tomorrow. The summer evening light lit the leaves of the trees that sheltered my third-floor flat and played upon the surface of the Ixelles lake, just visible through the gaps in the buildings. I had taken the flat at least in part because the lake was nearby. I did not know then that it was infested with botulism.

I picked up the phone.

"How's morale?" asked David.

"Not bad," I said. "Pretty much packed."

"Good," he said. There was a moment's silence, then: "Before you go, sit. In the hall. With your bags. That's what Russians do. Just for thirty seconds, a moment of stillness, before you leave."

I thanked him for ringing; it had been thoughtful. David was a polymath who had taught himself Russian, had been very active in London politics and was now writing a doctoral thesis on Jews and the opera. (He later defended it successfully, and eventually published it.[6]) In between he searched for the tombs of the famous and then uploaded pictures to a site called *Find a Grave*, to which he was a leading contributor.

I went back onto the terrace and had another *kriek*, or cherry, beer, deceptively moreish and sweet. Hangover juice. I picked up the Lonely Planet guide to Central Asia.

*

David and I had arrived in Brussels nine months earlier, in the autumn of 1998. We were on contract to the European Commission's Tacis programme. Tacis was Technical Assistance to the Confederation of Independent States – to wit, Russia and the rest of what had been the Soviet Union, plus Mongolia. We were to find out about the programme's projects and disseminate examples of good practice so that others could follow suit, either with or without Tacis assistance. (I naively thought we should also tell people what had *not* worked. I was quickly discouraged from this.) Tacis often took the form of making former Soviets do things the Western way. I came to question this. Give people money and they may do things that, in truth, they would rather not do. But sometimes, especially in the social sphere, much good was quietly done.

We recruited two Belgian colleagues, and took offices in the rue Breydel, a few yards from the Berlaymont, the awful 1960s EU headquarters building on the east of the city centre. Our office was in an attractive early-century house, sympathetically converted. We were lucky, for the EU's vast headquarters buildings were hideous warts thrust down in the midst

---

6 Conway, David, *Jewry in Music – Entry of Jews to the Profession from the Enlightenment to Richard Wagner*, Cambridge University Press, 2011. I seem to know a lot of people who have written books.

of 19th-century Brussels, large parts of which had been torn down to admit them. Fortunately the Berlaymont was encased in sheeting for the entire two and a half years that I was there, having been found to contain asbestos. It looked as if it had been wrapped by the Bulgarian artist Christo. But our own office had its drawbacks. On one occasion the office handyman removed the toilet to fix a plumbing problem; unable to find it, he left the toilet standing in our kitchen for nearly two months. I asked the office manager (who was his wife) if this was Belgian surrealism. She looked at me blankly.

The project was moderately successful, despite the hurdles that bureaucracy put in our way. We decided to build as many bridges as we could with the Tacis projects in the CIS. David, who had contacts in parts of Russia, travelled frequently. I did so less often, but visited Moscow and Kyiv; the latter turned out to be enchanting, studded with churches and monasteries, the city centre perched on a bluff above the great glistening expanse of the Dniepr, alive with shades of Vikings and of Kievan Rus.

One day in June David and I were in the slightly soulless Italian restaurant we often used in Brussels, eating a large closed pizza each. We also drank wine, as usual a small carafe, although there was always a bottle on the table that the restaurant hoped one would buy. It was, almost always, Aglianico del Vulture. This takes its name from Mount Vulture, a volcano in Basilicata, but always struck me as comic; I suppose not much else did in Brussels.

"That Vulture," I said, "goes well with grey meat."

"Yes, doesn't it," said David. He reached into his pocket for his diary. "I was thinking. Could you pop over to Central Asia next month? See a few people. A week or two should be enough."

Back in the early 1970s, when Soviet Central Asia, or Turkestan, was still largely closed to foreigners, I had read Fitzroy Maclean's classic *Eastern Approaches*.[7] As a young diplomat in Moscow in the mid-1930s, he was told he would never get permission to visit Central Asia. So he didn't ask for it. Instead, he bought a railway ticket to Novossibirsk, where he changed onto the then newly-built TurkSib Railway. He was shadowed all the way by NKVD officers, sweating in their city suits, who will have cursed him roundly. The Soviet authorities must have assumed he was a spy, and indeed he likely was in it up to his neck. He eventually reached Alma Ata (now Almaty), Tashkent, Bokhara and Samarkand, and even crossed the Oxus into Afghanistan, reaching what was then the North-West Frontier of British India. Spy or no, Maclean was a wonderful writer and ever since I had read the book as a teenager, the region had fascinated me.

"Yup, okay," I said.

*

My first stop would be Kazakhstan. I changed planes in Munich's sparkling new airport, all glass plate and steel-wire braces. I was struck by the coffee machines at some departure gates, each with a notice warning the traveller that their flight was too short for coffee to be served and they should take it now. I tried to imagine Germans, enraged by lack of coffee, rioting at 30,000ft.

Almaty was different. I queued for two hours at immigration and customs, then walked out into a dark, unsurfaced lot, deserted but for a single taxi. I was then asked for $50 taxi fare

---

7 Reissued by Penguin in 2010.

to my hotel. After some discussion this became $20, at which point I gave up and got in the car. The ride to the hotel took over half an hour through dark, bare streets. In the hotel, the clerk could not find my booking in the file although I could see it quite clearly, on top. Having reached my room on the 25th floor, I then did battle with the sheet sleeping-bag, a Russian invention which consists of a small aperture into which you insert yourself with difficulty. It resembles a straitjacket. I finally slept about three, to be woken a few minutes later and offered a massage, which I declined.

Everything improved in the morning. I threw back my curtains to find myself looking straight at the snowcapped peaks of the Tien Shan – the Mountains of Heaven – glistening in the sunshine; further down the slopes were bright green alpine meadows and thick woods. The mountains come so close to Almaty that a mudslide in the 1921 wrecked the city and killed 500 people. In the opposite direction, the ground sloped gently down to the brown, semi-arid steppe, stretching, featureless, for over 1,000 miles north into Siberia. It was a crucial resource, providing grazing for the sheep that vastly outnumbered people in this, the world's tenth largest country. Yet in the last decade the number of sheep had dropped catastrophically.

I had arranged, through a mutual friend, to meet a western World Bank official in my hotel first thing; he had been friendly in emails, but seemed oddly withdrawn when I greeted him in the lobby, and refused all offers of coffee or breakfast. He said very little. I never found out why. After a half-hour he left, and, disconcerted, I set about my business, making for the Tacis liaison office in the town. Here too I found an oddly strained atmosphere. The office consisted of a single large room; the young Italian in charge took me out into the corridor to talk, and I sensed that he did not trust the Kazakh staff. Yet he was friendly enough, and promised to set up appointments for me for the rest of the day.

Later, his English colleague, a bluffer, more relaxed type, took me to lunch. Almaty seemed to me to be still rather Soviet; the USSR, of course, was only eight years gone. All the street signs seemed to be in Russian. But there were also increasing signs of Turkish influence. There were Turkish restaurants, Turkish banks, Efes and Turkish Tuborg beer and frequent flights to Istanbul and Ankara. At that time, the Turks, as a matter of policy, were reaching out to their Turkic neighbours as the Silk Road reopened for business.

Almaty was an attractive place. In 1999 there were few high-rise buildings apart from the Kazakhstan Hotel (it's an earthquake zone). But there was much early-Soviet architecture, such as the Academy of Sciences, which, I was told, was magnificent within. There were many, many trees, watered by ditches fed from the Tien Shan above, and there was plenty of shade; the temperature was a balmy 30oC. Foreigners lived well, with trekking in the Tien Shan in summer and superb skiing in the winter. In the evening I went for a drink and a meal with my English colleague. We went to a restaurant that advertised itself as Tex-Mex; it had a choice of eight or nine beers and a very long menu. The tables were crammed with well-dressed young ethnic Russians armed with mobile phones.

But below the surface, I was told, all was not well. Unemployment had spiralled, especially in the dying industrial towns on the steppe; no-one knew the figures, but one source suggested a million (in a country of 10 million). One street in Almaty functioned as an informal labour market; the pavements were crowded with women carrying cheap grips, in which they carried working clothes for different types of jobs, from secretary to toilet cleaner – they'd take what was around. It was part of change. Everybody in the old Soviet Union had a job, but some of them did little in practice; those "jobs" no longer existed.

One European official told me bitterly that, as part of a poverty-alleviation scheme, they were helping to institute what was basically a 19th-century workhouse. This was an oversimplification, but it seemed it did provide indoor care for the families of unemployed workers in the steppe rust-belt, who would themselves remain outside and would work in the project's enterprises so that it would be self-supporting. I was told that there was considerable interest in this locally, because the state no longer had the funds to look after people the way it had. I was scandalized by the idea that the EU was helping fund a workhouse, but was unable to meet the people from the project or get further details.

It did not help that my contacts were mostly expats. Anyone who has travelled knows that they try to awe the visitor or the new arrival. I was told of much else that I could not confirm, but it is very hard for a foreigner to verify such stories, or to get an accurate picture of conditions in a country, in a short visit or even, sometimes, a long one.

*

Late on the afternoon of the second day I left Almaty in a hired car, bound for Bishkek, the capital of Kyrgyzstan. It was a three-hour journey. Like Maclean 62 years earlier we followed the foot of the Tien Shan, and I was reminded of a journey of my own some years earlier from Siliguri to Jaigaon, across the Bengal plain; the great massif formed by the collision of India and Asia rises quite suddenly from the plain, and equally suddenly, tumbles back into it on the other side. Once again I wondered at the fact that one can swelter on the plain in tropical summer heat, and see snowpeaks that seem so close one could reach out and touch them.

On the far side, in Bengal, the plain had been fertile. Here there was steppe, nearly as flat, but semi-arid. Land with perhaps 100-350mm annual rainfall is not desert, but to plant it is to ask for trouble, for sooner or later the crop will fail; by then the organic matter in the land will have been depleted, and the native vegetation will have been destroyed. This in effect was the fate of Kruschev's Virgin Lands scheme. Left alone, however, such land will support a shifting population of livestock. In Kazakhstan, some of it was in fair condition; better than some of the steppe land in East Asia and North Africa that had been grazed nearly to extinction, and was turning to desert. Nonetheless livestock production was falling.

We stopped once on the journey, where a Kazakh police officer had all the passing cars lined up on a quiet stretch of road and was calmly turning over the drivers for a few dollars each. My Kyrgyz driver simply took his slush fund out of the ashtray and went to pay up. He made no comment; his face was a mask, and I wondered about the future.

After a couple of hours we turned south, towards the mountains and Bishkek. There were no border formalities; one just drove straight through. Kyrgyzstan is about two-thirds the size of Poland. Unlike Kazakhstan, it is virtually all mountainous, with peaks of over 7,000 metres. There is only a small area of semi-steppe in the north. It is here – again, at the foot of the Tien Shan – that the capital is sited. Bishkek, known in the Soviet era as Frunze, had about 900,000 inhabitants. Again, it was mostly low-rise, with a series of parks and plazas in the city centre. And many trees; it claimed to have more natural shade per head than any other capital in the world. It was clearly an Asian city. Ethnic Russians, were still said to be about 40% of the population and there were also a fair few Koreans. The ethnic Germans, however, had largely gone, and many Slavs were planning to go; a recent survey had suggested that between 190,000 and 280,000 people expected to emigrate "at some point in the future".

The town was in good condition and seemed quite prosperous. There was a new Hyatt-Regency under construction. A splendidly loopy Soviet touch was a large, ornate opera house. Unlike most places in the CIS, they still had an enormous Lenin. He stood in the big modern square in the city centre, leaning forward, arm in the air, in a pose of fraternal exhortation.

Bishkek women dressed to kill. Typical outfits included Lycra cycling pants (I did see one bicycle) worn with much lipstick and big funky earrings. The Russians seemed to favour very, very short print dresses, and very, very high heels. A variation on this theme was the skirt that was ankle-length but split nearly to the waist and was so thin that it was almost completely transparent.

In fact, I liked Bishkek. As one now knows, some trouble did lie ahead; but in 1999 the city felt relaxed. There was freedom of speech. I called on the Kyrgyz editor of *The Times of Central Asia*, the excellent new English-language daily that covered the whole region and had correspondents in Kazakhstan and Uzbekistan as well as Kyrgyzstan. The government in Bishkek wouldn't stop her from publishing what she wanted, she said; indeed it tolerated a Russian-language paper which was heavily against it. Inevitably, she was subject to less formal censorship from the paper's owners. "They do set the general editorial policy," she said frankly. But it did not seem to bother her. She made a request for assistance which was revealing. She did not want staff training in newspaper production (the paper was extremely well-produced), but in Western attitudes to journalism. "We want to understand how you *think*," she explained.

In order to find out how *she* thought, I read the paper. It was well-written, lively, and covered a broad spectrum of politics, industry and the arts. One regular page carried quotes from the region's national assemblies. "The difference between erotica and pornography is understood by everyone to the extent of one's putrescence," thundered the Speaker of the Kazakh *Mazhilis* (Parliament). Quite. I turned to the small ads. "For sale: Genuine Kyrgyz yurt," said one.

An example of democracy in action was the public row about the national currency, the *som*, that was going on while I was there. The national bank was under heavy attack from the Government and the public for failing to defend the value of the *som*, which had been sinking. The national bank kept a dignified silence but allowed a British consultant working with it through Tacis to write a spirited defence of the Bank's policy. Emptying the national coffers by shoring up the *som*, he argued, would only destroy its credibility. He told me he was delighted with the article's reception; it seemed to be changing people's perceptions of the mechanics of currency and helping them to face up to reality.

Bishkek was not ideal. A consultant for a British firm, a very large Dutchman, had been badly beaten a few months earlier by a group of young men – one of them allegedly a policeman. I was strongly advised not to go out alone at night, and to avoid groups of youths. Exhaust pollution was dreadful. The transition to the free market, and the break-up of the Soviet system, had brought real problems. Electricity consumption by industry had dropped, but the number of private connections had risen, and although there was ample power from the country's big hydro-electric schemes, the grid could not deliver it. As elsewhere in Central Asia, the departing ethnic Russians and Germans were taking their skills with them. And no-one had had hot water at home for three months, since the communal heating system was switched off for the summer. (It was inefficient anyway, being a "total loss" system that delivered about 25% of the hot water to the consumer.)

In the countryside, the end of the state collective farms had left people with their own land. But few holdings were over 20 hectares and in the south of the country, few were over five. These were often not large enough to be viable, or to generate profits for investment. World Bank and EU projects had persuaded many people to form credit unions and to borrow communally, both for working capital for seeds and fertiliser, and for such things as storage facilities. New, more profitable crops had been introduced, such as leeks and red cabbage. But, for many people, life was a struggle to adjust and survive.

Yet somehow the atmosphere was much better than in Almaty, and the city seemed cheerful and open. (It helped that the Tacis office was clearly a happier place, run by a quiet and likeable Englishman.) Kyrgyzstan has had its troubles since, but on my brief visit, I liked it; and I wish it well.

I reserved judgment on my hotel. Sixties-built, once well-appointed, it had been allowed to slide. The towel-rack in the bathroom was heated, although it was 30-320C outside. The bathroom itself stank of diesel oil. The bed was rock-hard, and the bedside light had no chain; it was switched on and off with a piece of frayed string. There was an air-conditioner, but it made much noise and achieved little. Opening the veranda door instead simply let in the noise of the traffic nine floors below, along with clouds of exhaust fumes. And, worst of all, there were the whores. They sneaked into the lift with you on your way upstairs. They rang you at two in the morning. One knocked on my door after midnight.

None of this was funny. If I ever thought it was, I didn't after meeting George (not his real name). George was an American pharmacist, from deep down in the Bible Belt. I had met him the previous October in Moscow, where he was staying in the same hotel. He was about 45 and had one ear. He had come to Moscow for his annual sex tour; I forget where he'd been the year before, but he gave me a run-down on what/who you could get there and through which orifice, and how much it cost. He'd chosen Moscow that year after arranging to meet women on a Web site. The women were, ostensibly, looking for marriage. George attended social events with them during the day. At night he had the hotel whores. In between, he sat on a stool in the lobby bar and mused on picking up a Russian wife to take home. "I met quite a nice one today, but she'd be no good – she doesn't have any qualifications," he said one night. "I'm hoping to get a doctor. Her earnings would be useful." George was a friendly sort of chap but a bit dim, and there was not much point in lecturing him on sexual colonialism.

One night we got chatting to a tall, elegant whore, an ethnic Russian from Estonia. She was probably about 30. I liked her at once. As a very young woman she had trained as a pharmacist herself, and had been sent to Angola to help provide basic medical care. She was shocked by the poverty, the poor water and the extent of infection. She met an elderly Portuguese, married him and travelled with him to Portugal, where the family ignored her. Then he died, and they virtually kept her prisoner. She escaped back to Moscow. She could have become a pharmacist again, but it paid about $150 a month. In the tourist hotels, she could charge $90 for 45 minutes. "What would you do?" she asked me over her shoulder as she led a drooling George to the lift.

When I returned to Brussels I ran a Web search with the keywords Russian, dating, introduction; and turned up a host of sites, some very dodgy, others just sad. Usually there were panels and panels of attractive Russian and other Slav women, often with professional qualifications, all seeking Western husbands. Most had a child, and most were either divorced, had never been married – or, in a number of cases, were young widows. After 1991, Russian men lost their jobs and drank themselves to death, and their wives were carried off to the Bible Belt by men called George with one ear. Could this be why the Russians still don't like us very much?

*

After a few days I left Bishkek. Unable to find a flight to take me on to Tashkent, I had planned to hire a car and driver. Probably we would have gone through Osh and into the Ferghana valley, home of the Heavenly Horses sought by the Emperor in Bruce Chatwin's memorable article. We would also have crossed a bit of Tajikistan on the way. It would have been a beautiful journey, but gruelling; seven or eight hours to the Uzbekistan border, where I would almost certainly have had to leave the car and cross on foot, meeting another car on the other side in which to drive the remaining hour or two to Tashkent. So I was pleased when the travel agent told me she had secured a ticket on a flight from Bishkek. I told my English friend in the Tacis unit. "Kyrgyzstan Airways," he echoed. "Oh, well I've generally got there eventually, I suppose." We went out for a large Korean meal. The next day I got up at 5.15 and drove the 25 miles to the airport with a young man called Oleg in his Mercedes.

Oleg was about 25, short, stocky, with very high cheekbones, a shaven head and very light grey eyes. In fact Oleg was the sort you see on newsreels raising red flags on Reichstags. He was also one of the nicest, and most helpful, people I met on my journey. He had three children and was worried about the future; like so many ethnic Russians, he felt a stranger in his own country now, although he had been born in Bishkek and had always lived there. His parents, he said, had already gone "back" to Russia, and he was not sure what to do. Probably he would follow them.

I enjoyed the ride through the thin golden light of the early morning. Oleg helped me check in before he left me, and then we were driven out across the tarmac, less than 20 of us. Ahead of us was a small, very short trijet a little bigger than a Learjet, with a huge tail, and a round nose that stood higher off the ground than the rest of the plane. This was the YAK-40. We trooped up the tail stairs under the tailplane to find a large luggage rack; there was no hold. There were no doors to the rack, either. I pushed my briefcase as far in as I could, hoping it would not decapitate someone in an accident. The inside walls of the aircraft were unlined, and looked like the unfinished fibreglass you see on the inside of a kayak. The seats were very small, with low backrests and no head restraints. But they were covered with a very pretty chintz material.

I strapped myself in beside a large American evangelist in shocking pink. Three smartly-dressed crew members disappeared into the cockpit. The flight attendant stood up and did her safety briefing in Russian, then, noticing that there were foreigners aboard, smiled nervously and said something like this: "Well come on board, ladies and shentleman. Our flight time to Tashkent will be one whore, fifty minuets. Hev a, er, have a heppy plane!"

What followed was one of the most memorable flights of my life. There have been a few. Landing at dawn in Santo

Domingo, amongst the Stratocruisers and Super Constellations; a light aircraft in the Ecuadorian jungle; circling the cra-
ter of Cotopaxi; nosing down the Paro valley in Bhutan, looking for the airstrip during the monsoon. But the flight from
Bishkek to Tashkent was the best of them all. The little YAK-
40 rolled gently, and quite quietly, down the runway and eased
itself imperceptibly into the air at a very low speed, so that I
only realised we had taken off when I saw the fields falling away
from us. I have flown in many aircraft, and once I was learning how to glide; but never have I been in an aircraft that felt
so utterly at home in the air as this one did. They must have
had to tie it down on the tarmac. We seemed to float through
the air like a soaring bird, utterly stable, as we climbed up the
side of the towering Tien Shan. As we drew level with the first
high peaks, we drifted to the south, and the real magic began.
Snow-capped summits rose to meet us, then fell away into deep
valleys carved by glaciers. Long lakes snaked down the deeper valleys; mysterious tracks traversed the hillsides; here and
there was a square enclosure of drystone walls for animals, in
the middle of nowhere, that could have been there for one year
or five hundred. I saw a group of bright blue and green and
turquoise lakes like semi-precious stones in the morning sun.
Slowly we glided across the Tien Shan until, in the far distance,
I could see the gap where the Ferghana Valley must be. In the
very far distance beyond, I wondered if I could see the High
Pamirs at the junction of Tajikistan, Afghanistan, Pakistan and
India. Then I looked back a little and realized that I must be
looking into China. The mountains turned away from us; below was the northern slope of the Tien Shan, deeply scored by
erosion, and the fertile strip of land at its foot. Then the ground
started to flatten and turn brown; towns started to appear, and
factory chimneys. We were over Uzbekistan. But, just for an

hour, I had felt again that sense of wonder that I had thought I would not feel again, because I had been travelling too long.

*

Tashkent airport had a dire reputation, with rumours of three-hour queues for immigration, and customs declarations that required your great-grandmother's birth certificate to be attached in triplicate (with photographs). I left the happy plane with regret. I need not have worried. I have never got out of an airport so quickly. The immigration officer was young and pretty and she smiled at me.

The first person I saw as I left the terminal was a fleshy young Uzbek waving a placard with my name on it. "My name is Timur. My job is to take care of you, and if you like I will take you around Tashkent tonight and show you the sights. Now, this is our largest hotel. Note the excellent modern design of the buildings, the wide streets. That is Friendship Boulevard. Our people here are noted for their friendship. For their traditions..." Unremarked, a spectacular bright-blue Russian cathedral with silver onion domes flashed past. "...Which go back to the time of etcetera, down there is the Museum of Fine Arts, this is the park which we consider the centre of the city..." There was a large equestrian statue in the middle.

"Who's the guy on the horse, Timur?" I asked him.

Timur snorted with laughter. "The guy on the horse!" It was obviously the funniest thing he'd heard since Genghis Khan left sacks full of skulls all over Europe. "The guy on the horse! It's Amur Timur, of course. The guy I'm named after." Timur. Timur the Lame. Tamerlane. Ah.

Tamerlane would recognize little of Tashkent; neither, sadly, would Fitzroy Maclean. Indeed, the only older building I saw was the charming Romanov Palace in the central park, built for Grand Duke Nicholas Constantinovich, who was exiled to Turkestan in the late 19th century for womanising, swindling and generally being well dodgy. (He fathered a string of children by various mothers in the city.) Everything else was gone, for on April 25 1966 the city was shaken apart by an earthquake that left few buildings standing. So the Soviet authorities decided to rebuild this city of (today) 2.3 million as a showpiece of the system. In many respects they succeeded. To be sure, some of the blocks of flats I saw were depressing, but they were at least low-rise (for obvious reasons). And the city centre was one of the greenest I have seen. It was also one of the most alive. It was designed to be lived in, to be a meeting point, a social focus, for the city's people. It seemed to have succeeded.

I decided to explore without Timur, telling him as politely as possible that he would not be required until Monday morning, 48 hours hence. In the meantime, I decided to catch my breath. I had been intending to stay in the Uzbekistan Hotel, but when I mentioned this to a colleague in Tashkent he issued a whore warning. "I'll book you into the Meridien," he said. "Unless, of course..." "No," I said. The Meridien was totally lacking in character. It was also clean, cheerful and air-conditioned. And I arrived in time for breakfast. (Tashkent is an hour behind Bishkek.) So I sat down with a plate of ham and eggs. Then I tried to work out how to get to the park with the guy on the horse. It was not far away but of course, without Timur, I got hopelessly lost. Eventually, however, I turned a corner and found myself looking straight at the horse's arse. Still, that was better than being stuck with one all day.

Tamerlane stood at the post-Soviet centre of the city. The old centre was Lenin Square, about a mile away. Between the two ran Sayilgoh, also known as Broadway. It was a straight, narrow street through the park, closed to wheeled vehicles and bordered by trees and grass, full of small stands selling *shashlyk* and drinks and surrounded by tables with parasols where one might linger at will. On the path crouched traders of several kinds, selling cheap jewelry and related tat. But most sold paintings. It must have been one of the largest open-air art markets in existence.

Most of the art was a disappointment. There were gauzy young girls communing with nightingales; faux Monarchs of the Glen before stylised mountains; strangely static rushing rivers; crumbling mausolea of Tamerlane with dodgy perspectives and luridly blue domes; kitschy, busty nudes masquerading as tasteful eroticism. But it was cheerful enough stuff, God knows. I wandered slowly past the stands, stopping now and then, enjoying, after a hectic week, the sensation of not being in a hurry.

Then I saw a small, dark canvas, perhaps a foot square. It was conifer green, roughly finished; offset to its left, two figures scurried through the gloom, poorly-defined, but one clearly male, the other female; the man carried a candle which threw a luminosity around them. There were few details, but the sense of urgency and movement was such that one could almost feel a slight breath of air as their garments flowed around them and see the wisps of smoke from the candle drifting into the clear Central Asian air. I knew I must have it.

The artist's name was Bakhtiar. The matter was settled soon enough. He wanted 6,000 Uzbek *som*, about $40 at the official rate, perhaps $15 at the real one. I offered 3,500 *som*. (In Central Asia, unlike the Arab world, one does not demand extortionate amounts, or offer the derisory; opening bids will be about a third above or below the final price.) In the event, we settled on 4,000. Later I felt guilty. I had paid a man $10 for an oil he had painted, and had the nerve to shake his hand having done so. "I don't know what you are worrying about," someone told me later. "It's not much it's true, but I bet it's more than he'd got if you hadn't shown up." Maybe. Later I made a more prosaic purchase: a local cassette of Joe Cocker. An Uzbek Joe Cocker bootleg. Every home should have one.

That evening I stayed up long enough to watch the news on CNN and then I collapsed into bed, realizing as I did so that I had not slept properly for exactly a week. Confused images hopped through my brain, like a monitor that has been left on for too long. The tall blonde from Moscow was sitting on Timur's horse in the park waving at the passers-by; then it turned out the horse had only one ear and was grinning as it cantered off to leave a yurt standing on the plinth, then the flap of the yurt flipped back to reveal a Kyrgyz Airlines flight attendant standing demurely in the entrance, hands clasped in front of her. "I will now demonstrate the safety features of the YAK-40 yurt," she said. She faded away to be replaced by my English colleague from the EU office in Almaty, brandishing a bottle of vodka. I fell asleep.

The next morning I felt rested and ready to explore further. The soul of a city is best seen on a Sunday, when people are doing what they like doing, and not what someone else thinks they should be doing. I spent part of the morning with ex-colleagues from Syria at their office in the diplomatic compound; later, after three, I had nothing to do but wander through Tashkent (but slowly, mindful of the 40-degree heat).

Sayilgoh was just as busy. Everyone ambled through it in a relaxed fashion, dressed in an amazing variety of clothes. Like Bishkek, Tashkent is partly Russian and Orthodox, and partly Asiatic; but the Muslim influence is much stronger. There were plump, quiet Uzbek girls in black, unveiled but with their hair covered, their skirts below their knees. Tall blonde Russian

girls with high cheekbones strode along on block heels wearing light cotton summer dresses. Studeny girls of both races
stood on corners in jeans and tee-shirts. The constant, slight,
smoky whiff of *shashlyk* combined with the warmth and the
slight smell of dust in the air to remind me of Africa, but the
quality of the light – delicate, clear – was pure Central Asia.

At the end of Sayilgoh, a large circle of people gathered
round a barker who was introducing his teenage son, a contor-
tionist. Dressed only in tracksuit trousers, the boy stood on his
hands with his feet resting on his shoulders before cheerfully
twisting himself into less and less feasible forms like an exhibition of knots at a naval museum. It was too much to watch, so
I moved slowly on through the shade of the neem trees and
across to the concrete plaza across the road, where two large,
shallow lidos were separated by a narrow walkway; this walkway was sprayed by a row of water jets that shot ten feet or more
into the air and cast a fine cooling moisture through the sunlight. Crowds of people, mostly young, splashed about in the
lidos or sat together under the parasols by their side, next to the
inevitable *shashlyk* stands. Every now and then a group of children or teenagers decided to brave the walkway, shrieking and
giggling. A young Uzbek woman of startling beauty, dressed in
a simple white cotton shift, stepped along it like a cat, laughing
and holding her little boy by the hand.

Above the lidos, up a short ramp, was what had been, in
Soviet times, the town square. In a sense it still was, as the most
important Government buildings lay at its far side. But the
heart had gone out of its great windswept expanse and in the
soft summer afternoon it looked slightly forlorn, like a set for a
film that has long been made and forgotten. At one side was a
plinth, surmounted by a globe. Until 1991 it had held the largest
statue of Lenin in the Soviet Union. From below the ramp came

the sound of splashing and laughter. People preferred Sayilgoh, *shashlyk* and the lido to Lenin Square.

To the right of the square was some wooded parkland. In the distance amid the trees was a low wooden building. Policemen milled around it, but that was not unusual; there were policemen everywhere in Tashkent, a legacy of bombings by Islamic dissidents the previous February. When I came closer I found that the building was one of two attractively-proportioned structures of young, blond wood, still with a resinous smell; they enclosed a graceful ornamental garden. At the far end of the garden was a plinth on which a small orange flame guttered in the light breeze. The wooden structures were pavilions; on the inside walls were large, thin plates of steel inscribed with names. Above each plate was the name of a province, or *vilayet* (Uzbek is related to Turkish). The name Namangan caught my eye, as I had recently written a piece about a furniture manufacturer who worked in that town in the Ferghana valley. I remembered his name, and looked for it on the plates for Namangan Vilayet. Sure enough, there were four or five who shared his name, simply inscribed with their names and dates, 1919-1944, 1921-1942. I liked the memorial, with its flowers and grass and smell of fresh wood. It was not the Menin Gate, but sometimes less is more.

Behind the monument, a hundred yards or so away, the ground seemed to fall away sharply. I went over to the edge and found myself looking down a steep grassy bank to a pathway that ran beside a fast-flowing, yellow-green river, perhaps forty or fifty feet wide, between heavily-wooded banks. On the banks were young men in trunks, most sitting peacefully and watching the water. Now and then the water erupted briefly as someone belly-flopped into it and swam like crazy against the current for a minute or two, then grasped an overhanging branch and hauled themselves out, to sun themselves contentedly on the bank again. I wandered slowly down the riverside path and found that it ran right below and behind the grandiose buildings that fronted Lenin Square; they were even less impressive from this side, with dirty windows filled with junk, and surrounded by sheds.

The river was more interesting. Every few hundred yards there was a fountain stuck into the water so that great clouds of gossamer-thin spray drifted across the path and cooled me down. I rounded a corner to find a square of tennis courts where large numbers of young people were batting balls across the net. They wore trunks or sundresses, and made little noise, but they were laughing and smiling. I felt as if I had stepped back in time and was walking along the towpath of a river in a North British town in the 1950s, before there were computer games or Sunday supermarkets, and people strolled out after Sunday lunch to play with a ball and swim in the canal or take the sun. The atmosphere was contagious. And then I emerged from a fine cloud of spray from yet another fountain to find a kingfisher standing peacefully in the grass by the path, digesting its dinner. I came closer and closer but it made no move until I was five or six feet away, at which point it flew away, but slowly, not because it was frightened but because it thought it was somehow supposed to be. I liked Tashkent.

*

But the next day was Monday, and it was time to do some work. Timur was supposed to pick me up but of course he didn't, so an EU official called Mark came himself in his own brand-new right-hand-drive Land Rover with British plates. At the office Mark hired a driver called Hassan who drove a Lada with a front passenger seat that rocked backwards and forwards. I perched on this and tried to look like a European Expert.

Today, Uzbekistan has a very dark reputation in the West, but in 1999 this was not so, although the first signs of trouble – including Islamic dissidence, potentially violent – were beginning to be more visible abroad. I reserved judgment at the time. I did find that Tashkent reminded one far more of Moscow than Bishkek or Almaty, both of which were acquiring Western overtones. This was no disrespect to Tashkent. Indeed, the cars in the street were, if anything, newer and smarter than they had been elsewhere; it was just that they were all Russian, whereas in the other capitals they no longer were. It was a detail, but telling. And again, the trams and trolleybuses; they were a lot older than they are in other cities, but were a lot more numerous, were not sprayed with graffiti, and were moving. This did remind me of Moscow, where the Metro trains were ancient but swept into the magnificent stations every 90 seconds without fail. (Tashkent also has a Metro with similar marble halls for stations, but I did not go on it. I did see the ventilator shafts, the tops of which, to my delight, were disguised as large red mushrooms with white spots.)

However, Russian was no longer an official language of Uzbekistan. Uzbek is a Turkic language but is influenced by Russian, Farsi and Arabic and quite a few Turkish words are of Arabic derivation, too. (A project manager gently upbraided his tea lady for not bringing me water. "*Abadan moya?*" he asked.)

Westerners working in the curious admixture of nationalism and bureaucracy found themselves confused. A few said that they found working in Uzbekistan profoundly difficult, but people in Kazakhstan had told me much the same thing. Indeed, one Western expert told me that he had an excellent relationship with the responsible Uzbek minister, who knew a great deal about his work and provided constant guidance and support. I spent a pleasant hour or two with a Danish banking advisor who explained how his national counterparts had regarded him, at first, as a more-or-less useful way of getting their cronies onto overseas study tours. Danes are not noted for their patience but he found some, and after some months, a *modus operandi* emerged. He had a charming, attractive and very young Uzbek-Russian assistant who came to meet me at the front gate on heels like shooting sticks, wearing a dress that ended barely below her buttocks. It must have been awfully uncomfortable, but it certainly made an impression.

I called, too, at the temporary office of a new Swedish-run EU project. Their brief was to monitor the relationship between agriculture and the environment by means of remote sensing and Geographic Information Systems. However, the Swedes had little equipment so far; indeed, as yet they had no access to a toilet. "We hope to have the keys tomorrow," they told me, "but, being on the 13th floor, it's a bit inconvenient." I sympathized. "I expect you can hang on," I replied. They'd have their toilets tomorrow, or if not, soon thereafter; they were, quite rightly, not very worried about it.

I returned to the EU office to meet Mark for lunch. Afterwards, we were sitting at his desk when a water-pipe burst in the UN Development Programme office on the floor above. We charged around moving computers and pictures and siting buckets all over the floor, muttering about inter-agency cooperation. As the flood worsened, I developed a nosebleed, and had to slump down beside Mark's desk between the jets of water. The flow of water increased along with the flow of blood. I fled into the courtyard, handkerchief at my face, and headed for Hassan's Lada. Hassan, of course, had not been in it. He had been over the road reading the paper, and had left the windows up. We climbed into the fiery furnace and lumbered off down the track between the neem trees to my next appointment. I wondered what the kingfisher was doing.

*

Hassan appeared at the hotel at a quarter to two in the morning, just as I had asked him to. In the one day I had known him, I had come to like him a great deal. I settled into the Lada's rocking chair and watched the night streets of Tashkent flash by. We shook hands at the departure gate and then an Englishwoman and I helped a confused young ethnic Russian through emigration. "This is first time I do this. I frightened," she confessed.

We took off at half-past three, climbing in a rapid, tight spiral – I was told, for security reasons. Most of the passengers went to sleep. I watched the steppe appear below. We were flying west and it was a slow dawn, with ample time to admire the slow change of colour in the clouds and the orange tint spreading across the upper atmosphere. Below, huge salt pans drifted past at the north end of the Aral Sea, a wrecked, tragic landscape; two tiny gas-flares remained in sight for a long time, lost in the vast hazy plain. Slowly the steppe gave way to the Russian countryside with its great woods and patchwork of fields.

Later, flying over the Ardennes, their woods and gorges soft in the summer morning, I reflected that I had fulfilled a long-term ambition; I had seen, albeit briefly, a region that was effectively closed until I was in my thirties.

When I got back to my Brussels flat, my first action was to take Bakhtiar's painting from my briefcase and to set it on the mantelpiece. It stayed there until I left the city a year or two later, and today it hangs on the wall of my office in Manhattan. It is a little dark-green oil, about a foot square. Out of the gloom come two indistinct, flowing figures. They are in a hurry; that much is clear, but do they have an assignation? Or are they running from something in the green gloom behind them? Sometimes the painting catches my eye as I put on my coat at the end of the day, before I head out into the cold winter New York night, and I remember throwing back the curtains that first morning in Almaty to see great white peaks floating above emerald-green Alpine meadows. I remember Bishkek too, with its neoclassical opera house in the centre of Asia, and people in their summer clothes walking arm-in-arm under the shade of the trees past an enormous Lenin. I also remember that wonderful flight, gliding across the high yak-meadows past patches of snow with 7,000-metre summits in the distance, and glacial lakes set into the landscape like bright green and turquoise eyes. I can smell *shashlyk* and dust, and see a green city with pools and rivers and people swimming in the sunshine, a kingfisher in the city centre, and a beautiful laughing young Uzbek woman in white, stepping like a cat between the fountains, with her child in tow.

I've seen the *fusca*
and it works

It was last month's graduation ceremony that reminded me of Brazil. Several friends had completed PhDs and posted pictures of themselves in their finery, waving certificates and throwing hats in the air. It brought to mind a drizzly English summer day five years ago when I lined up to get my own scroll, wearing our absurd academic dress, which resembled something Thomas Cromwell might have worn. (It was designed by the photographer Cecil Beaton, who should have known better.) A few weeks later I left for a new job in New York, and for a long time I thought little about my PhD and the way I got it. In particular, I forgot the fieldwork. I had nearly failed; but in the end I did not, and the work was done now. We push things from our minds if they vex us, or if they no longer have a claim on our attention. So I hadn't thought in years of the bright sunlight, the lush vegetation, the heat or the drive across to Niterói on the long bridge; of the bare hills with their yellow grass and brown gullies, or the hard beds, or the flock of macaws that startled me late one afternoon as they took off from the Federal University campus and flew towards the city.

*

I had never seen a macaw in flight. I was walking down the un-made road between the bungalows where the scientists lived, as did the lecturers from the rural campus of the Federal University across the road. It was early May 2005, autumn in Rio de Janeiro, but very hot, and I moved slowly, weighed down with a bag full of empty bottles I was returning to the bar. As I came towards the main road, eight or nine large, bright-green macaws passed straight in front of me, flying in loose formation. Behind them the sky had just regained its colour after the heat of the day and was a gentle blue. By the side of the road in front was a tradesman's van piled high with intensely vivid oranges. Above the van a large silver full moon was rising into the pale blue sky above the first low hills of the Serra do Mar in the distance.

I had been in this small town, just outside the city of Rio de Janeiro, for a fortnight or so. I was deeply interested in something I had first discussed with scientist colleagues in Syria ten years earlier: the potential for agriculture to remove more CO_2 from the atmosphere, converting it to soil carbon and thus slowing climate change. In so doing, farmers would also increase the organic matter in the earth, which is, for a number of reasons, a good thing. The idea was not new. Farmers in the US, in particular, were interested. But few people had considered its potential for the developing world, and no-one had done much work with farmers there to see how it could be made to happen in practice. Now I was doing a PhD that I hoped would answer that question.

I had not thought through the wisdom of this. Most of my fellow-candidates were in their late 20s or early 30s. If they failed, their careers would have time to recover. I was 48, and mine would not. There was another problem: where to do the fieldwork. You cannot just dump yourself in a country and start talking to complete strangers in the countryside; rural people are cautious, and often rightly so, for in many cultures information is power and may be used against you. You must have an introduction through a project, or a mutual acquaintance.

I had planned to work with pastoralists in the grasslands of western China, under the auspices of a World Bank programme, but that had fallen apart. A further plan, to work with Swiss scientists in Kyrgyzstan, was abandoned when the Swiss did not respond to my proposal. (I found out a year later that they had said yes, but that their email had got lost.) Perhaps as a last resort, John, my supervisor at the University of East Anglia, put me in touch with an English-born scientist who lived in Brazil, where he specialised in soil fertility with the federal agricultural research institution, EMBRAPA. Receiving an enthusiastic reply, I decided not to hesitate. "I've booked a ticket to Brazil. I'm leaving in a week," I told John. "For how long?" he asked. "Dunno," I said.

I bought two items for the journey; a cheap new laptop, and *Nab End and Beyond*, William Woodruff's three-volume trilogy about growing up in the Depression. I would, I thought, need something to read during those long fieldwork evenings. It weighed more than the laptop, and would be used mainly to squash bugs. I packed a few shirts and jeans, some underwear, a tie for emergencies, a few medicines, printouts of one or two journal articles, and a Portuguese dictionary. I had the small copy of the *Rubaiyat of Omar Khayyam* that my boss had given me when I left for Africa 18 years earlier; for some reason I had always thought it a talisman, and I packed that too. I had the laptop and one small squashy bag. That, I thought, was enough. I had no idea how I was to mount a research project.

*

It was harebrained, but I had form for this. At 30 I had gone to a remote town in Sudan to do a job that I then found did not really exist. (I invented one, and stayed.) A few years later I had travelled to Ecuador to learn Spanish armed with a single overnight bag. Soon afterwards I went to Bhutan for two years, again taking only what I could carry. It was not hubris; rather, it was a sort of fatalism, in-for-penny, in-for-a-pound. I suppose I felt that things would work out this time too. Thus I found myself in Rio, wondering what to do next. The Brazilians were not unfriendly, but were nonplussed. I did not speak Portuguese; I had been told I would manage with Spanish, but this was not true. That, at least, I had anticipated. The two languages are far more different than most Anglophones realise, and the orthography of Portuguese is harder.

At a garden party in my first week I met L., a woman in her late 40s who offered to translate and to drive for me, both services I would need in abundance. Very short and thin and pale with bright red hair, she often wore white, and always wore it on Fridays; this was, she told me, part of her religion. She was an adherent of a branch of Candomblé, one of the Brazilian faiths that has evolved from a syncretic admixture of African beliefs and practices with Catholicism or occasionally Islam. Candomblé did, I was told, have adherents across the racial spectrum. Some of the rituals are beautiful, especially those connected with the sea-goddess Iemanja, the figure best known outside Brazil.

However, white was not going to be practical in farmyards churned up by cattle. Neither did she admit until too late that her ancient car wasn't taxed or tested, so could not be taken through the checkpoints on the main roads. I started to have misgivings about L., but it was too late for a plan B; my colleagues in EMBRAPA had identified a group of farmers I could talk to in the Muriaé valley near Itaperuna, seven hours' drive away up in the Serra do Mar, on the state border with Espirítu Santo. I needed a car. The cheapest answer seemed to be a Beetle. This was known as the *fusca* in Brazil, where it had once been built in large numbers.

It was clear that L. had increasing misgivings about me too. I think she expected a few days' light touring in an air-conditioned EMBRAPA twin-cab, interspersed with sightseeing and perhaps a little light flirtation. Instead she was going to ride for many hours in an ancient *fusca*, would be away from her beloved poodle for days and would be dragged through farmyards full of cowshit and flies. She must have needed the money badly, because instead of bailing out she trawled up a character who wanted to sell a 30-year-old *fusca*. We met. I drove the *fusca*; it sounded like a demented lawnmower, as Beetles do. But I liked it. The owner then told me he was desperate for money because his wife had cancer, and named a price. I went back to the office. "I've seen the *fusca* and it works," I said. A senior scientist, Segundo, said that sounded a hell of a lot for a *fusca* and settled the matter by calling the licensing office in Rio, who confirmed that a non-resident could not own a car. At this point an acquaintance recommended a car-hire firm on Copacabana Beach. They turned out to be very helpful, and I decided I would drive myself. One day in early May I put L. in the car; in the back was a taciturn young agronomist from the northern state of Maranhão, who had been working on soil fertility with farmers in the Muriaé valley, and who Segundo felt could help.

L. was navigating and got us lost straightaway. We found ourselves off the main road into central Rio de Janeiro and totally lost in the sort of streets that the police clear out, now and then, with teargas. This is not good in Rio. I made my displeasure clear. We then did find our way and I steered us onto the bridge that crosses Guanabara Bay between Rio and Niterói, its sister city across the bay, and capital of Rio de Janeiro State until the latter was merged with the city some years ago. The bridge is one of the engineering wonders of the world, with a length of over eight miles, more than five of them over water.

My spirits lifted. Guanabara Bay is one of the most beautiful natural formations on earth, shimmering in subtropical sunshine, the city of Rio rising above it, fronted by the strange Pão de Açúcar (Sugarloaf) mountain, with the outrageous Christ the Redeemer statue towering behind. Rio de Janeiro was scary, yet I never failed to appreciate is natural beauty, and I wonder what the Portuguese made of it when they first sailed into it in 1502. If indeed they were the first; the American explorer Robert Marx has claimed that there is a Roman wreck in the bay.

Past Niterói, we settled down to a five-hour slog on BR101, the two-lane blacktop that goes north from Rio de Janeiro, parallel to the coast. It was hot. Brazilian drivers are not the worst, but they do pull out to overtake and expect oncoming traffic to pull onto the hard shoulder to get out of their way. My eyes burned. L. chattered incessantly and I wondered if there was an ejector-seat button.

After a few hours we came upon an area of large sugar-cane plantations; then, in the town of Campos, we turned inland up the Muriaé valley. Bit by bit the landscape I had come to see unfolded along the road; low hills of scrubby pasture, scarred here and there by bare-earth gullies where water had concentrated and caused erosion, exposing the earth to the air and allowing its precious organic matter to rot, heating the planet instead of feeding it. A few fields were in much better condition, their bright green showing that the farmer had improved the pasture with *Brachiaria* species. For the most part, however, the grass was yellowish, suggesting nitrogen deficiency. Some of it, I learned later, was what farmers called natural pasture, with less productive grass species that the farmers sometimes took to be native. In fact it was mostly *colonião*, invasive species that had been brought in the bedding carried in slave ships.

The mention of slaves is apposite, for what I was seeing was the legacy of cheap labour and abundant land.

When we think of Brazil and forest, we think of the Amazon; but when the first Portuguese made landfall on Easter Day 1500 the *Mata Atlântica*, or Atlantic Forest, covered maybe 16% of what is now Brazil, including pretty much the whole of the east of the country. In the mid-1990s, Brazil's statistical institute, the IBGE, estimated that about 7% of the Atlantic Forest was left – down from about 1,363,000 sq km (847,000 sq miles) to 100,000 sq km (62,000 sq miles) today. It's said much of this has gone since. With it has gone much of the habitat of some rare plants and animals, for there was and is a high level of endemism. As I wrote later in my thesis, the forest was still a refuge for the maned three-toed sloth, the woolly spider monkey, the red-browed Amazon parrot, the black-headed berryeater, the solitary tinamou, the plumbeous antvireo and the buffy tufted-ear marmoset. ("Are you joking?" John wrote across the draft.)

The destruction had begun soon after the Portuguese arrived. It is recorded in depth in a wonderful history of the Atlantic Forest by Warren Dean of New York University.[8] Dean died in an accident in Chile in 1997, just before it was published; a serious loss, for the book is a first-class work of environmental history.

---

8 *With Broadax and Firebrand: The destruction of the Brazilian Atlantic Forest* (1997), Centennial/University of California Press.

Dean records that the new arrivals planted cereals, fruit trees and sugar-cane and that, within 30 years or so, they imported cattle. These had no natural predators – at first; then jaguars got a taste for beef. But cattle were the first big driver for forest clearance, and with ample land there was always somewhere else to go if the land became overgrazed and exhausted. This process was sped not only by the abundance of labour, but its nature, says Dean. "Not only were the short-lived slaves only briefly attached to the soil ... The conservation of natural resources was to prove irrelevant in a society in which the conservation of human life was irrelevant," he wrote.

But it was not cattle that really did for the Atlantic Forest, at least not then. A month or so later I would drive from Rio de Janeiro to Vassouras, about 30 miles to the north, through a series of very steep valleys. I found to my surprise that they were heavily wooded. The forest was an almost aggressive green in the sunlight and looked magnificent against the deep blue of the sky. I could have imagined that this was virgin Atlantic Forest, but it wasn't; that had been cut down and burned in the mid-19th century for coffee. The steeply-sloping land was perfect for it, with heavy rainfall but without waterlogging. However, the owners of the big *fazendas* had no idea that, with the right husbandry, coffee could be replanted. Instead, they tore every last berry from the land, planting downhill so that they could supervise the slaves more easily, and creating erosion. When crop and land were exhausted, they abandoned them, and planted anew on freshly-cleared land. When they finally ran out of new land they used their slaves as security for loans, and when slavery ended in 1888, they went bust.

In the Vassouras area, some forest regrew. Elsewhere, however, the wrecked and shabby land became poor-quality cattle pasture. Meanwhile coffee marched onwards across the Atlantic

Forest region and into the neighbouring states. It was a process that would not end until oversupply caused a market collapse in the late 1920s, and then many of the newer *fazendas* went bust, too. They left the land they had abandoned in the hands of smaller farmers who grazed their cattle extensively on this blasted landscape, and did little to help it recover. It was the end of that process that I saw as we drove up the Muriaé valley.

And yet there were a number of ways to replace the organic matter in the soil, burying carbon with it, producing more food, and fighting climate change. What I had to do was find out which options the farmers thought would or wouldn't work, and why. In that way I could build up a picture of the basic drivers of land use in the region, and work out what external aid could and could not do. The options included more rotations and crops, in place of cattle; combatting erosion, for instance by ploughing and planting on the contour; and many more. There were a couple of left-field options too. For example, I asked farmers whether they would be willing to grow *guandú*, known elsewhere as pigeonpea; it is cultivated very widely in south Asia but in Brazil it is not, although it grows wild on the farms and the farmers eat it. (Quite recently I mentioned my enthusiasm for pigeonpea to a friend in New York. "That sounds great," she said, then frowned. "But how do you get the pigeons to pee on the crops?")

*

We settled into a hotel in Itaperuna, a slightly soulless city of 75,000 or so people in the north-east corner of the state. For several days we visited farmers in the Muriaé valley. The hills were bare, with few trees. The farmhouses were mostly low concrete bungalows. Some had clumps of *guandú* growing nearby, or fruit trees, but the latter were few and were clearly for home consumption.

One or two of the farmers stand out across the years. There was the middle-aged woman and her teenage daughter on their very small farm of four or five hectares, deep in a valley, surrounded by hills of bare pasture. Their farm was much smaller than the others (which were typically 30 to 50 hectares), but they appeared to be growing more fruits and vegetables. They believed it was very important to take care of the soil, and were thinking of going organic. They were unusual, and nice. I remember that as we talked on the veranda, a neighbour's tractor was ploughing up the steep hillside opposite, going straight up and down the slope – a recipe for soil erosion. Farmers can not of course use a tractor along the contour unless the slope is very modest, or it will roll on top of them; it happens quite often. Farming is not always safe. But the slope looked so steep that I could not help but wonder whether the farmer should have left it alone altogether.

I remember another incident, quite close by. It was late afternoon and we were nearing the end of an interview with a farmer who lived beside a rough unmade road that wound its way into a narrow valley. I became aware of a disturbing sound, like fingernails being drawn across a blackboard. It got louder and louder until I could barely stand it. Neither the farmer nor my two companions appeared to notice it. Eventually I looked around and saw a high, square wooden cart being drawn by two oxen. The squeak was from the axles, which were of wood. It was a traditional ox-cart or *carro de boi*. The racket was incredible. I found out later that there were several local festivals in the neighbouring state of Minas Gerais, at which the *carro de boi* foregathered and wandered along the road in lines, making as much noise as possible.

For some days we went from farmer to farmer, sometimes in the company of the extension agent (the latter is a local agriculture advisor who works for local government, and is found in most developing countries). Because the agent was not immediately available, we returned to Seropédica for a few days. While there I replaced the car – a Gol, a Brazilian VW hatchback – with a rather smaller Brazilian Fiat Palio that I found much nicer to drive, especially over rutted farm tracks on which the Gol had flexed badly, making it very slow and awkward to handle. L. grumbled, because the Fiat was smaller, cheaper and had less status. Telling her that it was actually a better car made no difference.

This did not improve my mood. I had so far found Brazil rather cynical. It had started on the way in, when I had been changing planes; in desperate need of water, I had bought some for one or two reales at São Paulo airport, had paid with a large note (all I had), and been refused change. Speaking little Portuguese and having ten minutes to catch my connection, I had had to leave it. The attempt to rip me off with the *fusca* had worsened the impression, as had an incident with a local official in the countryside; I took him to lunch and he chose an expensive restaurant and ordered lobster, something that I would never have eaten. Moreover the countryside around Itaperuna and in the Muriaé valley depressed me; what had once been one of the great forests of the earth had been reduced to series of dull hills covered, for the most part, with mangy nitrogen-deficient fields scarred with gullies, grazed by bored cows that could find little shade. Not a solitary tinamou in sight.

The farmers, too, seemed cynical and rather despondent. They complained about the poor returns to cattle-farming, but there seemed to be so much more that they could have done with their land. A technician employed by a local farmers' association told me that they were deeply conservative and that attempts to interest them in new ventures, such as fish-farming, seemed doomed to failure. They were quick to explain why most of the options offered would not work. There was, they often said, no labour available, making extensive pasture farming the only way. I especially remember sitting on the veranda of a small concrete bungalow in the Macaé valley, talking to two middle-aged brothers; one, the owner of the 40-hectare (98-acre) farm, had injured his leg a few years earlier and could not work the land, but insisted that he could find no affordable labour to do so for him. I wondered if they could have shared the land with the landless, who sometimes did work as sharecroppers, or *parceiros*. But I was always told that everyone had gone to the towns. There were even some farms that were owned by doctors, lawyers or dentists from Rio de Janeiro, who basically used them as places for barbecues; the land was farmed lightly or not at all by caretakers, who were not allowed to spend money on fertiliser. I only visited one such farm, but the local extension agent told me that as many as 30% of the farms in the valley met this description. I did meet some farmers who were cheerful and wanted to try new things. But bit by bit I was getting a picture of farmers whose land was wasted on cattle when it could have grown more, was sometimes overgrazed, and was badly cared for, with a lack of manure or fertiliser, so that unimproved fields of yellowish *colonião* were all too common.

One night we were late at a farm, and left for Itaperuna, 20-odd miles away, when it was nearly dark. L. was beside me in the front seat; the agronomist from Maranhão was dozing in the back. I came round a bend into a stretch of road that had high, steep banks. Normally deserted even in the day, the banks were alive with people, their silhouettes visible against the last of the light above us, as were the forms of rough shelters that had been built for the night. Washing flapped between them.

"*Sem terras*," said L.

"What?"

"They will be planning an occupation," she said.

She was telling me that this odd camp had been made by members of the Landless Workers' Movement, or to give it its full title, the *Movimento dos Trabalhadores Sem Terra*, or MST. This movement, by then also well-known outside Brazil, had arisen in the 1980s, initially as a result of spontaneous occupations. The farmers' views on these people were, naturally, unprintable. They claimed that the *sem terras* never managed the land properly, and rarely tried to for long. A scientist told me that they sometimes occupied land being used for agricultural research. "If they seize land that does belong to real rich people, they get shot at," the scientist said. "We don't shoot at them, of course, so they pick on us." As with all contentious movements, it's hard to know the truth. What those people on the road to Itaperuna were doing, I do not know; I had a brief impression of an oddly silent crowd, watching the car. Children wandered in the road, and I slowed to a crawl to avoid them. Then they were gone, and there was only the empty dark road and the reddish glow from the Gol's instruments.

*

We returned to Rio. I worked quietly in the EMBRAPA office, where I borrowed the desk of a researcher who was in Britain; I am still grateful I was able to do this. I mapped my sample carefully onto the Brazilian statistical institute's data for family farmers in the region, and realised it was only partly typical. The farm sizes were a little too big, but also, they were not diverse enough; they really had nothing but cattle. People in the region usually made at least slightly better use of the land. I also felt I needed more data. I rang John in England and he agreed that I should do more. The question was how.

I pushed the problem aside for a week or two and ransacked the EMBRAPA library, which was full of first-class papers and journal articles on soil research in the region. Brazilian agricultural science is excellent. But it was all in Portuguese, and I had to learn more of it, and quick. I took lessons from the wife of a colleague. In the evenings I sat with a dictionary, glued to Brazilian TV, and bit by bit the words came into focus. I ploughed through the best Brazilian newspapers, *O Globo* and the *Folha de S.Paulo*, and the conservative but lively news magazine *Veja*.

One day, for a change, I bought the popular tabloid *O Povo* (*The People*), a sort of Brazilian equivalent of *The Sun*, *Bild* or the *National Enquirer*. I was holding it as I got into my landlord's Brazilian Renault in the town centre.

"Why are you buying this shit?" he asked. "This is the worst. This, the worst damn newspaper we have."

The front page splashed the death of a girl caught by accident in a shooting incident in some *favela* or other. It had been the morning of her *festa de quinze anos*. In Latin America a girl's 15th is a special coming-of-age celebration, known in Spanish-speaking countries as the *fiesta de quinceañer*, or *quince*. The pictures showed a cheap new handbag and plastic shoes scattered on a pavement against a wall; all were streaked or spattered with blood.

"That paper, God, it's rubbish," repeated my landlord as he pulled away. But now and then I still think of her, and her bloodstained cheap new handbag and shoes. She would be 23 now.

Paranoia about crime was a fact of life. A senior academic I met was mugged at gunpoint at his front door in Rio's classy Leblon suburb. A friend had me to dinner and insisted on driving me the 300 yards home. Garden furniture was of concrete and could not be stolen. One night Bob, the British-born scientist, and I went to visit EMBRAPA colleagues in Niterói, and arrived home at about eight. We found out the next day that there had been a carjacking 10 minutes later on the street we took from the main road. I asked an American how he liked living in Rio. "Beautiful and scary," he said. A nightly programme from São Paulo seemed to consist of little more than security videos of crime, with a hysterical voiceover. At São Paulo's internal airport, Congonhas, I was astonished to see a large glass case labelled "No weapons on plane. Deposit them here". In it was a large assortment of crudely serrated daggers, shivs, trench knives, breadknives and the like, some so vile that their owners should have been in a secure hospital.

Meanwhile a huge corruption scandal was brewing. This was the *mensalão*, the revelation that the governing party had been paying opposition members of the national assembly what amounted to a monthly salary in order to ensure they didn't oppose its legislation.

But what stood out was not that Brazilians accepted all this; it was that they didn't. There seemed to be a freshness about their anger that made me wonder if the cynicism had just peaked. In fact, the trend since I was there has been for crime to fall (albeit not by much), and the percentage who report being victims of crime is not especially high for the Americas. As for the *mensalão*, President Lula da Silva survived it but many of his close advisors and party bosses, including his chief of staff, did not. But I was conscious of being in a country that was a mass of contradictions: extreme violence and poverty coexisted with outstanding science and engineering (Brazil is a major producer of cars and has a globally important aircraft industry); politics and daily life seemed cynical, yet there was a lively and capable media, and an idealistic administration pressed for, and did achieve, change at home and status abroad.

My own life was not so bad, anyway. My landlord's large bungalow was split into two and I occupied the smaller part, with a living room, kitchen and bathroom mostly to myself. It was hot, even at midwinter, but I had a terrace where I could sit and read in the long evenings. The nearest shops were in the town centre, two miles or so away, but my landlord had lent me an old bike on which I could get to them; it was too hot at midday, but I would go when work finished at five, loading my rucksack with (among other things) quite agreeable Brazilian wine. Then I would take a shortcut home, crossing rough, bumpy meadows, the long grass catching in the spokes, the soft air cooling as the short subtropical dusk turned to night. In the evening I might go to a bar in town with Bob, or with an Australian scientist, Phil, who had had a career with the UN; as his wife was Brazilian, he had retired to Rio, but was working during the week at EMBRAPA. We celebrated my birthday, too, with far too many *caipirinhas*. If I had a problem, it was lack of sleep. Brazilian beds are very hard, to be cooler in the climate. There were also insects, mostly dispatched with *Nab End and Beyond*, of which I had still not read a word.

One day Phil and I drove to the Itatiaia national park on the border of Rio de Janeiro, São Paulo and Minas Gerais States. Here the wooded slopes of the Serra do Mar rose to a high plateau, capped by the Agulhas Negras (Black Needles), at over 9,000ft. We found ourselves in high uplands not unlike the moorlands of southwest England, with tussocky grasses and bog flowers, criss-crossed by fresh streams. From its edge the blue-green mountains of the Serra do Mar stretched away in the distance. In June I would read that some Brazilians had gone there to camp – it seemed they did so at that time most years, hoping to see snow. On the slopes below, steep rivers burst across waterfalls and filled clear rocky pools. On another day I went with Bob and his five-year-old son to a beach in a beautiful bay, surrounded by green hills, the sea a vibrant blue. I was starting to see how wonderful Brazil could be.

*

Workwise, however, I was still in trouble. I needed to talk to more farmers. I was very worried that I would leave Brazil without enough good data. Neither did I think my sample reflected the region properly, something I knew the examiners might ask me about (they did).

In fact, I had deeper concerns. I had been 46 when I started my PhD, in 2003, and knew I should be at least 50 before I finished. Now I thought I never would. One night in Itaperuna I lay awake all night on the hard bed, staring at the ceiling and wondering how I could have been such a fool. I was a middle-aged man who had wanted to do something that was for young people, at the start of their careers, and now I was lying on a hard bed in a dull hotel thousands of miles from home, financially compromised after years of study, staring failure in the face.

I was rescued by Eli de Jesus. A Brazilian researcher in his 30s, he had recently completed a PhD of his own on sustainable agriculture. Bob put me in touch with him and I liked him at once. He offered to take me to the area he knew well, in the state of Minas Gerais.

Minas is one of the largest, most important and developed, and yet also most beautiful states of Brazil. It is noted for its cuisine, which includes great rib-sticking stews and other comfort food. But its environmental history is even grimmer than

Rio's. The name of the state means "general mines", and the Portuguese colonists do not seem to have seen it as good for much else. The 18th-century gold miners had simply cut down all the trees and then diverted streams to carry away the topsoil. In some cases, even this was not done; using abundant cheap labour, they simply removed the soil until they found gold, with 50-100,000 baskets being carried away for a single gold-bearing one. In the first half of the 19th century, coffee arrived to finish the job. At the same time the population of the Zona de Mata (literally, "forest area"), which was where we were going, rose to 20,000 in 1828, 250,000 in 1870 and 548,000 in 1890.

We were bound for a small town in the Zona da Mata some miles north of the regional centre of Juiz de Fora. On a map of Brazil, the town was very close by – barely inland from Rio de Janeiro. But it would take us five or six hours to get there. I was beginning to understand the sheer size of Brazil.

As the light softened in the late afternoon, I started to enjoy the drive. North of Juiz de Fora a two-lane road twisted its way north through an endless parade of valleys and hills; I lost track of time as the little Fiat swept through curve after curve. A few buses, small cars and pickups passed the other way; white fences bound green meadows, and small farmsteads nestled in folds in the landscape; the light turned golden then orange then intense blue and then died, leaving us still on the road, the headlights probing the dark.

At length, we came to Rio Pomba. The name means, literally, "Pigeon River", and that may have been all it meant; or the pigeons referred to may not have been birds. According to Warren Dean, early settlers obtained slaves "through dealings with natives to whom they applied the same name as that they used in their African trade: *pombeiros* – referring to the pigeons set loose to lure others back to the cote."

But if Rio Pomba had had *pombeiros*, they were long gone now. We took rooms in a very basic but clean and friendly two-storey hotel opposite the church, on the corner of the town square. It was Sunday evening, and I opened the wooden shutters of my room to see worshippers streaming out from evening communion, very smartly dressed, the women in colourful frocks and very high heels, carefully coiffed. As they came down the steps the church bells rang, but there was another sound from what seemed to be a disco right next to the church wall in the square, where one or two elderly men in cowboy hats were dancing alone to *forró*. This is a distinctively Brazilian genre, a cross between folk and country that sounds like neither, having brisker rhythms and being led by the accordion. The loudspeakers fought with the church bells and the church bells fought back and no-one seemed to mind, the young women stopping to gossip below my window before teetering off on their six-inch heels, big hair swaying in the breeze, while the old men danced.

In fact the whole town seemed to me to be pleasantly mad. One morning, while waiting for Eli to transact some business, I took a walk around; the place was full of saddlers – yet there was not a horse in sight. (We went to see the artificial insemination people. "Don't you recognise me?" asked one. "I served you your pizza last night.")

Eli had been lecturing at the local technical college, and invited me to give an address on my research. The students were in their late teens, from local families. Beforehand Eli gave his own lecture, on his own subject (agroecological sustainability). I knew enough Portuguese to follow him now, and thought his lecture outstanding. He knew his subject well and presented it with clarity and concision, but without oversimplification. He was also clearly welcome on the farms and so, by extension, was I. The holdings here were smaller, maybe 15-30 ha, and the farming more varied.

The farmers were mostly friendly and cheerful, and were more interested in their land than they had been in Itaperuna, though – as so often in many countries – they complained that they could not get technical advice. I decided to interview the local extension agent, who should have been giving it. He was based in a nearby town, but he proved elusive. Eventually Eli, one of the farmers and I settled down in a bar opposite his office and drank beer until he arrived, and ambushed him. He was then friendly enough, and we talked for some time, but he did not seem to hold the farmers in high esteem. For one thing, he insisted, they were always over-using nitrogen fertiliser. (We had that morning heard from farmers that they found it hard to get information on how much to use.) But he also wondered why they did not band together to sell their produce; about this he was clearly right – the prices they were getting were awful. I thought they were nice men who needed information and an advocate.

Once again, we returned to Rio. My sample was now far more typical. Moreover I now had enough data to reach conclusions that were statistically valid. (I would later spend some weeks checking this, using something called the two-tailed test; let's not go there.) This is not the place to state my conclusions. They are discussed in depth in the book I later published.[9] But briefly, the land is a farmer's main capital equipment, and he is no different from any manufacturer; he must get sufficient returns on his assets, or he will be forced to run them into the ground. When that asset is farmland, doing that will have environmental outcomes that we need to understand.

---

9 *Crops and Carbon*, 2011 (Earthscan, now part of Routledge).

*

I spent a further week collecting literature. One Friday afternoon I said goodbye to the scientists at EMBRAPA; they had never really been involved in what I was doing, but they had been hospitable enough. I parted from Eli with genuine regret. He moved on shortly afterwards to a position at the Federal University of Paraná. I said goodbye to L., too; she had sometimes been a trial, but she had done what I had asked of her. My bag was heavy with papers in Portuguese. I threw it into the back of Phil's car and we drove downtown to spend the weekend at the flat he and his wife had bought on Copacabana Beach.

It was a good weekend. Phil and I walked the length of Copacabana and Ipanema beaches, and later his wife and I went to hear culture minister Gilberto Gil address a Gay Pride rally on the beachfront. There was much dressing up, much cheering and much colour. On Monday morning I flew to São Paulo to catch the flight to London. I picked up *Nab End and Beyond*, of which I had still not read a word. I read most of its 700 pages on the flight. As I began to read, the lights in the cabin went down, and Brazil too passed into darkness.

It stayed there, for me. I finished my PhD in 2007; it was examined at Christmas. Since then I have thought little about those months in Brazil, and with good reason. All my life I had begun major endeavours almost casually. But this was different. I had gone to Brazil ill-prepared, almost on impulse, and at 48 years old I had come far too close to failure. I never wanted to repeat that night in Itaperuna again. One day in 2008 I left England to start an office job in New York. It would pay for my old age.

Then last month I saw my friends in Cecil Beaton's medieval gear and I thought about my own PhD and how it had nearly ended badly but, in the end, had not. I thought about Brazil, and how lucky I had been to see a great nation of the earth at a time of change. I remembered the moon rising in a pale blue sky behind a cart piled high with ripe oranges and bright green macaws in formation, and thought that life was a chessboard, and that maybe every piece dropped into place in the end.

Uptown and the Bronx

I landed in New York in late August 2008. I wrote to a friend a few days later: "Anita Brookner once started a chapter set in London in the late summer with the words, 'The evening was livid and smelled of drains.' NY is livid and smells of drains, and other, worse, things that you would recognise from a tropical meat souk at the height for summer."

New York does not smell like a meat souk (though it can sometimes smell of drains). It was more my mood. I had not wanted to leave England, where I had lived very comfortably for several years. I had also had a lousy journey; Northwest had overbooked the flight and tried to kick me off it in Amsterdam. It would be fair to say that I was in a crap mood, and in no state to appreciate New York, which was sweaty and humid.

But, as I continued: "It becomes a much nicer city when the sun goes down; the concrete canyons become constellations of light and take shape slowly against an aquamarine sky that fades to orange."

A few days later I wrote to the same friend, Hazel: "Tonight I felt restless, so, although it was after 11, I went to a nearby

Irish bar for a pint. It is still hot here, humid and rather close. I was walking down 2nd Ave. and crossing 43rd Street, on a corner where there is a bar called Redemption (why?). The pedestrian lights were red and I stopped outside Redemption, which was crowded with people and spilling out onto the pavements and everyone talking very loudly, and there was a girl who wore a tiny skirt and her legs were incredibly long, and her heels must have been a foot high." There were few people about; Midtown is Manhattan's office district, and can be dead at night. The drinkers clustered outside Redemption formed a strange island of light and noise. As the girl stood there, and as I stood there, a garbage truck loomed suddenly out of the darkness towards Lexington Avenue. It roared and shook by, back open and stinking; a man in overalls clung to the back quarter. The girl stood there in her black cocktail dress, her flamingo-like legs bent by her weirdly high heels, and the man flew by inches away in overalls, greasy tee-shirt and thick gloves, hanging on to the back of the truck; then he was gone, and I thought of the medieval doom paintings in English churches, young men in their finery, their arms linked with a skeletal Death.

Ten days later Lehman Brothers filed for bankruptcy. As the months wore by the subway passengers thinned out, the panhandlers multiplied and scenes like that one outside Redemption became rarer. Over the next five years I watched New York go through a grim recession, a hurricane, a storm and tidal surge, and six winters, two of them appalling, another so mild it was like spring. Now and then I would write a friend, usually Hazel, about something I had seen in the city that had struck me. I called these my "New York moments". Here are a few.

*

I'm in a health-food store. It has mineral supplements, herbal medicine etc. and there are lots of rather gaudy pill-bottles on shelves. I go to the counter to pay for my bunch of bananas. At the counter in front of me is a stocky, badly dressed lady in her late forties, rather gone to seed, and literally down at heel (she is wearing either slippers or worn-out shoes, and her heels are sticking out of them at the back). She is showing the owner a leaflet with herbal remedies.

"I got something *like* that," he's saying. "Don't have that brand." He brandishes a pill-bottle. "Does the same thing. Gets your husband more interested in sex. More eager."

"I guess I better talk to him 'bout that," she says. "He's away but I guess I'll talk to him 'bout that when he gets back."

"Does the same," says the owner, "just like the one you got there, give him sekshal energy."

"I guess I talk to him when he gets back," says the woman.

She slopes off out of the shop without much energy of any kind. I pay for my bananas.

*

Walking to the subway station on a June morning, I take my usual route along the northern edge of Central Park. This isn't the quickest way, but I like to see the green trees on a hot summer day, and there is shade from the trees and from the scaffolding on the tall 1900s buildings, with their maze of painted fire-escapes that catch the sun and cast intricate shadows on the sidewalk.

On the way down Seventh Avenue to the park, I pause at a street crossing. Across the street, their backs to me, are a young woman and a young man. The woman is in her 20s or early 30s, slim, even lithe, with long glossy chestnut hair, and wearing a blue tee-shirt, short, tight white shorts and running shoes. The man is about the same age or a little younger, in a polo shirt and baggy shorts. Both have dogs on leads. The dogs are sniffing around each other excitedly, tails a-wag. The woman's dog is a thinnish black-labrador type thing; the man's, a sort of fun-sized border collie with a touch of spaniel. The man and woman clearly do not know each other, but the dogs have introduced them. Their tails are wagging too as they talk about their dogs and encourage them to get to know each other.

Later I chance to see a website called askmen.com; specifically, its page headed Dating & Sex. Under the title "9 Unusual Places to Meet Women", it volunteers the following: "...Many entrepreneurs are finding that our four-legged friends are natural-born matchmakers. *Leashes and Lovers* hosts cocktail parties for single dog owners... The company is based in New York for now, but it's soon to go national."

I must say that the name *Leashes and Lovers* conjures up something a little cruder, but perhaps that's just me. An article in the *New York Times* tells of another agency called Flexpetz, which rescues dogs from shelters and rents them out by the day (it does hope they'll eventually be adopted). As one customer says, "I'm single and moved here from Scotland two years ago, and it's been difficult to meet people ...But when I'm walking around with Oliver, I seem to get into so many conversations about him. It becomes a nice way to meet people." She certainly pays for this, at $279.95, or about £175, a month for four one-day rentals; extra days $45 each.

Americans in general do dote on their pets; they were expected to spend about $50.84 billion on them in 2011, and the State of New York told pet cemeteries to stop taking humans as too many people wanted to be buried alongside their loved ones. However, in New York it seems that dogs have a specific role in helping humans to mate. This conjures up a picture of dogs sitting quietly while the humans circle each other and occasionally recoil, growling.

It doesn't seem to happen today. The woman says a polite goodbye to the young man, and bounds off into the park, glossy hair swinging, the black dog jumping and leaping behind her.

*

I'm walking in Central Park; it's a Sunday evening about seven and heavily overcast. I decide to take a shortcut through the North Woods, and pick a wood-chip track that I think will cut through to the top of the hill and thence down to 110th Street. It doesn't, but before I find that out I find my way blocked by a very large Indian man who is talking on his mobile phone; his legs are splayed to either side of the path and he is urinating heavily onto the centre of it. All the while talking. This man must have a bladder the size of a zeppelin because he urinates heavily for what seems like several minutes, so that I decide to go past anyway. I have to clamber round him. He goes on urinating, talking intently on his cellphone, apparently quite unaware of me.

*

I am walking up 112th Street. It's early evening on a weekday, the sun is shining but it's very humid. Two young men are entering the ground floor of a brownstone, one with a bicycle, one carrying a cardboard box full of junk; the bike man is in long shorts and a sweatshirt and has a headcloth.

"I ain't staying in that house no more," says one of them. "It's got rats."

"Jeez, rats."

"Yeah, rats. Not mice, RATS."

"Rats," says the other. "Not mice, rats. Beeeeg rats."

As I walk on down 112th Street I hear their voices coming at me from behind. Raaaats. Not mice. Raaaats, man, raaats.

*

A very cold but snowless day in mid-December; I am walking back from the shop just as the last of the light is going. The sky is pink and dark blue and a moon has come up. As I get to my street, a Cadillac Escalade goes past. An Escalade is a huge, very long, very high SUV with lots of brightwork, like a sort of chrome-plated turd on wheels. It turns into my street, then stops abruptly; the driver has seen someone he knows. He winds down the tinted window and a great wall of bassy dub sounds billow out across the street. His friend on the sidewalk has a squat dog on a lead; it looks like a pit-bull. The two men greet each other very, very loudly. YO WASSUP HOWYR-DOIN' WASSUP. As I draw level I realise that there are deep bass sounds coming not just from the turd but apparently from the dog as well. The dog is standing patiently by its owner, blinking its pink, stupid eyes, and in its jaws it holds the handle of an enormous ghetto-blaster.

*

It's March 18 and nearly spring. But I've just looked out of my window to see light but steady snow falling out of a grey late-afternoon sky.

Four children run up the steps of the brownstone opposite. The reddish-brown stone of the building looks oddly purple in the grey light. There are three small children of about six, and a bigger boy of about 11. They're all dressed neatly in parkas and boots and have little backpacks. The older one rings the bell and as they wait for an answer, the young ones dance around on the lower steps as he looks down at them, a little sternly.

I wonder if they know that they are about to enter what was once the home of Irving Berlin, who moved in about the time he wrote *Alexander's Ragtime Band*.

*

A Thursday morning in mid-September; it's unusually dark and the sky is threatening. I'm standing in the crowded express subway on the way to Times Square. I get on through a door that won't open again on the journey, as the platforms are on the other side. If I can I will always stand and lean against the door, so that I can read without strap-hanging. Today I'm lucky; the train's packed but I can lean back on the notice that says *For Your Safety, Do Not Lean on the Door*, and open Camus's *The Plague*. For the first ten minutes, as the train rattles its way from Central Park North to 96th Street, I'm in plague-ridden Oran. I'm reading the passage in which the priest Paneloux mounts the pulpit and rails against the sins of the populace. There is a flail in the sky, he thunders, and it searches out the houses of those of you who have sinned.

As I read the train stops at 96th Street and a small middle-aged African-American woman gets on and stands a foot or so away from me, facing away from me down the train. She is wearing a bright purple top. She starts to preach at the top of her voice, which must penetrate to every corner of the carriage.

She bellows at us to abjure sin lest we be consumed by hellfire. I can no longer concentrate on Paneloux's flail for the one in the subway car. No-one says anything; this is not unusual; a few people shift from one leg to another and show signs of annoyance, perhaps thinking of becoming Wiccans or Druids or Satanists. I'm reminded of Goethe's comment: "Distrust all those in whom the urge to punish is strong".

In the street the sky is getting darker and a strong wind, cold for September, is blowing down Third Avenue. I get up to my office, in which I switch the lights out and use a desk lamp, so that I am sitting in a little island of light.

About 11 o'clock I get up and look down into the side-street six floors below. There's a man who runs a food cart; this is a portable kitchen in the street, a sort of aluminium mini-caravan with a gas bottle. He sells kebabs and chicken and rice. Two men are moving a second cart; it's heavy for them – one pulls, one pushes, and they swing out into the busy stream of Third Avenue and the traffic eddies round the cart, except for one big old-fashioned yellow cab that has to stop and move round it. It takes him 15 seconds but he honks loudly anyway. The men ignore him, bent over against the growing wind; one of them has no cap and his thin white hair blows this way and that as he bends over the handle of the food cart. This will not be his only job. He may have three. He may have papers. He may not. There are still more clouds now, light grey higher up, darker grey lower down, and the darker ones are chasing each other above the silvery-white Art Deco flanks of the nearby Chrysler building. The clouds build up through the day and at about 5.30, the light in my office suddenly drains away.

A clap of thunder comes down the gaps between the buildings. I look out and to the left at the Chrysler Building. It's *Metropolis*. Really. The sky above it is black but split with lines of lightning and the tip of the building pierces the clouds.

I remember that a friend's office is landlocked and she can't see the sky. "Come and see the storm," I say into the phone. I put down the handset and turn back to the window, and as I do so my hip catches my copy of *The Plague* and sends it spinning to the floor. I pick it up and put the bookmark back in the passage that describes Paneloux's sermon, then turn back to the window. The wind is driving clouds of spray up 41st Street. The lightning flashes catch the silver spurs that extend from the Chrysler's higher floors, far above me, like half-finished gargoyles on a medieval cathedral spire. My friend comes in. The storm is bad, but we do not know how bad; in Brooklyn there is actually a tornado that picks up trees and slams them onto cars, and it is very lucky that no-one has died.

After a while the storm abates a little and we make for the subway, but there are trains standing on either side of the platform, one for Times Square, the other for Flushing, and they are crammed full of bemused passengers who are going nowhere. An announcement is made but is so garbled that none of us can understand it. So we make for the Times Square shuttle train that leaves from below Grand Central, about 500 yards away through the underground passages that are crowded by hurried troglodytes laden with books and bags, often with wires snaking up from their pockets to the buds in their ears, so that every now and then you walk through clouds of someone's music as they pass you, like the diesel fumes from a bus going the other way. The shuttle trains are so full that each one groans away from the platform with people crammed up against doors that can barely close, and a voice booms around the hall THIS TRAIN IS FULL GO TO PLATFORM TWO FOR THE NEXT TRAIN THIS TRAIN IS FULL PLEASE GO TO PLATFORM THREE and masses of people divides this way and that like confused shoals of herring. We squeeze into the last carriage of a train and stand pressed closely together with the other passengers in the oddly stiff attitudes of those who are forced into close proximity when they are not intimate.

At Times Square we all tumble out and intersecting threads of passengers steer for the lines they need, for the A Train, the Port Authority, Penn Station. Here and there puddles have formed as the jets of rain in the street above leak into the passages below. The air is like wet cotton wool. A voice clangs at us: "We wish to inform you that due to weather conditions there are NO LONG ISLAND RAILROAD SERVICES At This Time." My friend has got a signal and is telling her husband that she will be late. We follow the signs saying UPTOWN AND THE BRONX and fight our way up to the uptown platform. As we reach it, there is a man standing in front of us, dressed in rough corduroys and a hooded jacket. His hooded face cannot be seen. His arms are outstretched and hanging around his neck is a placard that says NO HANDS PLEASE GIVE. He is in the middle of the platform and the crowds swirl around him. I notice that on the end of his arms there are stumps enclosed in the remains of knitted gloves, and then we're swept past him and a train comes in and its doors open and there are great gusts of hot and cold air, and we are lifted in with the crowd and the train pulls away, its wheels cracking and clanging on the worn track like a flail.

*

A warm afternoon in April, hazy milky clouds and patches of blue. I'm walking through the North Woods of Central Park to my favourite reading place, a common on a hill surrounded by trees, above the perimeter track. I love the spot although it is blighted by a young saxophonist who sometimes turns up and starts playing bad jazz on Sunday evenings. An unspeakable crime could be committed with a saxophone's mouthpiece.

I once passed the house where Adolphe Sax was born. It was a tiny cottage on a side-street, on a corner, in Dinant. I went to Dinant for the day because I wanted a day out of Brussels and thought it would be nice to spend it in the Ardennes. Dinant is built on a steep high hill in a gorge through which runs the Meuse. It was beautiful, but I mainly remember two things about it. The first was the waterfront, which was crowded by large numbers of Francophone African men, all trying to sell identical electric shavers with rather kitsch wooden handles. The second was reading in the guidebook that in the Middle Ages, 700 townspeople were drowned at Dinant by someone called Phillip the Good. I was not quite sure what to make of that. Anyway, I saw where Sax was born and if he hadn't been, my afternoons in the park would be more peaceful.

So anyway, I am walking through the woods on an unpaved path reinforced, here and there, by woodchips to prevent erosion. It's a strange path because at the weekend it's often full of rather gloomy-looking men, usually black or Hispanic, who sit on fallen logs looking vaguely confused, as if they were not quite sure what to do with their day off. I suppose it could be a pick-up area. But there's no-one around this afternoon.

I pass a tree with a slight hollow between two roots at its base. In the hollow is a fresh apple. Just sitting there for no obvious reason. In the evening the sax player appears so I give up reading and walk home for a beer. The apple is still there. For a moment I am tempted to pick it up; but there is a reason why it is there. It may even have been left by someone of animist beliefs who wishes to propitiate the gods. I leave it alone.

*

Today I have an appointment with the surgeon, Dr G, for 3.30; so out through the harsh January air, between the high-piled snow, being careful not to step in the deep pools that collect in the edges of the roads, where the snow had decayed to leave slushy water that won't drain away. It's nearly 3.30 when I get there, but the doctor's nurse tells me, unusually kindly, that he is running about 25 minutes late. I tell her I'm used to that and she laughs. (Last time he kept me waiting two hours.) She has a strong foreign accent and I wonder if she's actually his wife. (I was bitching about the cold to him once. "You should worry," he said. "My wife goes round the house turning down the thermostats all the time. She's French.")

But the waiting room, which is very small, is if anything overheated. It has a huge TV playing a non-stop loop of fish in a tank. The two doctors in this suite don't have much space; they are moving soon, to Fifth Avenue, but to an even smaller office. ("I don't know how the last doctor there managed with so little space," Dr G told me later. "She was a gynaecologist." I have a brief vision that I choose not to pursue.)

I look for the book in my bag. I left it in the office. I fish out another but don't really want to read it, and find myself looking out into the street two floors below. It is savagely cold out there, and the afternoon sky is just turning orange behind a spiders' web of naked branches. A few men fuss about with a delivery van that is drawn up hard against the snowbank on the sidewalk. A mother hurries by with a stroller – or perhaps she is a nanny; she looks very young and also has a small dog on a long lead *and you see she gets some fresh air and you dress her warm, and don't forget to walk the freakin' dog at the same time an I'll be back, I don't know, seven, eight, depends a dis Skype thing, there's loadsa stuff in da freezer but don't you give her no e-numbers she'll be up all freakin' night.*

I'm feeling mellow. My head leans back against the wall and I fall gently asleep.

I awake 30 minutes later to see the other nurse standing over me, telling me that Dr G will see me now. I'm undressed and ready in my surgical gown when Dr G comes in. He's a tall, bulky man of about my age, friendly and easy going.

One day last summer I was waiting in the consulting-room while Dr G finished with another patient. When he came in he saw that I was reading *Between the Woods and the Water*, the second of Patrick Leigh Fermor's trilogy on his walk across Europe in 1935. "Any good?" he asks, sitting down. "Yes, excellent," I say. "He walked across Europe. In 1935."

"My grandfather walked across Europe," says Dr G.

Patrick Leigh Fermor, I observe, seemed to have stayed in the house of just about every aristocrat in Austria and Hungary.

"My grandfather," says Dr G, "didn't."

He busies himself with implements.

"He set out from Odessa. In 1916. His parents gave him three gold coins and told him to walk to Palestine. No future for Jews, they said. Not round here. Walk to Palestine."

"He made it?"

"He made it. Not the three gold coins. They got robbed. In a barn. In Bulgaria. But he made Palestine. Wound up on horseback in the Frontier Force. Then came here. Had a few tales to tell."

Today he asks a few questions, examines me and sounds pleased. He's about finished when the phone rings; it's the ER (casualty ward) at a nearby very major New York hospital. A young doctor's on the phone; he has a woman who appeared to have appendicitis but, it turns out, doesn't. He wants to fill her with painkillers and send her home. Dr G's brow furrows. "I guess we oughta hold off on that awhile," he says. "You though-ta kidney - what? – no – KIDNEY stones. No. Yes. No. You do a UA, huh? You keep her right there and do a UA." He puts the phone down. "'Scuse me," he says. "They got a question, I got to answer it. We all gotta learn."

I say I come from a medical family myself, on my mother's side. When young, my two uncles lived partly in my grandfa-ther's granite house on the edge of Dartmoor. Some years af-ter he died the local police station received a phone call from a mildly hysterical owner, who said that two skulls had been found buried at the bottom of the garden. A placid policeman plodded round, examined the skulls and gave one of the jaw-bones a flick. It sprang back into place with a twang. "I believe, Madam, that before the War the young Seale gentlemen were preparing to enter the medical profession," he observed.

Dr G chuckles.

"One moment," he says, and leaves the room.

He returns a moment later with a skull. "This is the one I used when I was training," he explains. "I've had it, well 30 years I guess." He shows me the long, thin coil springs that fasten the jaw to the roof of the mouth. "And here's a wire I put in to show my students where to find the auditory canal. Now, this skull's a pretty good specimen and I paid extra, because you can see these bits here – and here..."

The skull, he explains, probably came from India. The teeth are long and their bases yellowed but they are all there, and I wonder if the man was young.

"I got it from Barnes & Noble," he says.

I say I thought Barnes & Noble was a bookshop.

"Sure, it's a bookshop but back then they got skulls also."

I try to imagine the big multi-storey Barnes & Noble opposite the Lincoln Center; it's just closed but I used to go there when I first came to NY. First floor, fiction, feminism, femurs. Third floor, skulls and biography. I'm thinking about the skull as I walk home. I remember travelling by bus across the Bengal plain late one afternoon as the day turned gold, watching the boys in the villages play cricket as we drifted past. Who were you? Did you play cricket when you were a child, and did you laugh? Did you lose your land and struggle in from Bihar or the Bengal plain to sleep below the platforms at Calcutta station? How long did you last there and where did they find you?

Twenty or so years ago, I was walking up Calcutta's Bentinck Street with an Irish friend. It was early one monsoon morning, when the heat was not yet too great. We passed a young man lying dead on the pavement in a torn T-shirt and stained *dhoti*. There were a few coins scattered around him. When Ronan and I returned an hour or so later he was still there but the piles of coins around him had grown, left by passersby to pay for the funeral. At the time, I thought how useless that was, when he needed the money when he was alive. I had missed the point. The coins were people's way of saying that they could do nothing for him and his kind, but took no pleasure in that fact.

I walk home through Central Park. It is nearly dark now and quite quiet, the hum of traffic coming from Fifth and Eighth Avenues some distance away. The snow shimmers in the dusk and the dying light bounces back off it. As I skirt the southern edge of the North Woods, the path climbs thirty or forty feet above street level, and I find myself looking south towards Midtown. The buildings shine a myriad of colours against a cold, darkening blue sky. I think about the long, strange routes that people have taken to reach this place.

*

I decide to walk home from work one night; it is cool for July, and anyway I like to do this when I'm in a bad mood, which for a couple of reasons I am. It's about an hour and a half, more or less if I dawdle or shop or have heavy books in my bag. I walk north up Madison Avenue, then west along 58th St., passing through some of the most expensive residential property on earth.

I cross Avenue of the Americas and am passing a solid old apartment block when I become aware that an old man is on the pavement, moving his legs as if trying to get up. Several people walk past and a girl is standing in the doorway, unconcerned. I walk past too; a Chinese couple beside me hesitate, look back, but continue.

Now, I'd like to say I hear a quiet still voice of conscience deep within me, but what I actually hear is a very loud voice (mine) saying "Go back and do something, you little shit." So I go back, and offer my help. He looks up.

I realise then that he is really old.

"Do you need a hand, sir?" I ask.

And really deaf.

"Euhh?" he says, looking up. Then he blinks, and said: "You have an extraordinarily civilised voice, you know. Now where are you from that you learned to speak like that?"

You'd think that'd be obvious, but New Yorkers often do not recognise English accents. There may be a reason. If you listen to Eleanor Roosevelt speaking, you may be surprised, as I was, to find that she spoke with something very close to an English accent. Maybe posh Americans did sound more like us 100 years ago.

The man has now managed to get to his knees, and is looking up at me with interest. He is certainly not drunk, and, although rather deaf, does not seem confused.

I say he has quite a nice voice himself (he does), and asked where he was from.

"Cleveland, Ohio, originally," he said, and then indicated the building behind with a stick: "But I've been living in this building for 62 years. And now I'm 92 years old."

I say that my father once taught at the university in Columbus, Ohio. This seems to please him.

"I went to university in Ohio," he told me, "and all my friends did, but I left. Yes, I left. I wasn't learning anything."

He thought for a minute. "You should do voiceovers," he said. "You'd be real good at voiceovers. And you'd make some money too. That voice, it's really quite extraordinary." And he reaches in his pocket and hands me up a smart if old-fashioned business card.

"I run a school of dance," he said. "Dance. In this building here. Dance and relaxation."

I chat a moment longer and then leave, shaking hands with him and saying that I enjoyed meeting him, which I have. He seems not to need assistance. His handshake is very firm. As I leave he remains on his knees and resumes performing the odd movements with his legs that had first drawn my attention.

Later I come across his card, and decided to see if the Milton Feher School of Dance and Relaxation exists. I find it certainly does, or at least has. It is named after Milton Feher, a successful actor and dancer in musical theatre in the first half of the 20th century. His career on Broadway was cut short by the onset of arthritis in 1941. Unable to obtain relief from conventional medicine, he explored movement and relaxation techniques that proved more helpful, and opened his school in the late 1940s to help both arthritis sufferers and people on the stage. In 1962 he released an LP of relaxation music and techniques that is today archived in the Folkways collection at the Smithsonian.

When I read all this, I realise that the elderly man's odd movements on the pavement had not been struggling attempts to get up, but exercises. I also realise that he was Milton Feher, sadly to die less than a year later at the age of 98 (he was 97 when we met, not 92 as he told me).

I have met a man who, a very long time ago, was afflicted with an illness that ended his career, but decided to confront it, and to share what he had learned to help others.

*

It's a weekday in January; there has been snow, there isn't now, and the streets are clear, but it's very, very cold, with a high blue-grey sky. I've been to get my sandwiches. I come back along the wide sidewalk on 42nd Street. Ahead of me, a mishmash of sky-scrapers of different eras rises up along the two sides of the street like markers of successive civilizations uncovered in the excava-tion of some ancient city; glass and steel, curtain walls, the jazz-age elegance of the wonderful Chrysler Building a block down. Closer to me, there is a row of crenellated castellated follies from a little earlier, dark with dirt and wreathed in steam. You just *know* that this is Gotham City and any moment now the Penguin will appear on a distant battlement, wheezing and evil.

Just in front of me are a row of bollards by the curb. Sit-ting on one is what looks like an old man. He has his back to me. He wears a dark wool coat and a sort of Homburg hat. He holds a stick, which is stretched out in front of him at an angle of 45 degrees, and planted firmly on the ground. He is look-ing along 42nd Street. There is a sort of space around him, the little crocodiles of passers-by on the busy sidewalk parting around him like a stream round a stone, and he seems oddly tranquil and otherworldly, and I think I have seen the ghost of Alfred Hitchcock.

*

A weekday, early evening, in Midtown, very hot and humid, really sticky. I'm crossing Third Avenue on my way to the subway. As the pedestrian lights change, there is a big surge on both sides of the street. A yellow cab has got too far forward at the lights and is in everyone's way. This happens all the time. He starts half-heartedly to reverse, then thinks the better of it. The crowd surging across from the other side are the usual Midtown commuters; men in shirtsleeves, sometimes with ties, often wearing yarmulkes; young and not-so-young women in light summer dresses and decorated sandals; tired young men with baggy trousers and handfuls of flyers they are handing out to make a buck.

There's a family coming towards me; dad, mom, son – and daughter. She is about fifteen, dressed in blue-grey shorts and a matching sun-top. She has long, vibrantly orange hair and a porcelain face and intense light-blue eyes with very long lashes; her mouth is open in a slight pout, her lower lip prominent, and on her feet she has gold sandals. She seems oddly unaware of her surroundings. But I'm aware of her, and I think others are too. The family makes the other side of Third Avenue and goes on down 42nd Street towards the Helmsley Hotel. I glance back and see her, still standing out, and I know that I've just seen Helen of Troy.

Atlantic crossing

I spent Christmas 2010 in England; it was fiercely cold and the country was blanketed in snow. On January 8 I travelled from my sister's home in the Oxfordshire countryside to my flat in New York's Harlem district. It seems a routine journey, but the Atlantic is never routine for me; my first memory in life comes from that journey, and the ocean has always fired my imagination. I had a notebook with me in the plane, and I jotted down random thoughts that spilled out on the Atlantic crossing, on the nature of travel and the movement of people. This is what emerged. If it makes no sense, don't worry; it wasn't meant to.

10.15am GMT

The blue sky is so pale in winter; everything was thrown into delicate relief, the intricate patterns of the bare twigs, and the ridges of grit on the country road. It was getting warmer, and the road surface was damp and black between the banks of snow on either side. I came round the bend at the bottom of the hill that leads out of the village of Combe and there was a magpie. I looked at once for its mate but it was alone. One for sorrow.

Over the brow of Stokenchurch Hill, and into the Chilterns. I was thinking of another journey to Heathrow on a November day nearly a quarter of a century ago, sitting beside my father in his silver Saab. Then as now I did not want to go. *I'm mad. I can't do this. I can't go to Africa. Hubris. Idiot.* The autumn weather was dull, with a low thin cloud stretched over the landscape. Then just for a minute a small patch of very wan sun lit up a field to the left of the road, and I saw that there was a dip in the land towards the far side of the field, the little island of sunlight lifting it from the dull landscape around. Then the sunlight was gone, and we were surrounded by murk again.

For some reason I never forgot that patch of sunlight on a dip in the field. It did not seem random. But I never could find that little hollow in the land again, and could not remember where I had seen it. Now this morning, as I hurtled over the crest of Stokenchurch Hill and down towards High Wycombe, I saw it again. The snow had melted here, and the field seemed greener than before; perhaps then it was fallow or rough pasture. Then I looked back towards the road and saw the traffic ahead dividing to the left and right round an object in the carriageway, and I veered quickly to the left myself. It was a swan. It lay in the middle of the road, on its breast, its wings spread to either side, its neck twisted and arched. Then a small wooded valley opened up to the right; it was hemmed in by busy roads, and there was a white Georgian manor standing there looking oddly out of place.

4.00pm GMT

Sitting in Gate 40 of Terminal 3, looking out at the aircraft drawn up beside us, the aluminium gleaming dully in the thin yellowish afternoon sun, a little desultory activity beneath the wings, a yellow cart scurrying here and there and the odd chap in orange dayglo vest walking purposefully across the tarmac with a clipboard. There didn't seem to be many passengers (there weren't; I would have a row to myself, with lots of room for long-flight detritus – books and jackets and customs forms and empty plastic glasses and little packets of biscuits that I would end up throwing away when I got home).

Once, this journey had a sense of occasion. I remembered a previous crossing; I was 11 and we were on the boat train. I wonder which was the last boat train, and when did it run? This one began at Euston and ran straight through Liverpool and into the dock. We got out of the train on one side of a huge shed-like building; on the other side of it I could see a mighty white wall that seems to stretch right across the horizon, studded with portholes. The shed was a heaving mass of steamer trunks and children and loud cheerful voices. There was a festive atmosphere. Lots of families had come to see people off. Looking back, I suppose many of our fellow-passengers were actually emigrating. These were the last days of the Assisted Passage, when "ten-pound poms" made the six-week voyage to Australia for that sum. Others went to Canada and would certainly have been aboard; flying was still extremely expensive.

We rid ourselves of a huge mound of luggage, all of it plastered with labels that said CANADIAN PACIFIC NOT WANTED ON VOYAGE (yes, really; we had those labels). Two or three hours later I was standing by the rail somewhere near the stern, sensing a growing motion as the great white wall moved slowly away from the quay. The water in the widening gap was churned up, probably not by the screws – tugs were pulling us out – but by the current flowing in to replace the 50,000 tons of steel as it pulled away. On the surface of the grey-brown water a solitary steamer trunk bobbed up and down; it had fallen in during loading, and now a trio of dockers peered down at it from the quay, waving grappling hooks. "I gather the chap's DPhil thesis was in it," says a jocular voice behind me. Someone else chuckled: "I say, I do hope he has a carbon copy!" I was hemmed in on both sides by fellow-passengers taking their leave of those on the quay; many were clutching the ends of long thin brightly-coloured paper streamers, the other ends held by their friends many tens of feet below. As the gap widened, the streamers parted, sometimes dropped, sometimes broken, and fell onto the rising and falling grey-brown water below.

We went below. In the morning I went back on deck. We had come up the Firth of Clyde in the night and were lying off Greenock. The engines had stopped and the late-summer day was dead calm, the Clyde estuary miles wide and as still as glass below a huge blue morning sky, greenish-brown mountains in the distance, an extraordinary feeling of light and space. All that moved was the tender, a small launch that nosed out towards us from Greenock with mail and a few last passengers for the New World.

It was almost the end of the North Atlantic liners. The *Empress of Canada* already sailed only in summer, and a year or so later the first wide-bodied jets entered service and the historic service from Liverpool to the St Lawrence was abandoned. The last two White Empresses fell into the twilight existence of cruise liners; but the *Canada* was one of the last survivors, and lived on, long-forgotten, until the end of 2003. Then she went to Pakistan, to Gadani Beach. This must be one of the strangest places on earth. They just run the ships straight onto the beach at full speed so that they plough deep into the sands, and then an army of thin men in white swarm aboard and break them with hammers and axes and the sweat of their brows.

I looked at the aircraft outside. There was a little more activity; a few more people with clipboards, a whine as a cargo door was closed. They won't break her. They will send her to the Boneyard. The Boneyard is in the Arizona desert and hundreds of ghostly aeroplanes stand there, preserved in the dry desert air; vast Boeing 747s, 777s like this one, B52s, transports from Vietnam, planes that once dropped napalm.

9.30pm GMT

There is an eerie tranquility in an aircraft in mid-flight at night. The lights are off and people are dozing; one or two are working on laptops; others are watching the screens set into the backs of the seats in front. Few read nowadays. I do though. Tonight I had an anthology of the best American travel writing from 2010 and it was rather good. It included a piece by Simon Winchester and I was reminded that he had recently written a 'biography' of the Atlantic. I haven't read it; I should, but I'm thinking about the Atlantic anyway, that great labile treacherous mass of water 40,000 feet below my arse.

I was trying to imagine that first flight in a fragile biplane, ending in an Irish bog. (I think it was probably just a field really. But it was in Ireland, so everyone decided they'd landed in a bog.) Leather jackets and thick woollens and leather flying-helmets, thick goggles; wind tearing through the strut wires; wooden propellors; engines forged from metals crude to us and badly fitting, sprays of oil in the slipstream, that sound from undamped exhausts that they used to say was like ripping calico, only nowadays no-one knows what ripping calico sounded like so perhaps there should be a new simile.

Some journeys on this ocean always have ended badly. You are in your cabin; it was a five-day voyage before, but now it's three weeks as you limp along at the pace of the slowest ship, and you zigzag and dogleg, and destroyers and corvettes fuss around like smoky sheepdogs. It's early morning and you're still in your bunk when there is a soft thud and a jolt and the ship falters and seems to have come to a stop. There is an odd silence. The lights flicker but stay on. You can hear the footsteps of a steward clanging on the steel floor of the passage outside so you open the door. No, probably nothing to worry about, but perhaps you wouldn't mind going topside, sir, do you have warm clothing? – good, sir, if you can get it on quickly. On deck everything's quite calm, but the other ships have moved on ahead, leaving a black smoke stain on the horizon; and you're alone in the early morning between a still, solid grey sea and a gunmetal sky, and there's a cool breeze. It's very calm and it must be only your imagination that the ship is settling slowly to starboard. In fact everything is calm and quiet and you know nothing of the jagged hole below and the cold water streaming in across the hot boilers and the screams of the lascars and stokers being flayed alive by superheated steam.

When I was young, many older people hated the sea.

1.30am GMT, 8.30pm EST

Yellow cabs have this floaty motion, the big heavy old-fashioned bodies swaying across bumps and centre-lines and potholes. A thick bulletproof steel wall divides you from the driver, but there is a sliding glass panel in it and it is always open. On the back of the steel wall is a little video screen, like the ones you get in planes. You can touch it to zoom in to the map and see your position, but mostly it plays a loop of what-to-do-in-NY and restaurants and cookery. Its clatter in the background merges with the sanitised rapping from the driver's radio and the murmur of his voice as he talks on his cellphone. He's talking to another cab driver, a friend or maybe a relative who is clearly a beginner, a fellow-African probably from Mali or Senegal, *no you gotta take the other slip, the second slip for La*

Guardia, where're you anyhow, no the second slip, the second you listening to me? and just then La Guardia drifts past on our starboard bow. A little later the cab slows for the tollbooths before the Triborough Bridge that links Queens with Manhattan. It's very long, the Triborough Bridge, and if you look left you can see the spires of Manhattan stud the skyline in the distance, lights shimmering in the great expanse of the East River that lies between.

Most times I do look left. I don't know why but I looked right that night. Another, unlit, bridge runs parallel to the Triborough Bridge, a thousand yards or so to the north. It's an old-fashioned bridge, desolate and lifeless, unlit; gantries show that it is a railway bridge. It rises to an elaborate iron cantilever that reminds me of the Forth Bridge; this must carry the central span, and then it runs downward to the shore, where its great length finally merges with the mess of sheds and concrete on the Manhattan bank. As it runs down it passes through an archaic arch and pediment, surmounted by ornate stone or concrete globes, just visible against the night sky. That night, nothing stirred on this old bridge. Any moment, I thought, I would see sparks and smoke, and steam white against the night, and an enormous engine with four or five driving wheels on each side would issue forth onto the cantilever, followed by dimly-lit carriages with slatted wooden benches packed with tired and sullen Swedes and Sicilians and Galicians, rocking gently with the movement of the train, fresh from a grimy floating coffin that has brought them to try their luck in the homesteads of Oklahoma and the stockyards of Chicago and the orchards of California.

Then the cab floated and swayed across the ramp at the foot of the Triborough Bridge. There were bright lights again, and fiercely-lit but deserted pizza parlours, furniture wholesalers, shoe repairers, small piles of grimy ossified snow, crushed hamburger cartons, liquor stores, overhead railroad tracks in latticed iron cages, congealed posters on boarded windows, short nuggety Hispanic men on bicycles delivering takeouts, and lots of African-American men in parkas and earphones, hunched against the bitter cold.

In November friends went to Sudan on business. "You must see the Mogren, where the Blue and White Niles meet," I said. "Especially at sunset. It's a huge expanse of water and there are oxen ploughing near it and date-palms, and it's where the big silver Short Empire flying-boats landed in the Thirties on their way from Southampton to the Cape." After a week, I got an email. They were sharing a modern flat near the airport, and every morning a car came to collect them and drive them from one side of the airport to the office on the other, past rows of identical modern flats lining wide treeless streets under a white-hot sky. "It isn't really charming," says my friend. At the office they worked 12-hour days, then did some more when they got home. "The Nile's only 300 meters away, apparently," my friend writes. "We haven't seen it." So it goes for six weeks, and then the day before they leave they finally get to the Mogren and stand beside it for five minutes. There's a picture someone takes, of two graceful but rather tired young women standing squinting beside a sheet of blue-grey water, the scene bleached of all detail by the midday sun.

If I look for long enough I see the sun start to set over the Mogren. Details emerge, trees, fields, the odd oxen driven across loamy earth by someone in a white headcloth and *djellabiya*. Orange rays lance across the water from the setting sun. There's a big silver flying-boat on the water, and someone is leaning from the nose with a grappling hook to push it away from the shore. On the jetty stand great tin drums from which fuel has been poured into the tanks, very slowly and carefully, filtered through muslin. There's one hell of a roar as first one engine, then the other three, start, black smoke jetting from crackling exhausts. The boat turns and taxis away, leaning down a little by the rear, its tall tail-fin standing up against the dark blue sky. After a mile or so it turns again; the engines pick up and it lumbers forward and the hull lifts slowly from the surface, and thin sheets of silver water cascade off the shiny aluminium surface and drop away, leaving a few flying drops to catch the setting sun behind. Then the plane goes higher and further away until it's just a dot, droning south towards Lake Victoria across Kordofan and the Sudd and great herds of animals and men with spears who stand on one leg in the shallows.

The future has yet to be created; it does not exist – but the past does. Those who came this way before are all around you. If you stop and close your eyes for long enough you can see them flowing past you like a river, and if you think hard you can make the river flow backwards so that aeroplanes rise from bogs and ships rebuild themselves on beaches strewn with steel detritus, and men and women stream back across the midwestern plains, through Ellis Island and back into steerage, and if you go back far enough you can see us all cantering backwards across the steppe on small, stocky, shaggy horses, back to wherever we began.